THE AFFLICTED

MW00533307

JOHN WILLISON

SOLID GROUND CHRISTIAN BOOKS
BIRMINGHAM, ALABAMA USA

OTHER SCOTTISH TITLES FROM SGCB

In addition to *The Afflicted Man's Companion*, Solid Ground Christian Books is delighted to offer the following Scottish titles:

The Life & Letters of James Renwick by W.H. Carslaw
The Sufferings of the Church of Scotland by Robert Wodrow
The Scottish Pulpit by William Taylor
Precious Seed: Discourses of Scots Worthies
The Doctrine of Justification by James Buchanan
Paul the Preacher by John Eadie
Greek Text Commentary on Galatians by John Eadie
Greek Text Commentary on Ephesians by John Eadie
Greek Text Commentary on Philippians by John Eadie
Greek Text Commentary on Colossians by John Eadie
Greek Text Commentary on Thessalonians by John Eadie
Divine Love: A Series of Discourses by John Eadie
Lectures on the Bible for the Young by John Eadie
Opening Scripture: Hermeneutical Manual by Patrick Fairbairn
Martyrland: A Tale of Persecution by Robert Simpson
The Preacher and His Models by James Stalker
Imago Christi: The Example of Jesus Christ by James Stalker
Sabbath Scripture Readings from the OT by Thomas Chalmers
Sabbath Scripture Readings from the NT by Thomas Chalmers
Lectures on the Book of Esther by Thomas M'Crie
The Psalms in History and Biography by John Ker
A Pathway into the Psalter by William Binnie
Heroes of Israel: Abraham – Moses by William G. Blaikie
Expository Lectures on Joshua by William G. Blaikie
Expository Lectures on 1 Samuel by William G. Blaikie
Expository Lectures on 2 Samuel by William G. Blaikie
Luther's Scottish Connection by James McGoldrick

THE

AFFLICTED MAN'S COMPANION;

OR,

A DIRECTORY FOR PERSONS AND FAMILIES

AFFLICTED WITH SICKNESS

OR

ANY OTHER DISTRESS.

BY THE REV. JOHN WILLISON,
DUNDEE, SCOTLAND, 1727.

REVISED EDITION.

PUBLISHED BY THE
AMERICAN TRACT SOCIETY,
150 NASSAU-STREET, NEW YORK.

Solid Ground Christian Books
PO Box 660132
Vestavia Hills AL 35266
205-443-0311
sgcb@charter.net
solid-ground-books.com

The Afflicted Man's Companion
by John Willison (1680 – 1750)

First Solid Ground Edition June 2009

Taken from a 19th century edition published by
The American Tract Society, Nassau Street, NY

Cover image by Borgo Design, Tuscaloosa, AL

ISBN: 978-159925-214-8

In this edition, a considerable part of the address to the reader
and a few lines in the body of the work, having mainly a local
application, have been dropped, and a number of words and
phrases used by the worthy author, which have become somewhat obsolete since the period at which he wrote, have been
changed for others more generally understood at the present time.
-The Editor for the American Tract Society

CONTENTS.

INTRODUCTION, · 25

CHAPTER I.

GENERAL DIRECTIONS TO ALL FAMILIES AND PERSONS VISITED WITH SICKNESS.

1. Diligently inquire into the ends and designs for which God usually sends sickness and affliction upon men, · 27
2. Let all who are visited with sickness or distress, search for the Achan in the camp, and inquire diligently what is the ground and cause of God's controversy with them, · 32
3. When any fit of sickness attacks you, think seriously upon death, and make diligent preparations for it, · 36
4. Be not anxious for recovery to health, but leave the issue of your present sickness to the will and pleasure of the infinitely wise God, · · · · · · · · · 40
5. Bind yourself with holy purposes and resolutions, in Christ's strength, to be more watchful against sin, more diligent in duty, and to improve the time of health better, if God shall be pleased to restore it again to you, · · · 42
6. Set your house in order by making your will and settling your domestic and secular affairs, while you have freedom and capacity for doing it, · · · · 43

CHAPTER II.

PARTICULAR DIRECTIONS TO THOSE WHO ARE SHARPLY AFFLICTED WITH SICKNESS OR LONG TROUBLE.

1. Justify God in the greatest afflictions which befall you, · · · · · · · · · · · · 47
2. Labor to be sensible of God's hand under heavy affliction, and beware of stupidity and unconcern under it, · 50
3. Beware of misconstruing God's dealings towards you, and of charging him foolishly, · 52
4. Under sore trouble and distress, labor to exercise a strong and lively faith, · 53
5. Labor to bear with patience whatever load of trouble the Lord appoints for you, · 56
6. Beware of envying wicked men, when you see them in health and prosperity, · · · · · · · : · 60
7. Guard against repining and murmuring against the providence of God, under heavy sickness and affliction, · 61

CHAPTER III.

SPECIAL DIRECTIONS TO THE CHILDREN OF GOD WHEN UNDER SICKNESS OR ANY OTHER AFFLICTION.

1. Let believers especially guard against fainting or desponding under God's afflicting hand, ... 70
2. Let the children of God be exemplary in patience and submission to him under their affliction, ... 78
3. Let believers be much employed in the praises of God, while they are under affliction by sickness or otherwise, ... 85.
4. Let the children of God, when visited with sickness, set about actual preparation for death and eternity, ... 89
5. Let believers in time of sickness endeavor all they can to glorify God, and edify those that are about them by their conversation and behavior, .. 96
6. Let God's children, when sick or dying, feel and manifest a great concern for the advancement of the kingdom of Christ, and of true religion among the rising generation, ... 102
7. Let the children of God labor to fortify themselves against all Satan's temptations and assaults, which they may expect to meet with in time of sickness and affliction, ... 104

CHAPTER IV.

SPECIAL DIRECTIONS TO UNREGENERATE PERSONS, WHEN AFFLICTED BY SICKNESS OR OTHERWISE.

1. Take a serious view of the miserable condition of a Christless person under sickness or heavy affliction, ... 109
2. Let unregenerate persons carefully improve their sickness and affliction, as a means to further their conversion, and pray that God may bless it for that end, ... 111
3. Be careful to obey God's voice in the rod, and beware of slighting it, · 113
4. Cast back your eyes upon the sins of your past life, and labor to be deeply humbled for them before the Lord, ... 114
5. Flee immediately to Jesus Christ by a true faith, and close with him as offered to you in the gospel, ... 116
6. Call for the elders of the church, that they may pray over you in your sickness, ... 116

CHAPTER V.

DIRECTIONS TO THE PEOPLE OF GOD WHEN THE LORD IS PLEASED TO RECOVER THEM FROM SICKNESS AND DISTRESS.

1. It is very proper, both under sickness and after it, to examine if the affliction be sanctified to you, and hath come from the love of God, ... 119
2. Make conscience of offering to God the sacrifice of thanksgiving, upon his recovering thee from sickness or any distress, ... 120

3. When the Lord is pleased to grant thee any signal mercy or deliverance from trouble, beware of forgetting the Lord's kindness towards thee, · 124
4. Inquire after those fruits of righteousness which are the genuine effects of affliction in the children of God, who are duly exercised thereby, · · · · 125
5. Be carefu. to perform those resolutions, engagements, or vows you have come under .n the time of sickness, and walk suitably to them, · · · · · 128

CHAPTER VI.

DIRECTIONS TO THE UNREGENERATE WHEN RECOVERED FROM SICKNESS AND RESTORED TO HEALTH.

1. Seeing the afflictions of the wicked are unsanctified, it is necessary you examine what sort of affliction yours hath been, and what fruits it hath produced in you, · 131
2. Consider the great danger of not being made better by sickness, and of not complying with the voice of God's rod, · 133
3. Wonder at the patience of God in sparing such hell-deserving sinners as you are, and be thankful for it, · 135
4. Study to improve the sparing mercy and goodness of God to you in a right and suitable manner, · 137

CHAPTER VII.

DIRECTIONS TO THE SICK WHO ARE APPARENTLY IN A DYING CONDITION, AND DRAWING NEAR TO ANOTHER WORLD.

1. Consider, when death stares you in the face, that now is the time, if ever, to exert the utmost activity in preparing to meet it, · · · · · · · · · · · · · · · 142
2. Continue to the last in the exercise of true repentance and humiliation for sin, · 146
3. Be mindful of all acts of justice and charity which may be incumbent upon you at this time, · 147
4. Labor to overcome the love of life and the fear of death, that you may attain to willingness to die and leave the world when God calleth you to it, · 149
5. Study to imitate the ancient worthies, by dying in faith, · · · · · · · · · · · · 158
6. Place the example of other dying saints before you, and study in like manner to shine in grace, and be exemplary in piety and heavenly discourse, for the glory of God and good of souls, when you are going off the stage, · 160
7. Let dying persons be much in prayer and ejaculations to God, · · · · · · · 200
Meditations and ejaculations proper for a sick and dying person, and especially for a dying believer, · 202
Meditations for drooping believers when death is near, · · · · · · · · · · · · · · 208
Additional meditations proper for any sick person in the view of death, · · 213

CHAPTER VIII.

DIRECTIONS TO THE FRIENDS AND NEIGHBORS OF THE
SICK, WHO ARE THEMSELVES IN HEALTH FOR THE
TIME.

1. Be very thankful to God for the great mercy of health and strength, and
   improve it to his glory, ································· 222
2. Make conscience of visiting your sick friends and neighbors, believing it
   your duty and interest so to do, ······················· 223
3. Let the friends of the sick, and those who visit them, deal faithfully with
   them about their souls, ······························· 224
4. Be earnest in prayer to God for your friends when sick or dying; pray with
   them and for them, ································· 231
Petitions for the sick,·································· 232
5. Be careful to furnish your friends with suitable company and spiritual converse, when they are sick or dying, ····················· 234
6. Be likewise suitably concerned for the bodies of your friends, when they are
   sick, ·· 236
7. When the sickness of your relations or neighbors doth issue in death, study
   a Christian and suitable behavior under such a dispensation,········ 236
8. Let the sickness and death of others be a warning to you in time of health,
   to make due preparation for the time of sickness and dying which is before you,·· 244
9. Let those who are in health set about the work of repentance and turning
   to God in Christ quickly, and beware of delaying this work until the time
   of sickness and of dying.····························· 252

THE AUTHOR'S ADDRESS TO THE READER.

THE subject of this book, however melancholy it may appear to some, is of vital importance to all, seeing the word of God and our own experience assure us that "man who is born of a woman, is of few days and full of trouble," and that he "is born to trouble as the sparks fly upward." Nay, God's dearest children are not exempted from this common fate. We see what is the character God giveth his church: "O thou afflicted, tossed with tempest, and not comforted!" Isa. 54:11.

If in this world then we must look for tribulation, it is highly necessary for every man to seek direction how to provide for it, and behave under it, so that he may glorify God, edify others, and attain to eternal happiness at last. The tribulations we have to look for here are manifold; but among those that are outward, I know none about which men ought to be more thoughtful and concerned, than bodily sickness, which often is the harbinger of death, and ushers the way to judgment.

This is a subject not much discussed in public sermons, which are delivered only to them that are in health, the sick being unable to attend them. Wherefore it seems the more necessary to treat of it in writing, that so the afflicted may have a book in their houses, and at their bedsides, as a monitor to preach to them in private, when they are restrained from hearing sermons in public.

And though sometimes ministers' sermons may be very

suitable to the case of the sick and afflicted, yet, alas, most men are careless and forgetful hearers of these things while they are in health and prosperity, reckoning the evil day at a distance from them. A book, then, such as the following directory, being with them in time of sickness or affliction, may, by the divine blessing, be useful to bring to their remembrance those counsels and admonitions which they very much neglected in the time of their health.

Again, ministers of the gospel, though never so much inclined to attend the sick, yet, by reason of disability, and a multiplicity of other work, cannot be always with them to counsel and comfort them. But such a book as this they may have ever at hand to consult with.

And since the afflicted, for the most part, are not able to read for themselves, it would be a most charitable work for friends or neighbors that attend them, to lay hold on proper seasons for reading such a book as this in their hearing, and especially such chapters or directions as they judge most suitable for them. Thus you might be helped in some measure to free your consciences, and do your last offices of kindness to your sick and dying friends, when you can serve them no longer in this world.   *   *

Seeing we all have many harbingers and forerunners of death before our eyes, it will be highly our wisdom to keep ourselves in a waiting posture, always ready and willing to die. What is there in this weary land to tempt us to desire to abide in it ? Is it not a land overwhelmed with sin and sorrow ? O, believers, are you tossed with tempests here ? seek the wings of a dove, that you may flee away and be at rest. Be habitually desiring to depart, that you may be with Christ. Surely for you to die is gain, yea, infinite gain. What are the imaginary pleasures of this world, to the real happiness of the next ? Though the struggles of death be grievous to nature, yet the gain of dying should reconcile you to it. You do not shrink from the trouble of putting off your clothes at night to gain a little rest to your bodies ; and why should you shrink from unclothing yourselves of the garment of flesh at God's call, to gain everlasting rest to your souls, and the fruition of Christ's glorious presence for ever ? Let the thoughts of this gain put you upon using all means to get your hearts weaned from the love of the world and its comforts. Keep the mantle of earthly enjoyments hanging loose about you, especially in these calamitous times, that so it may be easily dropped when death comes to carry you to the eternal world. O, for a more lively faith of that world, and of him who is Lord and purchaser of it. But seeing this subject is enlarged upon in the book itself, I shall add no more here upon it. I only subjoin a collection of some sweet and comforting texts of Scripture, very proper for dying believers to meditate and feed on by faith, to cling to and plead with God, and draw consolation from, when they have a near prospect of going through the dark valley and entering into the unknown regions of eternity. God's word will then be our hope.

COMFORTING TEXTS FOR DYING BELIEVERS.

Come unto me, all ye that labor and are heavy laden, and I will give you rest. Matt. 11 : 28. Him that cometh to me, I will in no wise cast out. John 6 : 37.

In my father's house are many mansions : if it were not so, I would have told you. I go to prepare a place for you. And if I go and prepare a place for you, I will come again and receive you unto myself; that where I am, there ye may be also. John 14 : 2, 3.

Because I live, ye shall live also. John 14 : 19.

Surely I come quickly. Amen. Even so, come, Lord Jesus. Rev. 22 : 20.

There remaineth therefore a rest for the people of God. Heb. 4 : 9.

I have waited for thy salvation, O Lord. Gen. 49 : 18.

Lord, now lettest thou thy servant depart in peace; for mine eyes have seen thy salvation. Luke 2 : 29, 30.

He is the Rock; his work is perfect. Deut. 32 : 4.

The Lord will perfect that which concerneth me. Psa. 138 : 8.

Being confident of this very thing, that he which hath begun a good work in you, will perform it until the day of Jesus Christ. Phil. 1 : 6.

I know that my Redeemer liveth, and that he shall stand at the latter day upon the earth. And though after my skin worms destroy this body, yet in my flesh shall I see God; whom I shall see for myself, and mine eyes shall behold, and not another, though my reins be consumed within me. Job 19 : 25, 26, 27.

Although my house be not so with God, yet he hath made with me an everlasting covenant, ordered in all things and sure; for this is all my salvation, and all my desire. 2 Sam. 23 : 5.

Into thy hand I commit my spirit: thou hast redeemed me, O Lord God of truth. Psalm 31 : 5.

For this God is our God for ever and ever; he will be our guide even unto death. Psalm 48 : 14.

Thou shalt guide me with thy counsel, and afterwards receive me to glory. Whom have I in heaven but thee? and there is none upon earth that I desire besides thee. My flesh and my heart faileth; but God is the strength of my heart, and my portion for ever. Psalm 73 : 24–26.

The sacrifices of God are a broken spirit: a broken and a contrite heart, O God, thou wilt not despise. Psalm 51 : 17.

O that I had wings like a dove; for then would I fly away, and be at rest. I would hasten my escape from the windy storm and tempest. Psalm 55 : 6, 8.

Though ye have lain among the pots, yet shall ye be as the wings of a dove covered with silver, and her feathers with yellow gold. Psalm 68 : 13.

The blood of Jesus Christ his Son cleanseth us from all sin. 1 John, 1 : 7.

Having boldness to enter into the holiest by the blood of Jesus. Heb. 10 : 19.

He hath said, I will never leave thee, nor forsake thee. Jesus Christ—the same yesterday, and to-day, and for ever. Heb. 13 : 5, 8.

He retaineth not his anger for ever, because he delighteth in mercy. Micah 7 : 18.

Though he slay me, yet will I trust in him. Job 13 : 15.

In his name shall the Gentiles trust. Matt. 12 : 21.

Blessed are all they that put their trust in him. Psa. 2 : 12.

He knoweth our frame; he remembereth that we are dust. Psalm 103 : 14.

I loathe it; I would not live always. Job 7 : 16.

We know that if our earthly house of this tabernacle were dissolved, we have a building of God, a house not made with hands, eternal in the heavens. We are willing rather to be absent from the body, and to be present with the Lord. 2 Cor. 5 : 1, 8.

For to me to live is Christ, and to die is gain. Having a desire to depart and be with Christ, which is far better. Phil. 1 : 21, 23.

And now, Lord, what wait I for? my hope is in thee. Psalm 39 : 7.

My beloved is mine, and I am his. His left hand is under my head, and his right hand doth embrace me. Awake, O north wind, and come, thou south; blow upon my garden, that the spices thereof may flow out. Let my beloved come into his garden and eat his pleasant fruits. Until the day break, and the shadows flee away. Make haste, my beloved, and be thou like to a roe or to a young hart upon the mountains of spices. Cant. 2 : 6, 16, 17, and 4 : 16, and 8 : 14.

O death, where is thy sting? O grave, where is thy victory? But thanks be to God, which giveth us the victory, through our Lord Jesus Christ. 1 Cor. 15 : 55, 57.

The time of my departure is at hand. I have fought a good fight, I have finished my course, I have kept the faith: henceforth there is laid up for me a crown of righteousness, which the Lord, the righteous Judge, shall give me at that day; and not to me only, but unto all them also that love his appearing. 2 Tim. 4 : 6–8.

The day of death is better than the day of one's birth. Eccles. 7 : 1.

And God shall wipe away all tears from their eyes; and there shall be no more death, neither sorrow, nor crying, neither shall there be any more pain; for the former things are passed away. Rev. 21 : 4.

This is a faithful saying, and worthy of all acceptation, that Christ Jesus came into the world to save sinners; of whom I am chief. 1 Tim. 1 : 15.

God so loved the world, that he gave his only begotten Son, that whosoever believeth in him should not perish, but have everlasting life. John 3 : 16.

For he hath made him to be sin for us, who knew no sin, that we might be made the righteousness of God in him. 2 Cor. 5 : 21.

Thanks be unto God for his unspeakable gift. 2 Cor. 9 ; 15.

Blessed be the Lord God of Israel; for he hath visited and redeemed his people, and hath raised up a horn of salvation for us in the house of his servant David. Luke 1 : 68, 69.

Them which sleep in Jesus will God bring with him. Then shall we be caught up together with them in the clouds to meet the Lord in the air; and so shall we ever be with the Lord. 1 Thess. 4 : 14, 17.

Unto him that loved us, and washed us from our sins in his own blood, and hath made us kings and priests unto God and his Father; to him be glory and dominion for ever and ever. Worthy is the Lamb that was slain, to receive power and glory. Rev. 1 : 5, 6, and 5 : 12.

We know that we have passed from death unto life, because we love the brethren. 1 John, 3 : 14.

I am persuaded that neither death, nor life, nor angels, nor principalities, nor powers, nor things present, nor things to come, nor height, nor depth, nor any other creature, shall be able to separate us from the love of God which is in Christ Jesus our Lord. Rom. 8 : 38, 39.

I know whom I have believed, and am persuaded that he is able to keep that which I have committed unto him against that day. 2 Tim. 1 : 12.

I count all things but loss and dung that I may win Christ, and be found in him, not having mine own right-eousness, which is of the law, but that which is through the faith of Christ. Phil. 3 : 8, 9.

Christ Jesus, who of God is made unto us wisdom, and righteousness, and sanctification, and redemption. 1 Cor. 1 : 30.

We rejoice in Christ Jesus, and have no confidence in the flesh. Phil. 3 : 3.

Giving thanks unto the Father, which hath made us meet to be partakers of the inheritance of the saints in light. Col. 1 : 12.

Behold, he cometh with clouds; and every eye shall see him. Amen. Even so, come, Lord Jesus. Rev. 1 : 7, and 22 : 20.

DUNDEE, 5th June, 1741.

DYING EJACULATIONS,

WRITTEN BY THE AUTHOR A FEW DAYS BEFORE HE DIED, AND LEFT WITH HIS BIBLE LYING ON HIS PILLOW, MAY, 1750.

O let me sleep in Jesus!

I would not live always in this evil world, that has little in it tempting, and seems still to grow worse, and where the torrent of sin and backsliding seems to grow stronger.

I would desire to depart and be with Christ, which is far better than to be here. I am willing rather to be absent from the body, and present with the Lord. Whom have I in heaven but thee? and there is none upon earth I desire besides thee: for though my heart, strength, and flesh fail, yet the Lord will be the strength of my heart, and my portion for ever.

Now, Lord, what wait I for? my hope is in thee; I have waited for thy salvation, O Lord.

O for Simeon's frame of mind, to be saying, " Lord, now lettest thou thy servant depart in peace; for mine eyes have seen thy salvation."

When Christ says, " Surely I come quickly ;" may my soul answer, "Even so, come, Lord Jesus."

I am living on the righteousness of Christ, yea, dying in the Lord. Even so, come. I am detained here upon the shore, waiting for a fair wind to carry me over this Jordan. I have waited, and will wait for thy salvation, O Lord. The Lord is a rock, and his work is perfect; Lord, perfect what concerneth me.

O, that I could say with Paul, "I am now ready to be offered, and the time of my departure is at hand. I have fought a good fight, I have finished my course, I have kept the faith : henceforth there is laid up for me a crown of righteousness, which the Lord the righteous Judge shall give me at his coming."

I am vile and polluted. O, how shall I be cleansed ? But that is a comforting promise, " The blood of Jesus Christ his Son cleanseth us from all sin." And so is that, " Though ye have lain among the pots, yet shall ye be as doves whose wings are covered with silver, and their feathers with yellow gold."

I resolve to obey, to submit to the Lord's will, to die like Moses and Aaron, the one at mount Hor, the other at mount Abarim. They went up and died there, at the command of the Lord.

O, that when my flesh and strength fail, God may be the strength of my heart and my portion for ever! When now the keepers of the house do tremble, O that God may be the keeper! When the grinders cease, because they are few, O that God would feed my soul with manna, that will need none of these implements! When the daughters of music are brought low, O to be fitted for the heavenly music above! When the lookers-out at the windows are darkened, O that my soul may be enlightened to see Jesus my Redeemer!

Lord, help the unbelief and infidelity of my heart; and

help to more of the faith of a risen Jesus, and an ascended Redeemer. O let me believe and feel the sweetness of that word of Christ, "I ascend to my Father and your Father, and to my God and your God."

O how shall such an unholy creature as I, presume to enter into such a pure and holy place? But the apostle has taught us, we may have boldness to enter into the holiest of all by the blood of Jesus.

O that when the time of my last combat comes with my last enemy death, I may be helped above all to take the shield of faith, whereby I may be relieved from the sting of death, and may quench the fiery darts of the wicked one.

O that I may be helped to adore the sovereignty of God, kiss his rod, and humbly submit to it. Save me from both extremes; let me never despise the chastening of the Lord, nor faint when I am rebuked of him.

Now the prince of darkness will study to raise tempests of temptations to shipwreck the poor weather-beaten vessel of my soul, when it would enter into the harbor of rest above: may Christ come to be pilot; take thou the helm, and all shall be safe.

O for more faith; may my faith ripen to a full assurance, that I may go off the stage rejoicing, and that an abundant entrance may be ministered to me into the kingdom of our Lord and Saviour Jesus Christ.

O for more faith, that I may die like Simeon when he had Christ in his arms, saying, Now let thy servant depart in peace; mine eyes have seen thy salvation.

Lord, one smile of thy countenance would banish away all my doubts and fears, and make me sing in pain.

Is my Redeemer gone to prepare a place for me? why should I be slothful to follow his steps, when he is saying, Come up hither; come up, dwell here; come up, reign here; come up, sing here?

O Lord, deliver my soul from death, my eyes from tears, and my feet from falling. O save me from the horrible pit, draw me out of the miry clay, set my feet upon a rock, and establish my goings, and put a new song in my mouth.

O give me grace to strive by faith and prayer to enter in at the strait gate. Lord, thou hast bid me Knock, and it shall be opened ; ask, and ye shall receive ; seek, and ye shall find. Lord, I knock—open unto me; Lord, I would be in, I must be in ; let me but in over the threshold ; let me in within sight of my Redeemer's face, within sight of the smiles of his countenance ; let me within hearing of the songs of the redeemed; let me but get to the outside of that praising company ; I shall be well enough if I get in. Lord, in I must be ; out I cannot stay. O shut me not out with swearers, Sabbath-breakers, and other profane persons. Lord, I never chose their company while in this world; do not gather my soul with sinners hereafter.

The redeemed thou art gathering, and the wicked also : Lord, gather me with thy flock ; they are fast assembling; the church's Head is gone; he has left the earth, and entered into his glory ; my brethren and friends, many of them, have arrived where he is ; I am yet behind. O how great is the difference between my state and theirs. I am groaning out my complaint, they are singing God's praise. I am in darkness and cannot see thy face, but they behold thee face to face. O should I be satisfied to stay behind, when my friends are gone ? O help me to look after them with a steadfast eye, and cry, O Lord, how long ?

O heavenly Father, draw me after Jesus; for none can come to him without thine aid. O Father, draw me up there where he is, and I will mount up as on eagles' wings. O draw me; and when thou seemest to fly from me, Lord, enable me to follow hard after thee.

O thou who rememberedst the dying thief, when on the

way to thy kingdom, O remember me now thou art seated in thy kingdom, and say to my soul when I am dying, "This day shalt thou be with me in paradise."

Lord, I am called to the work I never did; O give me the strength I never had. O strengthen me like Samson for this once, when at death, to pull down the stronghold of sin in me. Lord, wash away my sins in the blood of Christ, and then my soul shall not sink in the ocean of thy wrath.

O what is my life but a vapor; a sand-glass of sixty or seventy years! O how fast does it run down! O vain love of life! O give me grace to overcome the love of life, and the fear of death. O for more patience and less fretting. If the damned had hope of being saved from hell after a thousand years of my pain, how willingly would they endure it! Blessed be God, my pains are no hell, their state is not mine.

Lord, draw near to me; my body is full of trouble, and my life draws near to the grave. But, Lord, thy loving-kindness is better than life. O make thy loving-kindness sure to me, and I will willingly part with this dying life.

O that I could make all the world see the beauty of my precious and adorable Saviour.

Nothing but an interest in Christ can give peace in life, or comfort in death. He is the chief among ten thousand, and altogether lovely. My body is in part dead, but I know I cannot die eternally while Jesus lives. I must go down to the grave; but what is the grave? it is but a refining pot. Since my Saviour lay in it, it is but a bed of roses. "He is the rose of Sharon, and the lily of the valley."

It was his free grace that drew me and made me willing in the day of his power; no desire, no merit in me; it was all free and undeserved.

O let the chastisement of my body be the medicine of my soul, to cure me of sin and bring me to sincere repentance for it; for Christ was wounded for our transgressions, he was bruised for our iniquities : the chastisement of our peace was upon him.

Lord, remember the chastisement of Christ for sin, and let my pains be the chastisement of a father, and not the wounds of an enemy. Let Christ's sufferings mitigate mine.

I rejoice in the prospect of that glorious inheritance reserved in safety. I could not comfortably enter eternity any other way but in and through this God-man Mediator : if he was not God as well as man, I could not be supported ; but he is God.

Oh, this precious Saviour, he is my all in all ; he is my all-sufficient good, my portion, and my choice ; in him my vast desires are fulfilled, and all my powers rejoice : I am travelling through a wilderness to a city of habitation, whose builder and maker is God.

Oh, delightful thought! that I, who was going on in sin, should be plucked as a brand out of the burning. Oh, how will they lie on a death-bed who have nothing but their own works to fly to? with only this to depend upon, I should be the most miserable of all creatures ; but the long white robe of my Redeemer's righteousness is all my desire. They are truly blessed, they alone are happy, who are enabled to exult in the garment of celestial glory which never waxeth old—in the illustrious robe of a Saviour's consummate righteousness, which is incorruptible and immortal. This is a robe which hides every sin, of thought, word, or deed, that I have committed. Oh, how unspeakably happy are they who are justified by this all-perfect righteousness of the Lord Jesus Christ, and who therein can constantly triumph and glory '

Lord, I live upon Christ, I live upon his righteousness, I live upon his blood and merits; yea, I die also leaning wholly upon this Rock and Corner-stone. It is not past experiences or manifestations I depend upon; it is Christ, a present all-sufficient Saviour, and perfect righteousness in him, I look to.   All my attainments are but loss and dung beside him.

When I find myself polluted, I go to this fountain for cleansing.   Lord, give me delight in approaching to thee, delight to be at a throne of grace.   O that I could make my bed there, lie, and die there.

The kingdom of heaven suffers violence, and the violent take it by force.   O for strength to offer a holy violence by faith and prayer.

Thus the author died as he lived, testifying the power of religion upon himself; and that at a time when men have most need of its comforts.

DYING WORDS OF THE AUTHOR

TO HIS WIFE AND CHILDREN, FOUND AMONG HIS PAPERS AFTER HIS DEATH, DATED NOV. 10, 1749.

TO MY WIFE.

MY DEAR—My distress calls me to think of parting with you; the will of the Lord be done.   I thank you for your tender care of me ; may the Lord bless and reward you for it, and sanctify your own tenderness, and support you under it.   As you have studied to live a life of faith and prayer all your days, so I hope and believe you will continue to the end. In all your difficulties and fears, encourage yourself in the Lord your God.   Commit your ways to him ; trust Him that is faithful and true.   I resign you, my dear, to the HUSBAND of husbands, our dearest Lord Jesus Christ.

TO MY CHILDREN.

DEAR CHILDREN—Your earthly father must leave you : your heavenly Father is immortal.   O, cleave fast to him. Trifle not about your souls' concerns in time of health ; mind these things as the one thing needful ; this you will not repent of when you come within a near view of death, and endless eternity. O press for clear views of your interest in Christ, the only Surety and Saviour of sinners. Among other evidences of it, live by faith on him, and study holiness in heart and life. Dear children, think how you will be able to stand before Christ your Judge at the last day, unless you have Christ's image on you, and be made new creatures. The Lord make you all such, and bless you with his best blessing. My blessing be upon you all. What means God gave me, I have bestowed them on you, or left them to you. Be kind and careful of your mother while you have her. And let none of you forget, that though I go before you to the dust, you must all quickly follow me. O that we may all meet together at the right hand of our Redeemer, to see his face, and sing his praise. The time is near, be ye therefore also ready.

Now, my dear wife and children, remember what is above, as the words of your affectionate husband, and loving father, who, being dead, yet hereby speaketh to you for your eternal good and happiness. May they sink into your heart. So prayeth

JOHN WILLISON.

THE

AFFLICTED MAN'S COMPANION.

INTRODUCTION.

MAN, when he first came from his Maker's hand, was holy and innocent, pure from sin, and consequently free from sickness and trouble, enjoying uninterrupted health and prosperity, both in body and soul. But no sooner was he tainted with sin, than he became liable to all sorts of miseries, temporal, spiritual, and eternal; his soul being the residence of sins and lusts, his body turned the receptacle of sickness and diseases. And seeing God's own children have the relics of sin and corruption in them, while in this world they are not to expect exemption from such afflictions; and the infinitely wise God sees meet to make use of bodily diseases to correct the corruptions, and try the graces of his people, and to promote both their spiritual and eternal advantage. Hence it is said of Lazarus, "Behold, he whom thou lovest is sick." John 11 : 3. He was beloved, and yet sick. It is no rare thing for the dearest of God's saints to be put to chatter like cranes and mourn like doves, by reason of sore sickness, as Hezekiah did. Isa. 38 : 14. Sanctified and healthy souls may be matched with weak and sickly bodies, as was Gaius. 3 John, 2. Still, the case is sometimes most trying, even to the best of God's people; and they are never more ready to question God's love, or quarrel with his providence, than under heavy sickness and bodily distress. It is therefore highly the concern of all, whether families or private persons, to inquire how they ought to behave under or after afflicting sickness; and how they shall provide for such an evil time before it comes And for the help of all that desire instruction in this matter, I have written the following directory, which, for method's sake, I shall divide into several chapters.

1. General directions to all families and persons visited with sickness and affliction.

2. Particular directions to those who are sharply afflicted with sore sickness and long trouble.

3. Directions to the children of God under sickness.

4. Directions to unregenerate persons under sickness.

5. Directions to the people of God when recovered from sickness.

6. Directions to unrenewed persons recovered from sickness.

7. Directions to those sick persons who are, apparently, in a dying condition.

8. Directions to the relations, acquaintances, and neighbors of the sick, who are themselves in health for the time.

N. B. Let it be remembered, that what I say to those visited with sickness, is likewise applicable to all other afflicted persons, whatever their distress be.

CHAPTER I.

GENERAL DIRECTIONS TO ALL FAMILIES AND PERSONS VISITED WITH SICKNESS.

DIRECTION 1. Diligently inquire into the ends and designs for which GOD usually sends sickness and afflictions upon men.

AN infinitely holy and gracious God hath various and wise ends in afflicting the children of men, whether they be converted or unconverted, which ought to be duly considered by all, and especially by those who are visited with sickness ; some of which I shall mention.

1. God visits with sickness, to cause careless sinners to bethink themselves concerning their soul's estate, who, perhaps, never had a serious thought about it before. There are many who, when in health and strength, are so intent upon the pleasures and profits of the world that they mind nothing else ; all the warnings, exhortations, and counsels of ministers, teachers, and friends, are lost upon them ; they cannot endure to entertain a thought of God, of the soul, of death, of heaven, of hell, or of judgment to come, till God doth cast them into some sickness or bodily distress ; and then sometimes they begin, with the prodigal, to come to themselves, and bethink themselves concerning their souls and a future life. Now, this is God's design: " If they bethink themselves in the land whither they are carried captives, and repent." 1 Kings, 8 : 47. By sickness, God gives a man that before was wholly diverted from the care of his soul by business, company, and pleasures, occasion to bethink himself. The man is now confined to his chamber, is deprived of his former company and diversions, and so gets time and leisure to commune with his own heart, and reflect on his former ways, and to hear what conscience speaks concerning a judgment-day, and a world to come, and his need of a Saviour. And so, by the

blessing of God upon such afflictions, not a few have begun their first acquaintance with God and Christ, and serious religion.   Nay, it is in the furnace that Christ has usually formed the most excellent vessels of honor and praise.   " I have chosen thee in the furnace of affliction." Isa. 48 : 10. Manasseh, the prodigal, Paul, and the jailer, were all chosen there.

2. God visits us with sickness, in order to instruct and teach us things we know not.   Psa. 90 : 12.   It was the saying of Luther, *Via crucis est via lucis*—The path of the cross is the path of light.   And indeed the school of afflic- tion is the place where many of Zion's scholars have made good proficiency in spiritual and experimental knowledge. Now, there are several remarkable lessons which God would teach us by the rod.

One is the knowledge of God.   It is said of Manasseh, "When he was in affliction, then Manasseh knew that the Lord was God."   2 Chron. 33 : 12, 13.   Though Manasseh was well educated, and early taught the knowledge of God, yet till now he knew not the Lord; but now he knew him in his power and greatness, his holiness and hatred of sin ; now he knew God in his goodness and mercy, and wondered that he had kept him so long out of hell.

Another lesson is the knowledge of ourselves.   In time of health and prosperity, we are apt to forget ourselves and our mortality ; but sickness causeth us to know that we are but men, and frail men, Psalm 9 : 20—that God hath an absolute sovereignty over us, and can as easily crush us as we do a moth.

He teacheth us the emptiness of the world.   How vain a help is that which fails a man in the time of his greatest need ; and ofttimes we see, that worldly means and friends can neither give the least ease to the bodies, nor comfort to the souls of persons under sickness and distress.

Another lesson is the great evil of sin, which is the cause

of all sickness and diseases whatsoever. "For this cause many are weak and sickly among you." 1 Cor. 11 : 30. Ah, what a root of bitterness must that be, which brings forth such bitter fruit!

He showeth us the preciousness and excellency of Christ and his promises, ·which alone can enable a Christian to rejoice in tribulation, and be calm under the greatest pains and diseases. There are many who are indifferent about Christ in time of health, who, when sickness comes, through the blessing of God do change their note, and cry, O for an interest in Christ above all things!

3. God sends such trials and distresses, in order to mortify and kill sin in us. " By this shall the iniquity of Jacob be purged, and this is all the fruit to take away his sin." Isa. 27 : 9. And indeed sickness and affliction have a tendency to weaken and subdue our prevailing sins and lusts. O man, is thy heart turned hard, so that thou art not sensible of thy own sins or of others' sufferings? God sees meet to try the fire of affliction, to see if it will melt thy frozen heart. Hast thou undervalued health, and slighted thy mercies? Now God removes them from thee, that by the want of them thou mayest know the worth of them. Art thou turned proud and self-conceited? God sends thee a thorn in the flesh to prick the swollen bladder of pride, that thou mayest not be puffed up above measure; God lays thee low upon thy bed, that thou mayest be lowly in thy heart. Doth love to the world prevail in thee? God sends affliction to discover its emptiness, and wean thee from it. Art thou fallen secure, dead, and formal? God sends affliction to awake thee, that thou mayest not sleep the sleep of death.

4. God sends sickness to awaken in us the spirit of prayer and supplication, and make us more earnest and importunate in our addresses to the throne of grace. There is a great difference between our prayers in health and in sickness, between our humiliations in prosperity and in adver-

sity.   In prosperity we pray heavily and drowsily ; but
adversity adds wings to our desires.   " Lord, in trouble have
they visited thee ; they poured out a prayer when thy
chastening was upon them."   Isa. 26 : 16.   Though they
were backward enough to prayer before, yet they pour it out
most freely now.   The very heathen mariners cried aloud
to God in a storm.   What a famous prayer did Manasseh
make when he was under his iron fetters.   We find it thrice
mentioned.   2 Chron. 33 : 13, 18, 19.   And the voice of
fervent prayer is what the Lord desires to hear.

5. Another end is, to loosen our hearts from the things
of this world, and cause us to look and long for heaven.
When we enjoy health and ease in this world, we are apt
to say with Peter on the mount, " It is good for us to be
here ;" but when distress cometh, God's people will turn
their tongue, and say with the Psalmist, " It is good for me
to draw near to God."   Psalm 73 : 28.   When things here
go well with us, we are apt to think ourselves at home ; but
when trouble ariseth, we begin to say, Arise, let us depart,
this is not our rest.   Though heaven was much out of sight
and out of mind before, yet, when afflicting sickness comes,
the poor believer will sigh, and say with David, " O that I
had wings, like a dove : for then would I fly away and be
at rest.   I would hasten my escape from the windy
tempest."   Psalm 55 : 6.

6. God designs to make the world bitter, and Christ
sweet to us.   By such afflictions, he lets men see that the
world is nothing but vanity and vexation of spirit—that
riches avail not in the day of wrath ; then it is that they
may see the insufficiency of the world to relieve them—that
as one saith, " A velvet slipper cannot cure the gout, a
golden cap cannot drive away the headache, nor a bed of
down give ease in a fever."   And as the world turns bitter,
so Christ grows sweet to the believer.   In time of ease and
health, Christ is often very much neglected and forgot.   As

the disciples, while the sea was calm, suffered Christ to sleep with them in the ship, thinking they might make their voyage well enough without his help ; but when they are ready to be drowned, then they see their need of Christ, they awake him, crying, "Master, save us, or we perish ;" so the best of saints, when all is easy about them, are prone to suffer Christ to sleep within them, and thus neglect the lively actings of faith on Christ ; but when the storm of affliction begins to rise, and they are ready to be overwhelmed with distress, then they cry, " None but Christ, none but Christ."

7. God visits with sickness and distress, in order both to prove and improve his people's graces. Deut. 8 : 2 ; Rev. 2 : 10. Grace is hereby both tried and strengthened.

Such afflictions do *prove* both the truth and strength of our graces, as they serve to try if we love God for himself—if we can endure and hold out in serving him, waiting and depending upon him, notwithstanding discouragements. That faith will suffice for a little affliction, that will not suffice for a great one. Peter had faith enough to come upon the sea at Christ's call ; but as soon as the waves began to swell, his faith began to fail and his feet to sink, till Christ mercifully caught hold of him, saying, "O thou of little faith, wherefore didst thou doubt ?" Matt. 14 : 31. Little did Peter think his faith was so weak till now.

They tend to *improve* our graces also, by quickening and strengthening them. They serve as a whetstone to sharpen faith, so that the soul is made to renounce earthly shelters, and to clasp about God in Christ, as its only refuge and portion. They excite to repentance and serious mourning for sin ; for, like the winter frost and snows, they make the fallow-ground of our heart more tender. They prompt us to heavenly-mindedness, self-denial, and patient waiting on God. Yea, the experience of God's people can attest it, that grace is never more lively than under affliction.

David never found himself better, as to his spiritual state, than when he was persecuted and hunted as a partridge on the mountains ; and hence he says, "It is good for me that I have been afflicted." Psa. 119 : 71.

8. God's aim is, to awaken us to redeem time, to prepare for flitting, and clear up our evidence for heaven.   In the time of health we are apt to trifle away time, to loiter on our journey, and forget that we are pilgrims on the earth; wherefore God sends sickness as his messenger, to remind us thereof.

Now it highly concerns us, when sickness attacks us, to consider and meditate upon these ends for which God brings on distress, and pray earnestly that they may be accomplished in us; and so our sickness shall not be unto death, spiritual or eternal, but to the glory of God and the good of our souls.

DIRECTION 2.   Let all who are visited with sickness or distress, search for the Achan in the camp, and inquire diligently what is the ground and cause of God's controversy with them.

It hath been the practice of God's people in scripture times, to inquire into the cause and meaning of God's rods which have been laid upon them.   So David, when the land of Israel was three years under the stroke of famine, inquired into the meaning of it.   2 Sam. 21 : 1.   So Job is exceedingly desirous to know why God set him up as a mark for his arrows.   Job 7 : 20.   And hence it is that he makes that petition which is most suitable for every man in distress, "Show me wherefore thou contendest with me."   Job 10 : 2.

I grant, indeed, that God sometimes visits his people with affliction, for the trial and exercise of their grace and for their spiritual instruction, more than for the correction of sin.   But sin being the origin and foundation of all affliction, it is safest, when it is our own case, and most acceptable to God, to look on sin as the procuring cause.   Or if our sins have not immediately procured the present affliction, yet the best of God's children must own that they have at least deserved it. We see the sin of the Corinthians is mentioned as the cause of their sickness: " For this cause many are weak and sickly among you." 1 Cor. 11 : 30. The Psalmist concludes the very same thing : " Fools, because of their transgression and their iniquities, are afflicted; their soul abhorreth all manner of meat, and they draw nigh unto the gates of death." Psa. 107 : 17, 18. But, ordinarily, by sickness the Lord points at some one sin in us more than another—some Jonah in the ship, that hath raised the storm, which the Lord would have us to search out and throw overboard without delay.

QUESTION. But how shall we discover the particular sin for which God afflicts us with sickness or distress ?

ANSWER. 1. Study the Lord's word, and the chastisements there recorded, which he hath inflicted upon people for their sins, and inquire if you be guilty of the like. Observe what hath been God's mind to his people, and what sin he hath pointed out to them when they have been brought under such a rod, and so you may learn his mind to you. " For whatsoever things were written aforetime, were written for our learning." Rom. 15 : 4.

2. Consider what is the sin of which conscience doth most of all accuse thee, in thy most serious and solitary hours. Conscience is God's deputy and thy bosom-monitor, whose voice, perhaps, thou hast little regarded in the day of thy health ; wherefore God hath sent a sharper messenger to second the voice of conscience. Hear now the voice of the rod, for it is the same with the voice of conscience. In the day of prosperity, carnal profits and pleasures made such a noise that the voice of conscience could not be heard ; wherefore God hath brought on thee the silent night of adversity, that his deputy may obtain an audience. Well, then, give ear—what saith conscience now ? May you not hear it saying, as Reuben to his brethren in distress

Spake I not to you in the day of health, do not commit such a sin, and do not delay repenting for such a sin; but you would not hear. O man, let conscience get a hearing at last, as it got with the patriarchs, when they were brought to distress in Egypt, and made to confess their sin in selling Joseph: "We are verily guilty concerning our brother, in that we saw the anguish of his soul when he besought us, and we would not hear; therefore is this distress come upon us." Gen. 42: 21.

3. Consider what are the evils that others have observed in you, whether they be friends or foes. Hearken to what a Christian friend noticeth in you, either when speaking to you, or to others about you. "Let the righteous smite me," saith David, "and it shall be a kindness." Yea, do not disregard what enemies say of you; as David got good by the malicious reproaches of Shimei, in the day of his affliction, so may you in the time of distress: for sometimes malice itself will speak truth. Enemies are sharp-sighted to spy out our faults, and so may, through the divine blessing, prove monitors to us, both with respect to sin and duty.

4. Consider the nature and circumstances of thy distress. Ofttimes the affliction is so suitable to the transgression, that we may clearly read our sin written on the forehead of our punishment, as in the case of Adonibezek and many others. Judges 1: 6, 7. And also you may be helped to find it out by the Lord's timing of the rod to you. Was it sent when you were under much formality in duty; or when you were eagerly pursuing the things of the world; or when you were under the power of some prevailing lust? then the rod comes to reprove you, and awake you to see the evil thereof.

5. Consider what is the sin that hath been formerly most affrighting to thy thoughts, and perplexing to thy conscience, when thou hast been in the immediate view of death and

judgment. It is very likely, if thou hast not truly repented of it, that is the sin which God now intends to awaken thee to see the evil of, that thou mayest sincerely mourn for and turn from it, looking to God in Christ for pardon and mercy.

OBJECTION. Ah, saith one, it is my lot to lie under a dumb and silent rod; I do not understand its language, I cannot hear its voice, I cannot find out the sin that is pointed at by it; what course shall I take?

ANSWER. 1. Be deeply humbled under this trial, and bewail thy case before the Lord; for it very much aggravates the affliction to God's people, when they know not the language of it. Hence was it that Job lamented so heavily that his way was hid, and he knew not the reason of God's contending with him. Job 3 : 23.

2. A believer's case may be sometimes so dark that it requires a great deal of spiritual wisdom to enable him to hear the voice of the rod, and understand its language. Hence it is said, "The man of wisdom shall see thy name" upon it. Micah 6 : 9. Now, this wisdom can only come from above; therefore,

3. Go to God, and earnestly beg for wisdom, that you may know his mind, and the meaning of the rod. Do as Rebecca did, when she went to inquire of the Lord, saying, "Why am I thus?" Gen. 25 : 22. Cry to God to give you his Spirit, to teach and enlighten you to see sin in its evil, and the particular evils you are guilty of. This was Job's course in his affliction: "Show me wherefore thou contendest with me. That which I see not, teach thou me. Make me to know my transgression, and my sin." There is no better way for a prisoner to know the reason of his confinement, than to ask the magistrate who committed him. God is a wise agent, and can give the best account of his own actions.

4. If thou canst not find out the particular sin for

which God afflicts thee, then labor to repent of every known sin, and cry for pardon of every unknown and forgotten sin also. Do that out of wisdom which Herod did out of malice, who, because he could not find out the babe Jesus, killed all the little ones of Bethlehem that he might be sure to kill Jesus among them. Let us seek the utter ruin and death of all our sins, that we may be sure to destroy that sin for which God afflicts us.

5. Study to exercise a strong faith, and a humble submission, while God keeps you under the silent rod. Believe firmly that God is just, though you know not for what he contends. And however long he thinks fit to make you walk in the dark, resolve humbly to wait on him and commit yourself to him, who has many times guided the blind in a way they knew not.

DIRECTION 3. When any fit of sickness attacks you, think seriously upon death, and make diligent preparation for it.

I do not mean that any man may delay the work of preparation for death till sickness cometh. No, no ; this should be the great and absorbing business of every man in the time of his health and strength. But sickness and diseases being the harbingers of death, and messengers sent from God to warn us of its coming, every man is thereby called to renew the work of preparation for death with all earnestness and application. God's voice by every fit of sickness is that in Deut. 32 : 29 : " O that they were wise, that they understood this, that they would consider their latter end." God knows our folly and readiness to forget this great work in the day of health ; and therefore, in his mercy, he sends sickness and affliction to teach us to to number our days that we may apply our hearts to this piece of heavenly wisdom, of making preparation for death. And here I shall present some motives to press this duty, and some advice for the doing of it aright.

1. For MOTIVES, consider these things :

(1.) Consider God's mercy and patience towards you, in giving you so many warnings, and so many years to prepare for death, and in sending his messengers and warnings so gently and gradually to excite you to this work, when many younger and stronger than you are hurried into eternity, and little or no time given them to think where they are going. Have you not been spared many years, in the midst of dangers, while you have seen that bold archer, death, shooting his arrows, and killing thousands of your neighbors and friends round about you ? Sometimes the arrow hath glanced over your head, and slain some great man, your superior ; sometimes it hath alighted at your feet, and cut off a child or a servant, your inferior ; sometimes it hath gone by on your left hand, and killed your enemy ; at other times it hath passed on your right hand, and killed your near relations. So that you have seen friends and foes, superiors and inferiors, relations and strangers, dropping down dead around you; and all this for a long time, to give you warning to prepare for death. O let the goodness and forbearance of God towards you lead you to repentance, and persuade you to flee speedily to Christ for refuge and protection from wrath.

(2.) Consider how terrible death will be if it meet you in an unprepared state, in a Christless and impenitent condition. What a fearful change will it bring upon you! A change from earth to hell, from hope to despair, from pleasure to pain, from comforts to terrors ; a change from the offers of grace to the revelation of wrath ; a change from probabilities to utter impossibilities of salvation. Death will cut off all your hopes and expectations of mercy for ever. Job 27 : 8. There is no coming back to amend what hath been done amiss here ; and there is no work nor device in the grave, whither you go. As the tree falls, so it will lie, through all eternity.

2. I come now to give some ADVICES, in order to the right preparation for death.

(1.) Set about self-examination work. Inquire whether you are in Christ or not—whether you are yet far off from God, or have been brought near by the blood of Jesus. And see that you be impartial in this search, and willing to find out the truth on this important question. Be not foolishly tender of yourself, and apt to believe that you are safe, when it is not so; for in this way, thousands do ruin themselves. But be earnest to know the worst of your case, and thoroughly to understand your soul's danger, that you may be moved to take the right way to escape it. Wherefore take a view of the marks of Christless and unconverted persons laid down in God's word, and judge yourself by them; and consider also the signs of true grace there recorded, and see whether they are applicable to you or not.

(2.) If, after inquiry, you find your state is bad—that you have been a lover of the world more than of God, have minded your body more than your soul, have lived in the neglect of precious Christ, and allowed yourself in known sin, O then be convinced of your inability to help yourself, and your need of Christ to help you. Labor to be deeply humbled before God, under a sense of your sin and folly. " Ah, how foolishly, how rebelliously, how unthankfully have I lived! I have abused God's mercies, and left undone the work for which I was made and preserved, and enjoyed the gospel. Oh, I had all my time given me, to make preparation for eternity, and I have never minded it till now that sickness, the harbinger of death, is come upon me; and now what shall I do to be saved?" Then, in order to convince and humble you the more, cast back your eyes upon the sins of your nature, and of your past life; view them in their nature, number, aggravations, and deservings. O, do not so many years' sins need a very deep humiliation?

O, do you not stand greatly in need of such a person as Christ, to be your Saviour and Ransomer from such a vast number of sins ? O, but their weight will press you eternally down to the lowest hell, if left to yourself with them upon your head.

(3.) O, sinner, art thou deeply humbled, and desirous of mercy upon any terms ? Believe then that thy case is not remediless, but that there is a sacrifice provided for your sins, and an able and all-sufficient Saviour offered to you. Believe that the Lord Jesus Christ is the Son of God, and became flesh to be a surety for you ; that he is both able and willing to save to the uttermost all that come unto God by him. Though your sins, your danger, and your fears were never so great, yet he is able and willing to save. O, flee to this refuge city, whose gates are open to receive you. Trust your souls upon Christ's sacrifice and meritorious blood for mercy and salvation. Apply humbly to him, that he may teach you the will of God, reconcile you to his Father, pardon your sins, renew you by his Spirit, and save you from eternal wrath.

(4.) Give yourself up to God in Christ, by way of cove· nant and solemn resignation. * * Give a cordial and vol· untary consent to the covenant of grace. Acquiesce cheerfully in the gospel way of salvation through Christ and his righteousness, and accept of God in Christ as thy portion. Make choice of God the Father, as thy reconciled Father in Christ; and God the Son, as thy Redeemer and Saviour ; and God the Holy Ghost, as thy sanctifier, guide, and comforter. And likewise give up thyself, soul and body, and all that thou hast, to be the Lord's; engaging, in Christ's strength, to live for God, and walk with him in newness of life. And study to do all this deliberately, unfeignedly, and cheerfully. Though perhaps you have done this hypocritically, at former times ; though you have profaned God's covenant, and behaved unsteadfastly and perfidiously therein, yet now endeavor to be sincere with God for once.

(5.) Live daily in the exercise of faith and repentance: renew the acts thereof frequently, in proportion to your renewed sins and guiltiness. Cleave close to glorious Christ, your high-priest and surety, and be ever washing in his blood. As long as you are in the world, you will have need to wash your feet. John 13 : 10. Come death when it will, let it find you at the fountain, always looking to and making use of Jesus Christ. You have great need of Christ every day of your life, more especially in sickness, but most of all at a dying hour. O what need will you have of Christ as an advocate with God, when the question is to be determined where your mansion is to be assigned through all eternity, whether in heaven or hell. O then, be looking always to Christ, with the eye of faith. Live in the constant thoughts of this blessed Mediator. Let him be first in your thoughts in the morning, and last in your thoughts at night.

(6.) Strive to mortify every sin and lust, both outward and inward. Die to sin daily, that so you may not die for sin eternally. O that sin may be daily losing its strength and dying in you, so that it may be certainly dead before you. Pray earnestly that your sins may die before you die; for if they die not before you, but outlive the dying body, they will live eternally to sting and torment the never-dying soul.

DIRECTION 4. Be not anxious for recovery to health, but leave the issue of your present sickness to the will and pleasure of the infinitely wise God.

Remember, O man, thou art the clay and God is the potter; he is absolute Lord of thy life and times: therefore learn to adore his sovereignty over thee and all thy enjoyments. David did so, when he said, "Lord, my times are in thy hand." Psalm 31 : 15. And indeed they are only best in his hand, for he best knows how to dispose of them. The prophet saith, " The Lord is a God of judgment; blessed are all they that wait for him." Isa. 30 : 18. Judgment there signifies wisdom. The Lord is a God of wisdom, and will order and time all things well ; and therefore it becomes us quietly to wait for his pleasure, saying, " The will of the Lord be done." It is taken notice of as a great sin in the Israelites, that they waited not for his counsel, but limited the Holy One of Israel. Psalm 78 : 41. What an unaccountable folly and presumption is it, for the worms of the earth to seek to stint and limit the Sovereign of heaven to their measures ! It becomes us at all times, but especially in sickness and affliction, to have low, submissive thoughts of ourselves, and high, exalted thoughts of God's sovereignty, such as Nebuchadnezzar had : "And all the inhabitants of the earth are reputed as nothing ; and he doeth according to his will in the army of heaven, and among the inhabitants of the earth : and none can stay his hand, or say unto him, What doest thou ?" Dan. 4 : 35. We should therefore refer all to his wise determination, and be willing to die or live, as he shall be pleased to appoint. I remember to have read of a godly woman who, in her sickness, being asked whether she was most desirous to die or to live; answered, " I have no choice in that matter, but refer myself to the will of God." "But," said the other, " suppose God should refer it to you whether to die or to live; which would you choose ?" " If God," replied she, " should refer it to me, I would even refer it back again to him." It becomes thee, O man, to be entirely resigned to the will of thy Maker, and to stand like a sentinel in thy station, ready to move as thy great General and Commander shall give order concerning thee. It would be pleasant and acceptable to God, to see thee more desirous to be delivered from sin, than from sickness. Sin is a far worse disease than any sickness in the world; beg importunately that the great Physician may cure this woful

soul-disease, and let him do with the body what he pleaseth.
This was David's practice in his affliction : "Look upon
my affliction and my pain, and forgive all my sins." Psa.
25 : 18. As for his pains and afflictions, he asks no more
but that God would look upon them, and do with them as
he thought fit; but as for his sins, no less will satisfy him
than a pardon, and blotting them entirely out, so that they
might be remembered no more.

DIRECTION 5. Bind yourself with holy purposes and resolutions, in Christ's strength, to be more watchful against sin,
more diligent in duty, and to improve the time of health better,
if God shall be pleased to restore it again to you.

When God is visiting your iniquities with rods, and
pleading a controversy with you for your omissions and
slackness in duty, he expects that you will return from
your backslidings, and set about a serious reformation and
change of life. "I will go, and return to my place, till they
acknowledge their offence, and seek my face : in their affliction they will seek me early." Hosea 5 : 15. See then
that you open your ear to discipline ; study to answer God's
call and expectation, and in his strength resolve to enter
upon a new life. "Surely now it is meet to be said unto
God, I have borne chastisement. I will not offend any
more. That which I see not, teach thou me; if I have
done iniquity, I will do so no more." Job 34 : 31, 32. Now
is the season you should say with Ephraim, "What have I
to do any more with idols ?" Hosea 14 : 8.

Having duly examined yourself, and searched out your
sins, you ought to put a bill of divorce into the hands of
every one. Deliberately resolve against all your sins, whether
secret or open ; and especially resolve against your darling
and beloved sins, the sins which do most easily beset you.
Resolve also against all temptations to sin, and particularly
against the snares of bad company, whereby you have been
formerly enticed; say now with David, "Depart from me,

ye evil-doers; for I will keep the commandments of my God." Psa. 119 : 115.

You must not only purpose to forsake all sin, but also to mind every known duty; that you will make religion your one thing needful, and the pleasing of God the chief business of your life; that you will set the Lord always before you, give him your heart in all duties, aim at nearness and communion with God in every one of them, and press forward to the full enjoyment of God in heaven through eternity.

Resolve also, through grace, that you will in a special manner mind secret duties, which the eyes of men do not observe, and those duties which conscience doth most challenge you for neglecting. And you that are heads of families, resolve to make more conscience of family religion, of worshipping God with your families, both morning and evening; instructing your children and servants in the knowledge of Christ; and recommending religion and godliness to all about you, whether relations or strangers.

And if you would have your resolutions effectual, see that they be accompanied with a deep sense of your insufficiency to perform them in your own strength. Bear always in mind the corruption and deceitfulness of your own heart, and make all your resolutions in humble dependence on the sufficiency of Jesus Christ your Surety. Observe the apostle Paul's advice to his son Timothy: "Be strong in the grace that is in Christ Jesus." 2 Tim. 2 : 1. All your stock, O believer, is in his hand, so that without him you can do nothing; but, through Christ strengthening you, you are able to do all things.

DIRECTION 6. Set your house in order, by making your will, and settling your domestic and secular affairs, while you have freedom and capacity for doing it.

After the heart is set in order, the next work is to set your house in order, according to God's counsel to Hezekiah, Isa

38 : 1. It is recorded of the patriarch Abraham, that he was careful to settle the affairs of his family before his death. Gen. 25 : 5, 6. He disposed of his estate to Isaac, and legacies to the sons of his concubines. It is too general a fault, that men delay and put off making their wills, as they do their repentance, to the very last, and so too frequently never make them at all. Consider the evil of deferring or neglecting this necessary affair ; for if you, upon whom God hath bestowed means, shall die intestate, your estate may descend otherwise than you intended; much of it may be spent in tedious and expensive lawsuits ; such differences may fall out among relations, who should live in friendship and mutual affection, as cannot be healed ; some of them may be reduced to extreme want, when a small legacy might have put them in the way of a living : and many such inconveniences may follow. Now, if your neglect should bring on these evils, and involve your posterity in endless strifes and contentions, may you not justly fear that the guilt thereof will pursue you into another world, whose wretched carelessness was the occasion of all that mischief?

Pray, what is the reason that men put off this duty ? Is it not because they do not incline to think so seriously on death, as this will occasion them to do ? Doth not this neglect savor of abominable earthly-mindedness, as if a man desired all his portion in this life, and cared not for a better ; and that he is so far from preparing for death, that he cannot endure to think of it ? Alas, that this worldly disposition should so far prevail among us. But surely there is no wise man will say that the putting off the thoughts of death will keep death at the greater distance ; or that preparing for death and making our wills will bring on death the sooner.

It were surely best to arrange our affairs in good time, yea, do it in time of health, rather than delay it unto a sick-bed, or a death-bed ; for either you may be snatched off suddenly, and have no time for it ; or you may be taken with such a disease as shall seize your tongue, so that you cannot express your mind; or seize your understanding, so that you cannot rationally dispose of your effects. And though none of these should happen, yet certainly it proves a great disturbance to a dying man, to be casting up, ordering, and settling the affairs of his family, when he should be securing a heavenly mansion for his soul and clearing up his evidences thereto. It is great wisdom to attend to this affair in time, that you may have as little to do with the world as may be, and that all occasions of distraction to your immortal soul may be prevented, when it is near to its entering into an eternal and unchangeable state.

Moreover, in settling your secular affairs, observe these following ADVICES:

1. Make your wills cheerfully, and freely lay down whatever you enjoy, when God calls you to it. Praise God that you had these things while you needed them; and when you have no longer use for them, leave them without repining to those that come after you. Look not back to Egypt, when you are upon the border of Canaan.

2. See that you deal justly, in providing for your family, paying all your just debts, and making restitution if you have wronged any. Abhor all designs of defrauding any of your lawful creditors, for if your last act should be unjust, you leave a blot upon your name here; and since you cannot repent of this wickedness, it being among your last deeds, you expose yourself to a fearful doom in the world whither you are going.

3. In settling your estate, see that God and good uses be not forgotten nor left out. When you are leaving the world, and can glorify God no longer here by your words or actions, see that you honor the Lord with your substance, by leaving some part thereof to pious and charitable uses. It is a work of charity to give for maintaining the bodies of the poor, and especially the poor of God's people, who belong to his family

But it is much more pious and charitable to leave somewhat for propagating Christian knowledge in dark places,
for educating poor children to read the Scriptures, and instructing ignorant souls in the knowledge of Jesus Christ.
It is much to be lamented that so many rich men
among us die, and leave but little to such pious uses.
The liberality of papists on their death-beds, may give a
sharp challenge to many professed Protestants. O what a
shame it is to the professors of the doctrine of grace, that
the false doctrines of merit and purgatory should produce so
many donations and mortifications among the papists, and
the faith of Christ's most glorious gospel should not do the
like among true believers! Shall the proud conceit of merit,
and the imaginary fear of purgatory, prompt men to do more
this way, than the certain persuasion of the love of God in
Christ, and the well-grounded hope of eternal life through
the alone merits of Jesus Christ? O what a reproach is
this to our holy religion!

4. It might be much to the glory of God and the good of
souls, that our wills should contain many solemn charges and
exhortations and blessings to our children, or those to whom
we bequeath any legacy; so that they could never open our
wills, but they might see something adapted to make impressions on their souls, for their spiritual edification, and for
quickening them to the diligent practice of both family and
personal godliness.

CHAPTER II.

PARTICULAR DIRECTIONS TO THOSE WHO ARE SHARPLY
AFFLICTED WITH SICKNESS, OR LONG TROUBLE.

DIRECTION 1. Justify God in the greatest afflictions which befall
you.

THOUGH God should condemn you, see that you acquit
him, and say he is righteous in all his dealings. When the
church was under the heaviest distress, she found cause to
justify God. "The Lord is righteous, for I have rebelled
against his commandment." Lam. 1 : 18. So doth godly
Nehemiah: "Howbeit thou art just in all that is brought
upon us; for thou hast done right, but we have done wickedly." Neh. 9 : 33. The same doth holy David acknowledge: "I know, O Lord, that thy judgments are right, and
that in faithfulness thou hast afflicted me." Psa. 119 : 75.
Now, in order to bring you to this agreeable frame, and to
convince you of the equity and justice of God in his dispensations, however heavy and long your distress be, I shall lay
before you the following considerations.

1. Consider the infinitely holy and righteous nature of
that God who smiteth thee. "Righteous art thou, O Lord,
and upright are thy judgments." Psa. 129 : 137. We presume it of a righteous man, that he will do righteous things;
and shall we not much more believe so of a holy and righteous
God? We cannot be infallibly certain that a righteous man
will always do so, because a righteous man may leave his
righteousness, for the creature is mutable: but God is immu-
tably righteous; so that we may be confident that the Judge
of all the earth will do right, for it is impossible he can do
otherwise. "The just Lord is in the midst thereof; he will
not do iniquity." Zeph. 3 : 5. He will not, he cannot; for
it is contrary to his nature.

2 Consider that God never brings on any affliction

without a cause. "For this cause many are sick." 1 Cor
11 : 30. He hath just ground for the heaviest affliction, from
thy sins and provocations, and may always say to thee, as to
Israel, "Hast thou not procured this unto thyself, in that thou
hast forsaken the Lord thy God, when he led thee by the
way? Thine own wickedness shall correct thee, and thy
backslidings shall reprove thee ; know therefore and see that
it is an evil thing and bitter, that thou hast forsaken the Lord."
Jer. 2 : 17, 19. There is still ground enough for affliction to
be found in the best of God's people ; and therefore it is said,
"He doth not afflict willingly, nor grieve the children of
men." Lam. 3 : 33. No, it is our sins that oblige him to it.
As Christ whipped the sellers of oxen and sheep out of the
temple, with a whip, as is generally thought, made of their
own cords ; so God never scourgeth us but with a whip made
of our own sins. "His own iniquities shall take the wicked
himself, and he shall be holden with the cords of his sins."
Prov. 5 : 22. If we consider the mighty God as a Lord dispensing grace, then we find he acts sovereignly, and according to his will and pleasure. "Even so, Father, for so it
seemed good in thy sight." Matt. 11 : 26. But if we consider him as a Judge dispensing judgments, he never doth
it without a previous cause on the creature's part. God's
treasure of mercy is always full, and ready to be let out to
them that seek it; but his treasure of wrath is empty till
men fill it by their sins. "Thou treasurest up unto thyself
wrath against the day of wrath." Rom. 2 : 5. We always
provide fuel for God's wrath before it kindles and breaks out
upon us.

3. Consider farther this instance of God's equity, that
when there is a cause given, God doth not instantly punish,
but continues to threaten oft and warn long, before he exe-
cutes the sentence of his word. He sends light strokes as
warnings of heavier, if we repent not; and he repeats hi
warnings many times, both by his word and providence,

before he smites. Yea, even when repeated warnings are slighted, he delays a long time, and waits to be gracious. Isa. 30 : 18. And when men's obstinacy and incorrigibleness arrive to such a height that he can spare no longer, yet how loath is he to give them up to severe judgments. "How shall I give thee up, Ephraim? How shall I deliver thee, Israel? How shall I make thee as Admah? How shall I set thee as Zeboim? Mine heart is turned within me, my repentings are kindled together." Hos. 11 : 8. When the Lord hath sinners in his hand, ready to give them up to severe judgments, yet he makes a stand and would fain be prevented before he proceed to his "strange work;" for so he calls his acts of judgment. Isa. 28 : 21. Acts of mercy are conatural, most agreeable, and pleasant to God. "He delighteth in mercy," Micah 7 : 18; but judgment is his strange act, and his strange work.

4. Consider, that when at last he sends strokes on us, they are always short of the cause; he exacts not the debt that sinners owe to his justice, as Ezra doth acknowledge: "Thou hast punished us less than our iniquities deserve." Ezra 9 : 13. The stroke he there is speaking of, was a most heavy judgment: fearful ruin and desolation came upon Jerusalem and the whole land of Judah; the city and temple were burnt to ashes, the people carried captive to a strange land and treated as bondslaves among the heathen; yet the holy man saith, " Thou hast punished us less than our iniquities deserve." As if he had said, "It is true we have been carried to Babylon, but in justice we might have been sent to hell; our houses were burnt, but our bodies might have been burnt too; we have been drinking water, but we might have been drinking blood; we have had grievous burdens on earth, but we might have been groaning in hell; we were banished from the temple, but we might have been eternally banished from God's presence." We think it a great favor among men when any punishment is mitigated, when the sentence

of death is changed into banishment, or when banishment is
turned into a fine, or a great fine is made smaller; and will
you think that God deals severely or rigorously with you in
laying you on a sick bed, when he might justly have laid you
in hell and poured out all his wrath upon you there? You
but taste of the brim of the cup, when God might cause you
to drink of the very dregs thereof.

Have you not cause then to acknowledge God's justice,
nay, even his mercy too, in his dealings with you, however
rough they seem to be? May you not with good reason say,
Any thing less than hell is a mercy to such an ill-deserving
creature as I am? If even a hard-hearted Pharaoh, under
distress, went so far as to own the justice of God, "I have
sinned, the Lord is righteous," Exod. 9 : 27 ; shall any professed Christian fall short of that obstinate Egyptian?

DIRECTION 2. Labor to be sensible of God's hand under heavy
affliction, and beware of stupidity and unconcern under it.

It is a sin to faint under heavy affliction, but it is a duty
to feel it. "My son, despise not thou the chastening of the
Lord, nor faint when thou art rebuked of him." Heb. 12 : 5.
The apostle there cautions us against two extremes, which
every Christian under the rod should be careful to avoid :
these are, despising or making light of affliction, and sinking
or desponding under it. We are in great hazard of running
unto the one or the other. We may be said to despise the
chastening of the Lord when we do not observe God's hand
in our affliction, so as to abandon the things whereby he is
displeased ; or when we resolve to abide the trial by the
strength of our own resolution and stout-heartedness, without
looking to God for supporting grace; or when we turn stupid
and insensible under the heavy and long-continued rod. This
despising and slighting of the rod is not patience, but stupidity ; it is not Christian magnanimity, but a stoical temper of
mind, most sinful and provoking to God. We see how angry
God is with sinners when his strokes are not felt. " He hath

poured upon him the fury of his anger, and it hath set him on fire round about, yet he knew it not; and it hath burned him, yet he laid it not to heart." Isa. 42 : 25. "Thou hast stricken them, but they have not grieved; thou hast consumed them, but they have refused to receive correction : they have made their faces harder than a rock; they have refused to return." Jer. 5 : 3. There is little hope of a scholar's minding his lesson, that is regardless of whipping. It is a dreadful sign to be like Pharaoh, sleeping in our sins when God is thundering in his wrath. He that will sleep when his house is on fire, or lie still in bed, as if he was not concerned, may assuredly expect to be consumed in its flames. As David could not bear it, when the messengers he sent to the Ammonites out of good will, were affronted and despised; neither will God endure it, when the messengers he sends to sinners are slighted ; for he that slights a messenger, affronts his master. Those who make light of affliction, make light of God who sends it, and of sin that procures it.

Men are suitably concerned under a heavy rod, when they see God's hand, hear God's voice, are anxious to know his mind, desirous to do those things he requires, and forsake those things he is displeased with. Remember, every affliction is a messenger from God, and deserves a hearing from you. It comes to thee with such a message as Ehud did to Eglon: "I have a message from God unto thee, O king." Judges 3 : 20. I have a message from God to thee, O Christian, O sinner. Well, lend an ear, and hearken with reverence and attention to this errand : say, "Speak, Lord, for thy servant heareth ; what wouldst thou have me do?" Believe it that God speaks as really to you by his rod, as by his word; therefore he says, "Hear ye the rod." God spake as truly by his ten plagues to Egypt, as he did by his ten precepts to Israel. And if the calm voice of the word were more regarded, we should hear less of the rough voice of the rod. As Gideon took briers and thorns of the wilderness, and with them taught the men of Succoth, who would not be taught by fairer means, Judges 8 : 16 ; so God takes the sharp prickles of sore afflictions to teach you his statutes, when you will not be taught by softer methods.   Beware then of grieving God's Spirit, by turning stupid and insensible under sharp or long-continued trials ; but the more pains God takes with you by his rod, hearken the more carefully to his voice, and labor to make the greater proficiency in the school of affliction, where he thinks fit to continue you, that so you may inherit this blessing : " Blessed is the man whom thou chastenest, O Lord, and teachest him out of thy law." Psa. 94 : 12.

DIRECTION 3.   Beware of misconstruing God's dealings towards you, and of charging him foolishly.

We are apt to believe Satan's suggestions under heavy trials, and to entertain wrong thoughts of God and his dispensations.   Now these you ought to guard against.   For instance,

1. Beware of harboring atheistical thoughts, as if there were no Providence, no wise Governor of this lower world, no distinction between the good and the bad ; and that it is to no purpose to be religious, like those mentioned in Mal. 3 : 14 : " Ye have said, It is vain to serve God ; and what profit is it that we have kept his ordinances, and walked mournfully before the Lord of hosts ?"   Yea, even the psalmist, when he begins to compare his own sharp trials with the ease and prosperity of the wicked, is tempted to think all religion in vain, and say, " Verily I have cleansed my heart in vain, and washed my hands in innocency.   For all the day long have I been plagued, and chastened every morning."   Psa. 73 : 13, 14.   But these are nothing but the hellish suggestions of Satan, that irreconcilable enemy of God and precious souls, against which we should closely stop our ears.

2. Beware of charging God in your hearts with rigor or

injustice in his dealings, like those reproved in Ezek. 18 : 25: "Yet ye say, The way of the Lord is not equal." How highly unjust and injurious are such thoughts to him who is the Judge of all the earth, and cannot but do right!

3. Beware of thinking that heavy afflictions always speak wrath in God against thee. No; sometimes they speak forth love, and God may be carrying on a love-design thereby to thy soul, namely, to subdue thy strong lusts, and draw thee nearer unto himself. As for those who think that the smarting rod and divine love cannot dwell together, let them read that passage, "And ye have forgotten the exhortation that speaketh unto you as unto children, My son, despise not thou the chastening of the Lord, nor faint when thou art rebuked of him. For whom the Lord loveth he chasteneth, and scourgeth every son whom he receiveth." Heb. 12 : 5, 6.

4. Beware of desponding and distrustful thoughts of God, under sharp afflictions. Some are ready to raze the foundation, quit their interest in God and the promises, and cast away their hope and confidence, saying with Gideon, "Oh, my Lord, if the Lord be with us, why then has all this evil befallen us?" Judges 6 : 13. So David was ready to draw a hasty conclusion: "I said in my haste, I am cut off from before thine eyes." Psalm 31 : 22. But this was the effect of unbelief; for he that believeth will not make haste.

DIRECTION 4. Under sore trouble and distress, labor to exercise a strong and lively faith.

It was a noble and heroic resolution in that holy man Job, under his singular trials, "Though he slay me, yet I will trust in him." Job 13 : 15. Let his strokes be never so sore and heavy, yet I will not let go my hold of his word and promises; I will not raze these foundations of my hope. It was in this way the psalmist kept himself from sinking under his heavy burdens: "I had fainted unless I had believed to see the goodness of the Lord in the land of the living." Psa. 27 : 13. Consider but a little the noble influence that faith hath to strengthen and support the soul under sore trials:

1. Faith grasps the great gospel promise of salvation in and through Jesus Christ, and so secures the soul's main interest through eternity; which may make the soul happy in every lot.

2. Faith views God in Christ at the helm in the greatest storm, and so the believer endures "as seeing Him who is invisible." Heb. 11 : 27.

3. Faith casts the soul's anchor on the Rock of ages, and stays itself on God and the faithful promises, whereby the soul is eased and disburdened of its fears and melancholy · apprehensions. Psa. 22 : 4; Isa. 50 : 10.

4. Faith brings new strength and auxiliary supplies of grace from heaven, when the former supply is exhausted and spent; whereof David had the sweet experience. Psa. 27 : 13 As God doth plant and actuate grace in the soul, so he is pleased to come in with seasonable supplies and reinforcements to the weak and decayed graces of his people, according to their present exigencies; and thus he doth from time to time feed the believer's lamp with fresh oil, bestowing more faith, more love, more hope, and more desire; and hereby he gives more power to the faint, and strengthens the things which remain, when ready to die.

5. Faith keeps the soul from sinking under heavy trials, by bringing in former experiences of the power, mercy, and faithfulness of God to the afflicted soul; hereby was the psalmist supported in distress. Psa. 13 : 6; 87 : 4. O, saith faith, remember what God hath done both for thy outward and inward man; he hath not only delivered thy body when in trouble, but he hath done great things for thy soul: he hath brought thee out of the state of black nature, entered into a covenant-relation with thee, and made his goodness

pass before thee; he hath helped thee to pray, and many times hath he heard thy prayers and thy tears. Hath he not formerly brought thee out of the horrible pit and out of the miry clay, and put a new song in thy mouth, and made thee resolve never to give way to such unbelieving doubts and fears again? And how unbecoming it is for thee now to sink in trouble.

6. Faith supports the soul, by giving it a pleasant view and prospect of a happy release from all trouble, when it shall be admitted to see and dwell with Christ hereafter. Thus was Job supported in his greatest distress. "For I know that my Redeemer liveth, and that he shall stand in the latter day upon the earth: whom I shall see for myself, and mine eyes shall behold." Job 19 : 25, 27. A believing view of the soul's meeting with its Redeemer, and receiving a crown of glory from him at last, is an excellent support to a Christian under the heaviest affliction; and so was it to Paul. 2 Tim. 4 : 7, 8.

7. Faith gives great support, by the encouraging representations it makes of Christ, and of his present concern for the believer while under affliction. For example,

Faith represents Christ to a believer under trials, as sympathizing with him under his distress, feeling his pain, hearing his groans, bearing his burdens, and ready to relieve him in his own appointed time, which it well becometh him to wait for.

Faith represents Christ as putting his almighty arm under the believer's head, and conveying invisible strength to support and hold him up under his greatest burdens.

Faith represents Christ as pleading the afflicted believer's cause with God, and answering all the charges of the law, the challenges of conscience, and accusations of Satan against him.

Faith represents Christ as standing by the furnace, as a refiner where his gold is melting, carefully overseeing the trials of his people, that they may work for their good, and ready to bring them out thereof, when they are sufficiently purified from their dross.

Faith represents Christ as smiling on his people under the cross, whispering peace into their ears, and saying, "Well done, good and faithful servant."

DIRECTION 5.   Labor to bear with patience whatever load of trouble the Lord appoints for you.

You will perhaps observe some who are strangers to religion, contentedly enduring very painful evils; and this they may do by virtue of a natural hardness and resolution which some are endowed with, or by the aid of arguments furnished by human prudence. This is only patience as a moral virtue, which some attain to. But it is patience as a spiritual grace, or a fruit of the Spirit, which we must aim at under our trials, that we may bear them contentedly from divine principles, to divine ends. Now this grace of patience we must earnestly beg from God, under heavy afflictions, for it is only he that must work it in us; and therefore he is called the God of patience. Rom. 15 : 5. And in order to your attaining of this grace, I shall lay before you the following considerations, which may be useful, through the Lord's blessing, for that end.

1. Consider the patience of our Lord Jesus Christ under sufferings inexpressibly greater than yours. When it pleased the Lord to bruise him and to put him to grief, how patiently did he bear all, according to that remarkable word, "He was oppressed, and he was afflicted, yet he opened not his mouth; he is brought as a lamb to the slaughter, and as a sheep before her shearers is dumb, so he opened not his mouth." Isa. 53 : 7. Now Christ suffered as an example of patience, though it was not his chief end; and surely all the members of the body should study to imitate the head in patience. Did your blessed Saviour patiently endure such agonies and

burdens of wrath for you; and will you decline to undergo some short pains or sickness in obedience to his command?

2. Consider God's sovereignty over you. He is the great Potter, and you are his clay; and why may he not do with you as he pleaseth? If your children offend you, you punish them, and perhaps do it sometimes without reason; yet how ill do you take it when they refuse to submit. How will you drive and spur your horses under you, and sometimes perhaps unreasonably. Yet they bear all quietly, and make no resistance. Shall they take blows from their master, and will not you from your Maker, that has far more power over you? If any challenge you for cruelty to your children or beasts, you take it not well, because you think you may do what you will with your own and no man hath a right to quarrel with you. But hath not God a greater property in you, than you in your children or cattle? And will you not patiently submit to your wise and absolute Sovereign?

3. Consider thy sins as the just cause of all thy afflictions, however heavy they be. If thou hast right thoughts of thy sins, and their aggravations, thy mind may be composed to a patient submission to God's hand; if sin be heavy on thee, all thy afflictions will be light. Luther gives this as a reason why he slighted the rage of the pope and emperor, and all his outward troubles: "They are all little to me, because sin is so weighty on me." Hence it was that Paul complained not at all of his sufferings, great as they were, but he cried out much of his sins: "O wretched man that I am, who shall deliver me from the body of this death?" Rom. 7 : 24. The sense of sin doth swallow up the sense of affliction, as the ocean doth little brooks. For with whom shouldst thou quarrel but thyself, when thou bringest troubles on thyself? This consideration should bring thee to resolve and say with the prophet, "I will bear the indignation of the Lord, because I have sinned against him." Micah 7 : 9.

4. Consider, that however sharp the pains are you are called to bear, yet they fall infinitely short of what you have justly deserved at God's hands. It is of his infinite mercy that death and everlasting destruction have not been your portion long since, and that you are not now wailing under the extremity of his indignation in the bottomless pit, together with the devil and his angels. And consequently, whatever falls short of this is truly a great mercy, and is so far from being a ground of quarrelling, that the greatest sufferer on this side of hell hath just cause to admire God's clemency, in dealing more favorably with him than he hath deserved.

5. Compare thy case with others that have been, or now are in distress. Do not say there is no one so hardly dealt with as thou art, for thou knowest not the affliction of others. Consider duly the trials of that eminent saint Job, in all the circumstances thereof, and see if you can say that your sorrow is near so great as his was. Again, compare your case with that of the damned in hell, who lie in endless and ceaseless flames, so that they have no rest day nor night, but the smoke of their torment ascends for ever; and think what a blessing it is that you are yet in a state of salvation, and not delivered over to these everlasting burnings, which were the due deserts of your sins, and to which you would long ago have been justly condemned, had it not been for the patience and long-suffering of Almighty God, who waiteth to be gracious to guilty sinners. When you consider these things, instead of being dissatisfied with the divine dispensations, you have cause to bless God that matters are not worse with you, and that you are kept out of hell to this day, where thousands, no more guilty than you, are even now groaning in endless desperation.

Unto these considerations I shall subjoin some few helps or advices, in order to the attaining of patience under sore troubles.

6. Labor to get pardon of sin and peace with God secured to thy soul, and this will enable you to bear the heaviest cross with patience. Hence it was that Luther cried, "Smite, Lord, as thou wilt; I take it all in good part, seeing my sins are pardoned. Oh, pardon of sin is the crowning blessing, therefore will I bear any thing; I will swallow up quarrelling into admiring; I will welcome the pruning-knife, seeing there is no fear of the bloody axe to fell me down."

7. Labor to see God's hand in thy affliction. Do not, like the dog, snarl at the stone, but look up to the hand that throws it. And surely a view of the hand of a holy God may serve to calm all the boisterous waves of thy corruption; so did it with David: "I was dumb, I opened not my mouth, because thou didst it." Psa. 39 : 9. When he looked to the instruments and second causes of his afflictions, his heart waxed hot, and the fire of his inward passion began to burn and break out; but when he once espied God's hand and seal to the warrant for his correction, he became silent, and patiently submitted to the divine will.

8. Get a humble and self-denied frame of spirit, that you may have low thoughts of yourself, and of all your attainments whatsoever. A proud man cannot think of submitting to the divine will, but will break before he bow. Hence we see a vast difference between a proud Pharaoh and an humble Eli, under the rod : the one says, "Who is the Lord, that I should obey him?" but the other saith, "It is the Lord; let him do what seemeth him good."

9. Get love to Jesus Christ. Love is an enduring principle. 1 Cor. 13:7. It endureth all things. It makes the soul, like the kindly child, draw nearer to Christ, the more it is beaten. Interpret God's ways and dealings with you always in the best sense; and be earnest in prayer that God may conquer your rebellious will, and subdue those mutinous risings of heart within you against himself.

DIRECTION 6.   Beware of envying wicked men, when you see
        them in health and prosperity.

The psalmist, when he was chastened every morning, and
in great adversity, fell into this error.   "I was envious at the
foolish, when I saw the prosperity of the wicked." Psa. 73:3.
Corrupt nature doth strongly incline us to this sinful disposition, especially in the day of sore affliction; for "the spirit
that dwelleth in us lusteth to envy." James 4:5.   But, did
we rightly consider the state of wicked men, we would see
greater ground to pity than to envy them in their most pros·
perous condition.   Why?   "The prosperity of fools shall destroy them."   Prov. 1:32.   It makes them forget God, and
turn hardened and secure in sin, which hastens their ruin.
Who would envy a malefactor's going up a high ladder, and
being mounted above the rest of the people, when it is only
for a little, and in order to his being turned over and hanged?
This is just the case of wicked men who are mounted up
high in prosperity; for it is so only that they may be cast
down deeper into destruction.   "Fret not thyself because of
evil-doers, neither be thou envious against the workers of
iniquity; for they shall soon be cut down like grass." Psa.
37:1, 2.   "When the wicked spring as the grass, and when
all the workers of iniquity do flourish, it is that they shall be
destroyed for ever." Psa. 92:7.   It would be a brutish thing
to envy an ox his rich pasture, when he is only thereby fitted
for the day of slaughter.   Who would have envied the beasts
of old the garland and ribbons with which the heathen adorn-
ed them when they went to be sacrificed?   These external
ornaments of health, wealth, pleasures, and preferments, with
which wicked men are endowed, cannot make their state
happy, nor change their natures to the better.   Whatever
appearance these things make in the eyes of the world, they
are but like a noisome dunghill covered with scarlet, as vile
and loathsome in God's sight as ever.   How quickly is the
beauty of earthly things blasted!   "The triumphing of the

wicked is short." Job 20 : 5. "They live in pleasure on the earth," for a while; but God sets them in slippery places, from whence they soon slide into perpetual pain and anguish. They have a short time of mirth, but they shall have an eternity of mourning. The longer their prosperity is, their sins are the greater, and their sufferings will be more grievous. But, O believer, it is in mercy to thee that God doth hedge up thy way with thorns, that thou mayest not find thy paths; while he turns the wicked loose, and suffers them to stray and wander whither they will, to their eternal ruin. God takes this method with you, to make you meet for an inheritance, and prepare you for a crown of glory; but he takes a contrary way with the wicked, to fit them for destruction : therefore you ought not to be fretful under his hand, but thankful. We read of queen Elizabeth, when she was in prison, how she envied the poor milk-maid she saw passing by, and would have thought herself happy to have been in her condition ; but had that afflicted princess known the glorious reign of forty-four years she was soon to enter upon, she would not have repined at the happiness of so mean a person. But O, afflicted believer, it is not a glorious reign for a set number of years, that is provided for thee; it is even a reign with glorious Christ thy Redeemer for ever and ever: and hast thou any ground to be discontented or envious?

DIRECTION 7. Guard against repining and murmuring against the providence of God, under heavy sickness and affliction.

We see that murmurers and complainers are classed with those that walk after their own lusts. Jude 16. I know the people of God are liable to murmuring and impatience also under affliction; but there is a great difference between them and the wicked. I shall have occasion to speak of believers' murmurings afterwards, when I come to speak of their case in particular; but here I shall handle the sin of murmuring in general, and as it appears mainly in the unregenerate, under heavy affliction.

This sin of murmuring is the froth of impatience, and scum of discontent; it is first cherished by repining thoughts, and then vented by unsuitable complaints and expostulations, taxing the administration of providence, as if God dealt too hardly with us. Our very thoughts are audible with God, yea, as loud in his ears as words are in ours; but it is yet worse when repining thoughts are not crushed, but suffered to break out into words tending to the dishonor of God.

Observe here that humble complaints are not murmurings, nor sinful in themselves; otherwise there would be no room for prayer, and for spreading out our distressed case before the Lord. We find God's children making complaints in affliction, but then they do not complain of God, but to God, with an humble inquiry into the cause and meaning of his dispensations, and laying all the blame upon themselves, as did Job. "I will leave my complaint upon myself; I will speak in the bitterness of my soul. I will say unto God, Do not condemn me; show me wherefore thou contendest with me." Job 10 : 1, 2. Thus the blessed Son of God himself did in his distress, when he cried, "My God, my God, why hast thou forsaken me?" But there we may observe, he complains to God, not of God; he hath not a hard word or thought of God, but expresseth a holy confidence in God: "My God, my God;" he hath two words of faith for one word of fear; he humbly inquires into the cause of the dispensation, and desires to bring up his will to God, not that God should bring down his will to him. "If it be possible," says he, "let this cup pass;" however, glorify thy name, provide for thy own glory, and do with me what thou pleasest. In this matter our Lord doth set himself as an example of patience to us, teaching us to beware of impatient murmuring and quarrelling with God's providence in our afflictions, which many times we are guilty of, either when we harbor harsh thoughts of God's dealings, or break forth into rash and unadvised speeches; when we charge God foolishly, and complain either of too much severity, Ezek. 18:2, 25, or of too long delay, Isa. 49:14, or when our complaints are mixed with unbelief and distrust, Psa. 78:19, or when we complain more of our punishment than we do of our sin, and nothing will satisfy us but deliverance from trouble.

Now, to deter you from these murmurings and complaints in trouble, I shall lay before you the following CONSIDERATIONS:

1. They who deserve worst commonly complain and murmur most, and are most ready to think they are hardly dealt with. The unthankful Israelites were always murmuring; ambitious Absalom was discontented; bloody Haman, in the midst of all his greatness, cries out, "What doth all this avail me?" But humble Jacob saith he is not worthy of the least of all the mercies and truth which God had showed him. And holy Job blesses God and patiently submits, when he took from him as well as when he gave him.

2. Murmuring is a sin that God takes special notice of, and looks upon as an injury and affront done immediately against himself. "I have heard the murmurings of the children of Israel, which they murmur against me." Num. 14:27. He that gives ear to the "groanings" of his own Spirit, doth also hear the grumblings of thine, and will reckon with thee for them.

3. It cannot benefit or relieve us in distress. I may say of sinful complaining, as Christ did of sinful care, Which of you by complaining can add one cubit to his stature? What ease or relief can you get by contending with God? Nay, instead of easing you of your burden, it will make it the heavier; as the more a child struggles with his parents, the more he is beaten. The Israelites were once within eleven days' journey of Canaan; but by their murmurings

they provoked God to lead them forty years' march in the wilderness before they could reach it.

4. Whatever be your distress, there is no just ground for complaints while thou hast thy life for a prey.   Remember that word of the afflicted church, "Wherefore doth a living man complain, a man for the punishment of his sins?" Lam. 3 : 39.   A man living, a man upon the earth, a man out of hell, has no cause to complain, whatever be his afflic tion.   For, let him compare his sin and punishment together he will find there is no proportion ; sin is a transgression against the infinite God, punishment is but an affliction upon the finite creature ; sin strikes at the very being of God, but temporal punishment only at the comfort of the creature. So that whatever your punishment be, you have more cause to give thanks than to complain, and to say with Ezra, "Thou hast punished us less than our iniquities deserve." It would have been a thousand times worse if strict justice had been the rule.   "It is of the Lord's mercies we are not consumed."

5. When you murmur under sickness, you quarrel with the messenger of that sovereign God who gave you your life and can take it again when he thinks fit ; and we know messengers ought not to be maltreated or abused, whatever be their commission, and far less when they are sent upon a good design.   Now, if you consider the design of this messenger and his errand to you, instead of fretting and quarreling at his coming, you ought rather to bless God that sends such a suitable harbinger and forerunner to tell you that death is approaching, and that he vouchsafes to take so much pains with you to wean you from the world and make you willing to be gone by long-continued trouble, when he might have seized you in a violent manner and driven you away by main force, without using any means to obtain your consent.   Have not many, who at the beginning of a sickness were most unwilling to die, been brought by the in-

crease and continuance of it to be well satisfied to leave the world and long to be with Christ? And was not this for their advantage?

6. Consider the great evil and sinfulness of impatient murmurings, complaints, and quarrellings under affliction.

Murmuring hath in it much *unbelief* and distrust of God. "They believed not his word, but murmured in their tents." Psalm 106 : 24, 25. They could not believe that the wilderness was the way to Canaan, that God would provide and furnish a table for them there, and relieve them in all their straits. So it is with us in trouble : we quarrel with God's providence because we do not believe his promises ; we do not believe that this can be consistent with love, or can work for good in the end.

It hath in it *unthankfulness.* While we complain of one affliction, we overlook a thousand mercies. The Israelites murmured so for what they had not, that they unthankfully forgot all they had ; whereas a thankful person is so far from fretting that God doth not give him every thing, that he wonders that God should give him any thing. "I am less than the least of all thy mercies," said Jacob. "We are perplexed," said Paul, "but not in despair :" we have God to go to, which is matter of praise. But the murmurer unthankfully overlooks all his present, and forgets all his former mercies, and gives not God thanks for any thing. Because God removes his comforts, his health and strength and ease for a time, all the years he formerly enjoyed them, though most undeservedly, are quite buried in oblivion.

It implies much *pride* and *self-conceit.* He that complains of God's dealings, secretly applauds his own deservings. Only by pride comes contention. When men have a conceit of themselves, they pick quarrels with God's providence, being apt to think they deserve better treatment at his hands : whereas the humble soul is sensible he deserves nothing but wrath, and therefore lays his hand on his mouth when the Lord afflicts him.

It involves men in *rebellion* against God. When God strikes men for sin, murmurs fly in his face, and they kick against his strokes like bullocks unaccustomed to the yoke. They in some respect resemble that desperate apostate Julian, of whom it is written that he shot up his darts against heaven when he was in distress. They fulfil that word of holy writ, "The foolishness of man perverteth his way, and his heart fretteth against the Lord." Prov. 19 : 3. The repining heart boils with rage against God and his dispensations, like those wicked Jews when hungry and distressed: "They shall fret themselves, and curse their king and their God, and look upward." Isaiah 8 : 21.

It imports much *impenitency* and unhumbledness for sin, and that we have seen little of the intrinsic evil of sin, and of our ill-deservings for it. Can we truly believe that our sins deserve hell-fire, and yet impatiently repine at sickness and lesser strokes upon our bodies?

It includes much *atheism* and blasphemy against God, and his infinite perfections, in several respects.

By our impatient murmurings, we either virtually deny that things here below are governed by God's providence; or else,

We tax his providence with unrighteousness in the managements thereof; as if God did withhold from us what is due, or inflict on us what we have not deserved. O, what atheism is this; shall not the Judge of all the earth do right? May he not, upon the justest ground, answer every murmurer, "Friend, I do thee no wrong?" Matt. 20 : 13.

We in effect grasp at the sovereignty and usurp the throne of the most high God, and would have the disposal of things in our hands; yea, we presume to summon God to our bar to give account of his administration, when we take upon us to quarrel with any of his dispensations. Alas, we little remember the woe that is pronounced against so doing: "Woe unto him that striveth with his Maker; shall the clay say to him that fashioneth it, What makest thou? or thy work, He hath no hands?" Isa. 45:9.

We on the matter take sin's part against God; we either justify it, or extenuate its evil, and allege, by our murmurings, that God is unrighteous to punish such small sins with such heavy afflictions.

We virtually question God's power to reach us a greater blow. When we enter the lists with God, and contend with our Maker, is it not in effect to say, we know how to reduce him to our terms, or make our party good against him?

We disparage his wisdom, and take upon us to be his counsellers, as if we could instruct him better in the management of affairs, and teach him what is fit to be done with his creatures. Hear what the Lord saith, Job 40:2 "Shall he that contendeth with the Almighty, instruct him? He that reproveth God, let him answer it." Murmuring is a reproving of God, and a charging him with ill-conduct, saying, in effect, with Absalom, "There is none that takes care to order men's affairs: O that I were king of the world; then should things be better ordered than they now are." So blasphemous is the language of our impatient murmurings. Let us therefore be ashamed of them, and abhor ourselves in dust and ashes for our foolishness in censuring the actions of the only-wise God. Shall a poor ignorant passenger, that understands not the use of the compass, be angry that the skilful pilot will not steer the vessel according to his pleasure?

We hereby slight and undervalue the riches of divine goodness, of which we have formerly shared, and do still partake: as foolish and pettish children, if they cannot have their will, or get some things they want, do presently throw away the things which they have, saying, with unthankful Haman, "All this availeth me nothing."

This sin hath some resemblance to hell itself; for there the damned do continually vex and torment themselves with their fretting and impatient thoughts, which cause them to break out in fearful rage and blasphemy against God.

QUESTION. But how shall we prevent such discontented murmurings? for sometimes trouble is so great we cannot bear it patiently.

ANSWER. God hath given you reason to bear rule over passion, and furnished you with strong arguments to prevail against discontent. Why then should you be so brutish as to dethrone reason, and suffer sense and passion to govern in you? Are you not Christians, and sworn to live according to the rules of the gospel of Christ? Why then do you act so contrary to your profession and engagements?

Besides what I have already said, I shall add some few remedies more for the cure of this murmuring distemper.

1. Look on thy murmurings as worse than all thy pains and troubles whatsoever; those are but afflictions from God, but these are sins grievous and provoking unto God.

2. Remember the judgments which murmuring hath brought down from heaven upon sinners. Miriam was smitten with leprosy for it; Dathan and Abiram were swallowed up alive; fiery serpents, plagues and exclusion from Canaan, were Israel's judgments for this sin. "Neither murmur ye, as some of them also murmured, and were destroyed of the destroyer." 1 Cor. 10 : 10. The arrows which murmurers shoot up against heaven quickly return upon their own heads.

3. Whatever thy sufferings are for the present, yet still believe thy case might be worse. The troubles that light upon the body are nothing so terrible as those that light on the soul. "A wounded spirit who can bear?" Prov. 18 : 14. They are nothing to what thy innocent Saviour suffered upon the cross; yea, nothing to what some martyrs have endured for the truths of the gospel.

4. Get very low thoughts of yourself, and a deep sense of your ill-deservings for sin. O, should a firebrand of hell murmur for temporal afflictions?

5. Be employed in examining thyself, rather than in censuring God. Doth God seem to neglect thee? say, then, Alas, it is most just; have not I neglected him, and given a deaf ear to his calls many a day?

6. Bear in mind that these troubles will not last : there is a great change near ; they will issue either in life or in death. If in life, you will be ashamed you had no more patience when sick. If in death, then if you belong to Christ, it will give a finishing stroke to all troubles and complaints, and heaven will make amends for all. But if you be not in Christ, whatever your afflictions be now, troubles a thousand times worse are abiding you in another world : death will turn thy crosses into pure unmixed curses ; and then, how gladly wouldst thou return to thy former afflicted state, and purchase it at any rate, were there any possibility of such a return. You now fly out in a passion, and say you are not able to bear what you complain of. But consider, if you will not obediently bear God's rods now, you will then bear more, whether you will or not ; and God will make you able to bear more, when there will never be any hopes of relief.

7. Study to give vent to thy sorrows in a way of prayer and praise. An oven stopped, is the more hot within ; but the breath of prayer or praise gives ease. If we complained more to God, we should complain less of God. What a mercy is it that you still have God to go to. Improve the privilege, confess your unworthiness, and beg the grace of patience and submission out of Christ's full treasures. Praise God also for mercies received ; and however bad thy case is, bless God you are not in hell ; you are in the land of hope.

CHAPTER III.

SPECIAL DIRECTIONS TO THE CHILDREN OF GOD WHEN UNDER SICKNESS, OR ANY OTHER AFFLICTION.

DIRECTION 1. Let believers especially guard against fainting or desponding under God's afflicting hand.

THIS is an exhortation which God in a special manner directs to his children: " My son, despise thou not the chastening of the Lord, nor faint when thou art rebuked of him." Heb. 12 : 5.   There are two extremes mentioned, despising and fainting.   I have spoken of the first in Chapter II., Direction 2.   It is a duty to feel our affliction, but a sin to faint under it.   God's people may be said to faint under their trials when they sink or despond, or give way to fretting or repining under them.   In the preceding direction, I spoke of the evil of murmuring in general; here I shall speak of believers' faintings in particular, and inquire whence their fainting under affliction doth proceed, bring some arguments and helps against this evil, and answer some objections of fainting believers.

I. Whence these faintings in believers proceed.

1. They proceed from the grievousness of their affliction and the heaviness of their burden, which is ready to amaze and stagger their thoughts, and sink their spirits with fear and despondency.   Hence did the psalmist complain, "Thou hast showed thy people hard things : thou hast made us to drink the wine of astonishment."   Psalm 60 : 3.   "I sink in deep mire, where there is no standing ; I am come into deep waters, where the floods overflow me."   Psalm 69 : 2.

2. From the smallness of their spiritual strength, and particularly the weakness of their faith : " If thou faint in the day of adversity, thy strength is small."   Prov. 24 : 10. Whence was it that Peter fainted and began to sink in the waters, but from the weakness of his faith ?   Matt. 14 : 30.

31. We know not our strength till it is tried. Sometimes we have such a conceit of it, that we think, like Peter, we can walk upon a sea of trouble ; but soon, behold, some sudden blast assaults our confidence, and then we faint, or cry out with him, "Help, Lord, or we perish." Peter reckoned only upon the sea, he did not think of the boisterous wind; and he looked to dangers more than to the power that was to carry him through them.

3. From their impatience of delay. When deliverance is long in coming, it is not easy to wait God's leisure, and to keep the heart from desperate conclusions. " I said in my haste, I am cut off from before thine eyes." Psa. 31 : 22.

4. From the power of Satan's temptations, and furious assaults. When Satan is let loose in time of affliction to throw in his fiery darts, the believer is ready to faint and say, " Will the Lord cast off for ever; and will he be favorable no more ? Is his mercy clean gone for ever ; doth his promise fail for evermore ? Hath God forgotten to be gracious ? Hath he in anger shut up his tender mercies?" Psalm 77 : 7–9.

5. From their wearisome conflicts with a body of death and an ill heart. These, in time of trouble, add affliction to the afflicted.

6. From long and great desertions. When God hides his face from the believer in affliction, his soul faints under it. "Zion hath said, the Lord hath forsaken me, and my Lord hath forgotten me." Isa. 49 : 14.

7. From the consciousness of their guilt and ill-desert before God, on account of old sins, abuse of mercies, and not walking humbly before God. Affliction doth revive old sins, as with Job : " Thou writest bitter things against me, and makest me to possess the iniquities of my youth." Job 13 : 26. His old sins, and the guilt of his youthful follies, now revived upon him and sat close to his conscience, which occasioned his fainting under his burden.

8. Great afflictions frequently cloud believers' graces and evidences for heaven, and disclose their corruptions, whereby they are made to sink under their trials. They see more unbelief, impatience, distrust, and enmity to God in themselves, than they saw before; they see more of their weakness of grace, and of their want of faith and love, than before; whereby they are sometimes tempted to raze the foundation, and say, all their former attainments were but delusions, and their professions but hypocrisy. These things make afflictions sometimes very heavy and sinking to the people of God.

II. For preventing and helping this evil of fainting under affliction, let believers consider,

1. These heavy trials are all needful for you. Deep waters are not more needful to carry a ship into the haven, than great afflictions are to carry the vessels of our souls into the port of bliss. Strong winds and lightning are frightful, but they are necessary to purge the air. One of the sharpest calamities that ever befell Israel, was the Babylonish captivity: yet even this was in mercy to them; for the Lord saith, "I have sent them out of this place into the land of the Chaldeans for their good." Jer. 24 : 5. Strange! of freemen to be made prisoners, and that in a strange land, among the heathen—to be removed far from their own houses, vineyards, friends, nay, from the temple of God and his ordinances; and yet all this for their good! Why? They were hereby effectually weaned and broken off from their darling sin of idolatry.

2. Consider that your affliction, however heavy it be, will soon have an end. "For I will not contend for ever, neither will I be always wroth; for the spirit should fail before me, and the souls which I have made." Isa. 57 : 16. The goldsmith will not let his gold lie longer in the furnace than until it is purified. The wicked have a sea of wrath to drink; but, O drooping believer, take comfort, you have

but a cup of affliction, which will soon be exhausted. The time is near when all thy trials shall have an end : in heaven there is no cross, no complaint, no tears nor sorrows for ever.

3. Faint not, O child of God, for these afflictions are all the hell which thou shalt have; thou hast nothing to fear hereafter. Judas had two hells, one in time, by terror in his conscience, another after this life, which shall endure to eternity; but all the hell that a believer hath is but this light affliction, which is but for a moment.

4. Desponding or murmuring in affliction is evil in any, but in none is it so bad as in the children of God. It doth very ill become their covenants, their privileges, their hopes. Have they resigned and given up themselves and all they have to God by a solemn covenant, and will they fret when he disposeth of them? Didst thou not say, O believer, in the day when thy heart was stung with sin, and the terrors of God made thee afraid, O let me have Jesus Christ for my Saviour and portion, and I will be content, though I should be stricken with boils like Job, or beg my bread like Lazarus. Now, God tries thee if thou wilt stand to thy word : O beware of retracting. Hath not that soul enough, who hath an all-sufficient God for his portion? If God be thine in covenant, that comprehends all things.

5. It doth discompose and unfit the soul for any duty. It is ill sailing in a storm ; so it is ill praying when the heart is in a storm of disquiet and despondency.

6. Your fainting under affliction, and acting as if the consolations of God were small, is enough to stumble others at religion, and make them call the truth of it in question. When they see those fainting that profess religion, and have often declared that their rejoicing is in Christ Jesus as their portion, O may they not be tempted to say, " Where is the truth of religion ? Where are those divine supports and consolations we have often heard of?"

7. O then seek to get faith revived and strengthencd, and resolve with Job to trust in God, though he should slay you. This would be of noble use to keep the heart from sinking under the pressure of affliction, as the psalmist found it to his sweet experience: "I had fainted, unless I had believed to see the goodness of the Lord in the land of the living." Psa. 27 : 13.

III. I come to answer some objections or excuses of fainting believers, which they commonly allege as the ground of their discouragement in their afflictions.

OBJECTION 1. O, saith one, my afflictions are not ordinary; they are sore burdens I lie under, and of various kinds too.

ANSWER 1. O believer, God hath taken the ordering of your lot in his own hand, and he knows what is fittest for you. Should a man be left to carve out his own portion, it would soon appear he would be his own greatest enemy. We would all be for the dainties of pleasure and prosperity, which would not be for our soul's health—as children think green fruit the best diet, because it pleases their taste ; but their parents are wiser to keep it from them.

2. God may see you have many and strong lusts to be subdued, and that you need many and sore afflictions to bring them down. Your pride and obstinacy of heart may be strong, your distempers deeply rooted, and therefore the medicine must be proportioned to them, as with the Israelites : "Because they rebelled against the words of God, and contemned the counsels of the Most High, therefore he brought down their heart with labor." Psa. 107 : 11, 12. O believer, your God and Father, that hath the mixing of your cup and portion, is a wise and skilful Physician, who knows your constitution and your need. "If need be, you are in heaviness through manifold temptations." 1 Pet. 1 : 6. And as he knows your need, so he understands your strength. "God is faithful, who will not suffer you to be tempted above that ye are able." 1 Cor. 10 : 13.

3. God sends great and sore troubles, that you may have the more experience of his wisdom and mercy in your support and deliverance : " Thou which hast showed me great and sore troubles, shalt quicken me again, and shalt bring me up again from the depths of the earth." Psa. 71 : 20.

OBJECTION 2. But, saith another, my affliction is singular, there was never any in my condition.

ANSWER 1. It is very common for a man in great distress to reckon his case singular, because he feels best what is nearest to himself, but is a stranger to what his neighbor feels.

2. This suggestion is one of Satan's devices, that he may tempt the child of God to question his Father's love ; but he is a liar, and not to be credited in what he saith ; for others of your brethren have been afflicted in the same kind and degree, if not worse : " Knowing that the same afflictions are accomplished in your brethren that are in the world." 1 Pet. 5 : 9.

3. Whatever your case be, you must own your sufferings are not so great as your sins. The trials of God's people in Babylon were singular ; yet Ezra owns, " Thou hast punished us less than our iniquities deserve." Ezra 9 : 13. If our provoked Judge shall in his clemency send us to Babylon instead of hell, we have no cause to complain.

4. But, O child of God, however thou complainest of the singularity of affliction now, all such complaints will be taken out of thy mouth ere long; and the time is near when thou shalt be made to wonder at the wisdom of God in guiding so many sons and daughters to glory, through such a variety of trials, exercises, afflictions, and temptations ; and you shall be made to say, like those in Mark 7 : 37, " He hath done all things well."

OBJECTION 3. But, saith one, my affliction is long continued, and I see no way of escape ; and how can I but faint under it ?

ANSWER 1. It is not so long as your sins deserve : for in justice it might be for ever; it might be "the worm that never dieth, and the fire that is never quenched."

2. Your sufferings on earth are not so long as your reward in heaven. "For I reckon that the sufferings of this present time are not worthy to be compared with the glory which shall be revealed in us." Rom. 8 : 18.

3. No length or continuance of affliction here should hinder a believer's comforts. If we take a view of our head and pattern Jesus Christ, how long did his afflictions continue! No end was put to them, till he cried with a loud voice, and gave up the ghost. Though he was the Son of God, yet from the hour of his birth to the moment of his death, from his manger to his cross, his afflictions still increased, and he ended his days in the midst of them. Now, Christ is the Head of the church, and your great Representative, O believers, into a conformity with whom you are predestinated ; be content, then, to be like your Head and Pattern, and have no ease or rest from afflictions till you lie down in the grave. It is "there the wicked cease from troubling, and there the weary be at rest." Job 3 : 17.

4. Remember, that your afflictions are a part of Christ's cross, which your loving Redeemer hath contrived for your good, and hath appointed you to take up and bear with him. Now, love to Christ should keep you from wearying to bear a part of Christ's cross, especially when he himself bears the heaviest end of it ; nay, bears you and your cross both. It is said of Jacob, that "he served seven years for Rachel, and they seemed to him but a few days, for the love he had to her." Gen. 29 : 20. And shall we not endure a few years' affliction for our Lord Jesus Christ, who lived a life of sorrows, and died a cursed death for our sakes ? Had we more love to Christ, his cross would not be so irksome to us.

5. Should it not be good news to thee, that there is a deliverance for thee at death from all thy troubles, and that

this time is hastening, and very near? Be not anxious for
deliverance here in time, for that savors too much of unbelief and love to the world. Doth it not seem to say, that
you would be better content to be turned back again to the
stormy tumultuous sea of this world, than to be safely landed
at your rest above; that you would be happier of a few temporal mercies on earth, than to enter upon your eternal in
heritance with Christ?

OBJECTION 4. No wonder, saith one, that I faint under
my affliction, for I want those consolations and supports
which God useth to reserve for afflicted saints.

ANSWER 1. If God be now chastening you for your sins,
you must be content to feel the bitterness of sin, before you
can taste of the sweetness of God's consolations.

2. Can you say that your afflictions have duly humbled
you, and fitted you for comfort? Have they yet brought
you to a willingness to quit and renounce all your beloved
sins, and even to part with all your earthly enjoyments and
comforts at God's call, and be content with God in Christ
alone for your happiness and portion? If this be not done,
your afflictions have not had their due effect to prepare you
for comfort, and till then you cannot expect it. You are in
the hands of a wise and skilful Physician, who will not too
hastily heal and bind up your sores, so as to let them spoil
and fester at the bottom.

3. Though you should have no sensible consolations from
God in your present trials, yet you must still labor to keep
in the way of duty, and live by faith on his promises. Believe firmly that God is good to them that love him, and
that there is forgiveness with him for the penitent sinner.
And if all stars withdraw their light while you are in God s
way, then assure yourself the sun is near the rising.

OBJECTION 5. But my affliction is such that it disables
me from duty, and makes me useless and unprofitable; and
this makes me faint under my burden.

ANSWER 1. God sends afflictions not to unfit, but to quicken you for the performance of duty—to make you repent more thoroughly, pray more fervently, flee to Christ more earnestly, and mind heaven more intensely.

2. If it be your duty to others that your affliction incapacitates you for, then remember, if God in his providence disable you for that, it is no longer a duty incumbent on you, and you must not grudge if God take you off, and put others in your room. God is a free and sovereign agent, and will be tied to no means or instruments whatsoever for carrying on his work.

DIRECTION 2. Let the children of God be exemplary in patience and submission to God under their affliction.

I treated of patience, and gave some motives and helps to it, to all afflicted persons in general, Chapter II., Direction 5. But here I shall bring some special arguments to Christian patience and submission proper for believers. You for whom God hath done so much beyond others, ought to shine in this grace of patience, and be examples to others in it when God chastens you, though it be with very sore affliction.

1. Study patience under affliction; for it is the common path and beaten road to heaven that all the saints have trod, who have gone thither before you. Behold the print of the footsteps of all the cloud of witnesses in this road; and would you be singular, and choose a way of your own? When God solemnly renewed his covenant with Abraham, and he had prepared the sacrifice whereby it was to be ratified and confirmed, God made a smoking furnace to pass between the pieces of the sacrifice, Gen. 15 : 17, to let him know that there was a furnace of affliction attending the covenant of grace and peace, and all that entered thereinto. God has appointed that all the stones of this spiritual and heavenly building shall be hewed and polished by affliction

here; and we are not to think that God's ordinary way will be changed for us. We must not think to walk on roses when so many worthies have marched through briers and thorns to heaven.

2. Consider, that the greatest afflictions you meet with are consistent with the love of God, nay, spring from his love to you. Every sanctified rod is a gift and royal donation sent by the hand of God to you. "To you it is given, in behalf of Christ, not only to believe on him, but also to suffer for his sake." Phil. 1 : 29. Now surely, if we look on the cross as a gift, an honor, an advantage, and blessing, we should bear it patiently. "Blessed is the man whom thou chastenest, O Lord." Psa. 94 : 12. O believer, thy temporal cross comes from the same love that thy eternal crown comes from, according to Rev. 3 : 19, 21. Men will not take pains to correct stubborn servants, but will turn them out of doors; but love constrains them to chastise their sons. God lets many a sinner go unpunished in this world; for why should he prune or dress the tree which he will cast into the fire? The malefactor that is condemned to the gallows escapes scourging. "The wicked is reserved to the day of destruction; they shall be brought forth to the day of wrath." Job 21 : 30. But it is far otherwise with the children of God. That is a strange word which Job hath, chap. 7 : 17, 18, "What is man, that thou shouldest magnify him; and that thou shouldest set thy heart upon him; and that thou shouldest visit him every morning, and try him every moment?" Now, if we compare this place with others in the context, we shall see how he acknowledgeth that the most overwhelming distress proceeds from the love and care of God, yea, from his fixing his heart on a man, to magnify him and do him good; and that for this end he doth chasten him every morning and try him every moment; and that with such afflictions as for the present are so far from being joyous, that they give the soul no rest, but even make the

man weary of his life—as he expresseth what effect his affliction had on himself. Yea, it may be observed in the providence of God from the foundation of the world, that those who have had most affliction, have had most grace and the most eminent testimonies of acceptance with God. Jesus Christ the Son of God had the most afflictions of any, and yet the Father always loved him and was well pleased with him.

3. Consider the bright examples of patience which God sets before you in his word. Besides that of his dear Son the Lord Jesus Christ, of which I spoke before, consider the patience of Job, when he was stript of all earthly comforts, and laid under the greatest afflictions; yet, he calmly falls down and worships God, and says, "Naked came I out of my mother's womb, and naked shall I return: The Lord gave, and the Lord hath taken away; blessed be the name of the Lord. In all this Job sinned not, nor charged God foolishly." Job 1 : 21. Consider the patience of David when he was driven from his throne, from his house, and from God's sanctuary, and all this by his own son ; yet how submissive is he to God : "Behold, here am I; let him do to me as seemeth good unto him." 2 Sam. 15 : 26. And when Shimei cursed him and threw stones at him, he pa- tiently bore it and would suffer no harm to be done him for it, saying, "Let him alone, and let him curse, for the Lord hath bidden him." 2 Sam. 16 : 11. Consider the patience of holy Eli, when, though he heard such news as, like a sud- den clap of thunder, made the ears of such as heard it to tingle and their hearts to tremble, yet he calmly and quietly submitted to it: "It is the Lord; let him do what seemeth him good." 1 Sam. 3 : 18. He doth not fly in God's face in a passion, but falls down at his feet in humble submis- sion. Observe also the wonderful patience of Aaron, when God afflicted him very sore : he is silent and submissive under the Lord's hand. "And Aaron held his peace."

Lev. 10 : 3. If we consider the greatness of the punishment, we shall see the more cause to commend the greatness of his patience. Aaron lost his *children*—not his estate or worldly substance, but his children ; these are a part of a man's bowels : other earthly losses are not comparable to this ; therefore it was that Satan, that cunning enemy, reserved the loss of Job's children to the last onset, as his great masterpiece and sharpest attack. How sadly did Rachel lament and weep for her children. Matt. 2 : 18. Yet Aaron held his peace. Aaron lost his *two sons at once.* How pathetically did David bewail the loss of one son : " O my son Absalom ! my son, my son Absalom ! would God I had died for thee, O Absalom, my son, my son !" 2 Sam. 18 : 33. Yet Aaron lost both his sons together, and saith not one word : " He held his peace." Aaron lost them *by a sudden death,* of which he had no warning. Sickness usually prepares men for the stroke that is coming by death ; but Aaron met with a surprising blow, yet he held his peace. Aaron's sons were not taken away by an ordinary stroke of God's hand, but *by an extraordinary supernatural rod ;* for it is said, " There went out fire from the Lord, and devoured them, and they died before the Lord." Lev. 10 : 2. He lost them in such a manner as might speak forth God's anger. Now a religious father had rather lose all his children in the favor of God, than one child in his anger ; yet, whatever were the bitter ingredients of this cup, Aaron was not impatient against God that mixed it for him, but held his peace because God did it.

4. To engage you to patience under your trials, do but compare your case with that of others. Do not say, there are none afflicted as you are ; for there are many plunged far deeper in the waters of Mara than you are : some are still upon the rack, and spend their whole days and years in continual fighting and struggling ; as in Psalm 31 : 10 . " My life is spent with grief and my years with sighing."

Have you sore distress in your body ? others have grievous wounds in their souls. Do you bear the wrath of man ? others bear the wrath of God. You have but one single trial ; others have many twisted together. Some are stript of all comforts; you have comforts still remaining. You may have many sad things in your trial, but you have not ground as yet to complain as the psalmist doth : " All thy waves and thy billows are gone over me." Psalm 42 : 7. Take a view of what the Son of God, what the apostles, and what the martyrs and other worthies have endured. They had trial of cruel mockings, scourgings, bonds, and imprisonments : they wandered in deserts and mountains, and in dens and caves of the earth, being destitute, afflicted, tormented. They were tempted, they were crucified, stoned to death, sawn asunder, slain with the sword, etc. And yet, how well did they bear the cross ! Saith Paul, " We glory in tribulation." Rom. 5 : 3. And what saith James ? " My brethren, count it all joy when ye fall into divers temptations." James 1 : 2. As if he had said, Rejoice, aye, more and more, that you are afflicted ; God is magnifying you, he is visiting you, doing you good, taking the more pains with you, and fitting you for glory.

5. The consideration of God's former mercies and kindnesses to you should engage you to patience in trouble, and make you blush to take any thing ill out of God's hand. Thus Job taught his impatient wife : " What ; shall we receive good at the hand of God, and shall we not receive evil ?" Job 2 : 10. O believer, let not thy afflictions cause thee to bury thy mercies in oblivion. Has not God brought thee from Satan's family and put thee among his children ; and will you forget or undervalue that honor ? Hath he struck off your fetters, taken off your prison-garments, and set you at liberty ; and will you be unthankful ? Hath he given you Christ for your treasure and portion, entitled you to his unsearchable riches ; and will you be discontented ?

Hath he given you the graces of his Spirit, which are more precious than rubies ; and will you quarrel when he smites in some outward things ?   Hath he made you an heir of glory, and provided eternal mansions above for you ; and will you be fretful for want of some trifles here ?   The view Moses had of the recompense of reward in heaven, caused him to choose to suffer affliction patiently with the people of God.

6. The time of affliction is usually God's gracious season of meeting with his people, the time of their rarest comforts and sweetest foretastes of heaven, according to 2 Cor. 1 : 5. Paul and Silas did never sing more joyfully than when they were laid in the inner prison, with their backs torn with scourges, and their feet fast in the stocks.   Acts 16 : 24. And when was it that Jacob saw the angels of God ascending and descending upon the ladder that reached between heaven and earth, but at the time when he was in a destitute case, forced to lie in the open field, having no canopy but the heavens and no pillow but a stone ?   When was it that the three children saw Christ in the likeness of the Son of God with them, but when they were in the furnace, and that when it was hotter than ordinary ?   When was it that Ezekiel had a vision of God, but when sitting solitary by the river Chebar in the land of his captivity ?   When was it that John got a glorious vision of Christ, but when he was an exile in the isle of Patmos ?   And when was it that Stephen saw the heavens opened, and Christ standing at the right hand of God pleading for him, but when they were stoning and bruising him to death ?   So that the most remarkable experiences of God's kindness that believers get in this world, have been reserved to the time of affliction ; and this consideration should move every Christian to wait on the Lord, and bear his cross with patience.

7. When you are helped to Christian patience and submission under God's hand, it doth contribute much to the

credit of religion, and to the conviction of the world, that there is a reality in the truths of the gospel, and a great efficacy in the grace of God, which bears you up and carries you through beyond the strength of nature.

8. O believer, bear up with patience under the cross, for thou hast not long to bear it. God's wrath abideth on the church but for a moment, yea, a little moment. " Come, my people, enter thou into thy chambers, and shut thy doors about thee ; hide thyself as it were for a little moment, until the indignation be overpast." Isa. 26 : 20. Surely a moment, a little moment, which is the smallest part of time, will soon be over ; and wilt thou not have patience for a moment ? The psalmist supported himself with this consideration : " He will not always chide, neither will he keep his anger for ever." Psalm 103 : 9. The time of indignation will soon be overpast, and the time of consolation will succeed. O believer, the end of all thy trials is near ; think on it, and look for it. Is it bodily pain or sickness that is thy affliction ? Then consider, the end of it will be either life or death ; if death, then what thou sufferest is the last brunt, bear it patiently. These enemies you now see, you will see them again no more. In the mansions above there is no pain nor crying : the inhabitants there shall never say they are sick ; and one hour with them will make thee forget all thy momentary afflictions. If the issue shall be life, you will be ashamed, when well, that you had no more patience while sick.

I shall close this direction with the words of the apostle James : " Take, my brethren, the prophets who have spoken in the name of the Lord, for an example of suffering afflic tion and of patience. Behold, we count them happy which endure. Ye have heard of the patience of Job, and have seen the end of the Lord ; that the Lord is very pitiful, and of tender mercy." Jas. 5 : 10, 11.

DIRECTION 3. Let believers be much employed in the praises of God, while they are under affliction by sickness or otherwise.

As we should bless the Lord at all times, and keep up good thoughts of God on every occasion, so especially in the time of affliction. Hence we are commanded to glorify the Lord in the fires. Isa. 24 : 15. And this the three children did in the hottest furnace. So Job blessed God when he had taken away his greatest comforts. Job 1 : 21. And this is agreeable to the command, "In every thing give thanks." 1 Thess. 5 : 18. I grant, indeed, we cannot give thanks for affliction as affliction, but either as it is the means of some good to us, or as the gracious hand of God is some way observable therein towards us. In this respect there is no condition on this side of hell, but we have cause to praise God in it, even in the greatest calamities. Hence it was that David, when he speaks of his affliction, Psa. 119 : 67, adds presently, "Thou art good, and doest good." And he declares, verse 65, "Thou hast dealt well with thy servant, O Lord, according unto thy word." Hence Paul and Silas praised God when they were scourged and imprisoned. Well then, O believer, obey the command of thy God, and imitate his worthies by praising God under thy affliction. For,

1. This practice would be very pleasant and acceptable to God ; for as music is sweetest on the waters, so praise is most agreeable to God from an afflicted soul on the waters of trouble. It is a sign of a noble and generous spirit, to sing the praises of God's goodness while his hand is afflicting us. Distress and danger will make the most wicked man pray ; but it is a principle of love and gratitude that makes the troubled soul to praise.

2. It would bring credit to religion, to see saints thankful and praising God under the cross : it would make people say, Surely they find sweetness in God and his ways, that we see not ; they have meat to eat that the world knows not of.

And this would invite strangers to come and try a religious life. The joyful praises of the martyrs at the stakes and in the flames, made people go home with love to religion in their hearts.

3. If the issue of your affliction should be death, this employment of praise would be a sweet preparative to fit and dispose you for the work of heaven. Use yourself much to this heavenly life, and be oft trying to sing the song of Moses and the Lamb in the time of sickness and trouble; and this would sweeten the thoughts of death, and make you incline to be there, where praise is their constant work.

QUESTION. What should be the subject of a believer's thanksgiving and praise under affliction?

ANSWER 1. He hath ground of praise on account of God's mercies to him through his past life. His mercies to thee, O believer, cannot be numbered: compare thy mercies with thy crosses, and thou wilt soon see thy receivings are far greater than thy sufferings. Thou hast had many days of plenty for one day of scarcity, many days of liberty for one day of straits, many days of health for one day of sickness. And are not these to be remembered with praise?

2. And more particularly in thy greatest affliction, thou hast ground to praise God, O believer, that thou wast born in a land of light, where thou hadst the means of conversion to God and acquaintance with Jesus Christ; and especially, that God of his free grace made these means effectual to work a saving change in you, when others were passed by. Is not this matter of praise, that he opened your eyes and humbled your soul and renewed your heart; that he gave you Christ, forgave your sins, and adopted you into his family, and made you an heir of heaven? Oh what a sad case would it be if you were yet in your sins, and in the bondage of Satan—if you had the work of conversion to begin, if you had your faith and justification and interest in Christ all to seek, and all your preparation for heaven to make—if you

had all this to do with a sick and pained body, and a disordered mind that cannot command one settled thought, with the terrible views of death and eternity before your eyes: this is the case that God in justice might have left you to. Well, then, ought you not to praise God, that sent his Holy Spirit in time to determine your heart to close with Christ, and be reconciled to that God before whom you are shortly to appear; and that the sins which now would have been your terror, are all forgiven and washed away through the blood of Jesus Christ?

3. Is it not matter of praise in thy greatest trouble, that thou hast a great High-priest, that is passed into the heavens to provide a mansion with the Father for thee, and to receive thy soul when separated from the body; that where he is, there you may be also?

4. You have cause to bless God that he sends such suitable harbingers as sickness and trouble to tell you that death is approaching, and that he should take such pains with you to wean you from the world, and make you willing to be gone. Many of God's people, that at the beginning of a sickness have been averse to dying, by the increase and continuance of it have been brought to be well satisfied to depart, that they may be with Christ.

5. You have ground to bless God for timing your afflictions so well, that he sent them not till he saw you stood in need of them. He saw a "need be" for them, as in 1 Pet. 1 : 6, and he would not let you want what was needful.

6. You ought to praise God that he mitigates your trials, and proportions your burden for your back; that when he takes the rod to you, he hath not made it a scorpion; that when he deprived you of one comfort and enjoyment, he did not strip you of all, and leave you wholly comfortless; that when you suffer in one thing, he hath not made you to suffer in every thing—in soul, body, estate, relations, and all together; that instead of afflicting you for a few days, he hath

not made your whole life a scene of misery and affliction. Bless God that he punisheth you less, unspeakably less than your iniquities deserve; that your sick-bed is not hell, your fever is not everlasting burnings, your pain is not the gnawing of the worm that never dieth.

7. You have cause to praise God that your affliction is not so great as that of some others, and even of some that were very dear to God, and had not grieved him so much as you have done. Remember the trials that some have endured of whom the world was not worthy, which I mentioned before, as recorded Hebrews 11. Yours are nothing to theirs, nothing to those of Job, that eminent servant of God. Observe the difference with thanksgiving and praise.

8. You have reason to bless God for the strength and support he hath given you under affliction. You would soon sink and succumb under a small burden, if he did not support you by his grace; but when he bears you up, the heaviest trial shall not sink you. Have you not met with some afflictions, which you thought at a distance you would never be able to bear up under; yet when they came, you have found them light, by reason of the strength God bestowed on you?

9. You have ground of thanksgiving, because the mercies and blessings which God hath continued with you are far greater than those he hath taken from you. For though he hath taken this and that temporal blessing from you, yet he hath not taken Christ from you, nor his Holy Spirit. He hath not separated you from his love, nor cut you off from all hopes of heaven. However great your trials may be, yet still there is a mixture of mercy in your lot, which should be a matter of praise.

10. You have cause, O believer, to bless God that all the afflictions he brings on you are in love, and for your profit. All his ways are mercy and truth to you. If he smile, it is in mercy; and if he smite, it is in mercy. God

may change his dispensations towards his children, but never his disposition. His heart is still towards them, and the cords wherewith he scourgeth them are cords of love. Their profit is the great thing he aims at in all his chastisements. Heb. 12 : 10. He designs thereby to reclaim them from their wanderings, cut off provisions for their lusts, make them pant and long for a better state, and cause them to mend their pace towards it. Hence David saith, "It is good for me that I was afflicted : for before I was afflicted I went astray, but now have I kept thy word." Psa. 119 : 67, 71. From all which it appears, that you have manifold grounds of praise, even in time of affliction.

DIRECTION 4. Let the children of God, when visited with sickness, set about actual preparation for death and eternity.

Every believer hath his main work done, and is always in a gracious state, by reason of his union with Jesus Christ, his reconciliation with God through the merit of his blood, and the universal change that is wrought in him by regenerating and sanctifying grace ; upon which account every child of God hath habitual preparation for meeting with death. Yet, because frequently when sickness cometh there are many things out of order with them, that make death frightful and undesirable, they must set about actual preparation for death, and seek to have their souls made ready for the bridegroom's coming. And here I shall show wherein this actual readiness of believers doth consist, which should be their proper work and exercise in time of sickness, especially when sickness is lingering and doth not destroy the use of reason. But beware of thinking that this should be delayed till sickness come. No, no ; the time of health is the main working season, and all should be finished then as far as possible. But seeing even the best generally find much to do at the very last, I shall give the following advices for your actual preparation.

1. Seeing sickness is a means appointed of God for his

people's good, and particularly for fitting them for a better world, labor earnestly to reap the benefit of sickness; seek God's blessing upon it, that thereby you may be helped to discover more of the evil of sin, that you may hate and abhor it the more, and that you may see more effectually the vanity and vexation of the world, and get your heart loosed from all the things of time, and brought to a willingness to depart, that you may be with Christ.

2. Seeing the time of sickness and death is the time of your greatest need, beg earnestly of God, for your Redeemer's sake, such special assistance, influences, and operations of his Holy Spirit, as he knows needful for you in your present low and weak condition, in order to carry on and complete your actual readiness for meeting with himself at death, and entering into the invisible world, and being unalterably fixed in your everlasting state.

3. Renew the exercise of repentance, and of faith in the blood of Christ, for removing all grounds of quarrel and controversy between God and your soul. And in order thereto, review your past life, and look into your heart also, and search out every predominant sin and idol of jealousy; for if there be any iniquity regarded in your heart and unrepented of by you, it may occasion no little anguish and bitterness of spirit in a dying hour. When thou hast discovered sin, humbly confess and bewail it before the Lord, and ask forgiveness for it through the blood of Jesus Christ the Son of God, which cleanseth from all sin. Yea, make confession of all thy own sins, and particularly reflect upon the fountain and spring of them, thy *original sin*. Know the plague of thine own heart, and mourn over it; mourn for the loss and misspending of much precious time. Mourn for the unprofitableness of thy life. Now, when the axe is laid to the root of the tree by sickness, it is high time to mourn for your unfruitfulness under the grace and waterings of the Holy Spirit. Mourn for your sinning against such light and

love as have been many days displayed to you in the glorious gospel; and in a special manner mourn for your sins
of omission, which commonly are but little minded by us.
Thus mourn for all thy sins, till thou dost water thy couch
with tears.   It is most suitable that death should find every
man, even every child of God, in the exercise of mourning
and repentance; for they that thus sow in tears shall eternally reap in joy.   But see that your tears run much in the
gospel channel, and flow from believing views of a crucified
Christ, whom you have pierced by your sins.   And in the
midst of your mourning, be still aiming to take faith's grasp
of the clefts of this rock, for sheltering thy soul from the
guilt of by-past sins; say, "Lord Jesus, I have no refuge
but thy wounds, no fountain but thy blood, no covert but
thy righteousness.   And seeing thou freely makest offer of
thy merits for my protection, and invitest even the chief of
sinners to come unto thee, saying, 'Look unto me, and be ye
saved,' Lord, I embrace the offer, and flee to thee to cover
me."   O believer, do this, not once or twice, but do it a
hundred times over; do it as long as thou hast breath to
draw in the world.   Be still breathing to the very last after
a crucified Jesus for relief against the guilt of sin, which
thou art always contracting, and wilt be till the earthly
house of this tabernacle be dissolved.

4. In order to your actual readiness to go forth to meet
the bridegroom, when coming to you by death, you must,
as the wise virgins did, arise and trim your lamps.   Matt.
25 : 7.   As it is not enough to have a fair lamp of a profession, so it is not sufficient to have only the oil of grace in
the lamp; nay, to have it burning in some degree.   There
is more requisite at this time, that the soul may be actually
ready; the lamp must be *trimmed:* which imports, first,
a supplying it with more oil.   You must seek to have your
grace increased, to have new strength and new supplies of
grace given you from God; to fit you for the last conflict

with your spiritual enemies, and especially the last enemy, death. Secondly, it imports a stirring up of the oil, and raising the wick higher. So there must be an excitation of grace, which may be in a low, declining condition; you must endeavor to stir and raise it up to a more lively exercise, and more elevated acts. "Stir up the gift that is in thee;" make the oil burn clear and shine bright. Bring faith, love, repentance, and holy desires to a lively exercise. Thirdly, this trimming imports the cleansing of the lamp, by taking away the dead ashes that hinder the light, or prevent its burning so clearly as it otherwise would. So you must labor to take away the dead ashes of corruption, that hinder the shining of grace; remove all unbelief, earthliness, deadness, self-seeking, and formality, and whatever else doth suppress the exercise of faith, love, and heavenly-mindedness: let all these dead ashes be snuffed away by repentance and mortification. As you ought to strive earnestly against all these heart evils in time of health, so now labor to give them a deadly stroke when death's harbinger gives you a summons.

5. Be diligent in gathering and summing up all your evidences for heaven and eternal life, that so you may not venture into the dark valley at an uncertainty. The comfort of dying will much depend on the clearness of your evidences. It is therefore your wisdom to examine them carefully, and see if you can say, "I know in whom I have believed; I have consented with my soul to the method of salvation laid down in the covenant of grace. I am desirous that the glory of it should be eternally ascribed to the free grace of God, and the creature be wholly abased in his sight; I have chosen God for my portion, and Christ for my only Saviour; and the happiness which I aim at, is to enjoy God in Christ for ever. And in order thereto, I depend on the Holy Spirit to apply the redemption which Jesus Christ hath purchased for me, and to sanctify me perfectly. There is

no sin but what I hate, and desire to part with. I would rather have more holiness, than to have health and all the pleasures in the world. I earnestly desire the flourishing of Christ's kingdom, and prefer Jerusalem's good to my chiefest joy." If these your evidences be clear, you may cheerfully take death by the cold hand, and welcome its grim messengers, and long to be gone that you may be with Christ. You may say, "Yea, though I walk through the valley of the shadow of death, I will fear no evil, for thou art with me." Psalm 23 : 4. You may go off the stage with the psalmist's words in your mouth, "Into thy hand I commit my spirit; thou hast redeemed me, O Lord God of truth." Psalm 31 : 5.

6. Labor earnestly to overcome the love of life and the fear of death, so as to be content to part with all things here at God's call. O believer, what is there in this earth to tempt thee to hang back, when God calls you to depart? While you are here, you may lay your account with many losses, crosses, disappointments, griefs, and calamities of all sorts. Friends will fail you, enemies will hate you, lusts will molest you, Satan will tempt you, and the world will deceive you. Death is the way that the dearest of God's saints and all the cloud of witnesses have gone before you; yea, the Lord Jesus your Head hath trod this path, and hath taken the sting out of death, and hath paved a way through the dark valley that his people may safely follow him. Hath the Captain of your salvation gone before you, and will any of his soldiers shrink to follow him? Are you content to remain always at the same distance from him, and to enjoy no more of his presence than now you have? Are you satisfied to live for ever with no more holiness or heavenly-mindedness than at present you have? Do you not groan under your remaining ignorance, deadness, wanderings, pride, passion, unbelief, selfishness, worldliness, and other sins and lusts that here beset you? And are you not

desirous to go to the place where you will be eternally free from them all, and where you shall never complain of a dull, dead, and senseless frame of heart, or of any heart-weariness or wandering in duty any more? For the heart shall then be as a fixed pillar in the temple of God, and shall go no more out: the eternal adoration and praises of God shall be the soul's delight and element for ever. By such considerations strive to conquer the fears of death and desires of life, which are often great clogs to the people of God in their preparations for the eternal world.

7. Be oft meditating upon the heavenly glory which all believers will shortly see and enjoy. Be much in the contemplation of the glorious company above; behold Christ upon his glorious throne at the right hand of God, and Abraham, David, Peter, Paul, and all the rest of the faithful ones, with their crowns of righteousness, triumphing in the presence of their Redeemer. Think, O believer, how happy that day will be, when thou shalt meet with thy father and brethren, and shalt see thy elder Brother on the throne ready to pass sentence in thy favor. With what melody will that sentence sound in thy ears: "Come, ye blessed of my Father, inherit the kingdom prepared for you from the foundation of the world." What frame wilt thou be in, when he sets the crown of glory on thy head? "O eternally free love," thou wilt cry, "O Saviour, thou didst wear a crown of thorns, that I might wear a crown of glory; thou didst groan on the cross, that I might now sing. Wonderful free love, that chose me when thousands were passed by; that saved me from ruin, when my companions in sin must burn in hell for ever." Think how ravishing it will be to meet with your godly acquaintances in heaven, with whom you prayed, praised, and conversed here. Will you not then cry out, "O my brethren, what a change is here; this glorious place is not like the poor dwellings we had on earth; this body, this soul, this state, this place, our clothes, our company, our

language, our thoughts, are far unlike those we had then. The bad hearts, the body of death, the corruptions and temptations we then complained of, are all gone. We have no more fear of death or hell, no more use for repentance or prayer, faith or hope; these are now swallowed up in immediate vision, eternal love, joy, and praise." And for thy help, O believer, in meditating on these things, read some parts of the book of Revelation, or cause them to be read to you; and suppose with yourself that you had been a companion with John in the isle of Patmos, and had got such a view of the glorious majesty, the bright thrones, the heavenly hosts, and shining splendor which he saw—the saints in their white robes, with crowns on their heads and palms in their hands—and heard them singing the song of Moses and the Lamb, and trumpeting forth their eternal hallelujahs; what a heavenly rapture wouldst thou have been in. Well, O believer, thou shalt shortly have clearer and sweeter sights than all these which John or any of the saints ever saw here upon earth. Surely that heavenly glory is a subject worthy of thy thoughts, and most suitable for thee to meditate on in time of sickness, and when in the view of death.

8. It would be also very suitable at this time, in order to your actual readiness for death, to be frequently looking out and longing for Christ's coming. As Abraham stood in his tent door, ready to go forth to meet the angels that were sent unto him, so should the believer keep himself in a waiting posture at this time. He should be like the loving wife, that longs and looks for the coming of her absent husband, according to his letters to her. By this time, thinks she, he will be at such a place, and against such a time he will be at another place, and so in a few days I shall see him. It is a character given of believers, they are such as love his appearing. 2 Tim. 4 : 8. They desire his coming. " Make haste, my beloved." Cant. 8 : 14. " Even so, come, Lord

Jesus, come quickly." Rev. 22 : 20.   Believers should look
upon themselves as pilgrims here, wandering in a wilderness,
absent from home, and at a distance from their father's
house ; and in time of affliction it is very proper for them to
be crying as David doth, " O that I had wings like a dove,
for then would I fly away, and be at rest ; I would hasten
my escape from the windy storm and tempest." Psalm
55 : 6, 18.   " O when shall the time of my pilgrimage, and
the days of my banishment be finished, that I may get home
to my country and friends above?   O, my Lord is gone, my
Saviour hath left the earth and entered into his glory ; my
friends and brethren are gone to their blessed rest, where
they see God's face and sing his praise for ever: and how
can I be willing to stay behind, when they are gone?   Must
I be sinning here, when they are serving God above ?   Must
I be groaning and sighing, when they are triumphing and
dividing the spoil ?   Surely I will look after them and cry,
O Lord, how long ? when may I be with my Saviour and
my God ?"

DIRECTION 5. Let believers in time of sickness endeavor all they
    can to glorify God, and edify those that are about them, by
    their conversation and behavior.

If ever a child of God be active to promote the honor
and glory of God, it should be in time of sickness, and when
death may be approaching.   And there is good reason for
it : for,

1. This may be the last opportunity that ever thou shalt
have to do any thing for God on earth ; and therefore thou
shouldst study to improve it to the uttermost.   Heaven, to
which thou art going, is the place where thou shalt receive
thy reward ; but thou canst have no access there to advance
God's glory, by commending God and Christ and religion to
sinners or weak believers.   Upon this account many of God's
children have been content to suspend their heavenly happiness for a while, and to stay upon the earth for some longer

time. I have read of a certain martyr who, when going to suffer, expressed some sorrow that he was going thither, where he should do his God no more service ; that is, in the sense above explained. And of another that said, " If it were possible there could be place for any grief in heaven, it would arise from the Christian's considering that he did so little for God while he was upon earth." Now is the working season ; O believer, be busy while it lasts, according to the example of thy blessed Saviour : "I must work the work of Him that sent me, while it is day : the night cometh, wherein no man can work." John 9 : 4. This consideration should make thee bestir thyself with the greatest activity, like Sampson before his death ; who, when he could have no more opportunity to serve God and his church, cried to God and said, " O Lord God, remember me, I pray thee, and strengthen me only this once." Judges 16 : 28. And then he bowed himself with all his might to pull down the pillars of Dagon's temple, being willing to sacrifice his life to the ruin thereof.

2. The holy language and conduct of dying believers may, through the blessing of God, make a deep impression upon the hearts of unregenerate men that are witnesses to them. Many who have derided the people of God for the strictness of their lives, and despised their counsels and reproofs as proceeding from ill-humor or preciseness, have begun to notice their words and actions when they have seen them on sick-beds and on the borders of eternity, and to have other thoughts of religion and holiness than formerly they had. Now, they think, the man is in good earnest, and speaketh the thoughts of his heart ; and, if ever he can be believed, it must be now. It is most convincing to carnal persons to see believers bearing up with patience in their sickness ; to hear them speaking good of God, commending his ways, and rejoicing in God as their portion in the midst of their sharpest pains : to see them behaving as those that are going to dwell with Christ ; smiling and praising God,

when friends are sighing and weeping about them. This inclines them to think, surely there must be a reality in religion; there is a visible difference between the death of the righteous and that of the wicked. Hence a wicked Balaam wished to die the death of the righteous, and to have his last end like his. It left a conviction upon that young man's conscience, who said to his loose companion, after they had visited godly Ambrose on his death-bed, and seen how cheerful he was and triumphing over approaching death, "O that I might live with thee, and die with Ambrose." Nay, such sights might draw them not only to desire to die the death of the righteous, but also to resolve to live their lives. If carnal men saw believers going off the stage with such confidence and joy as becomes those that are entering into eternal rest with Christ, and those that are going out of a howling wilderness to a glorious Canaan, it might be a powerful invitation to them to go and seek after the same felicity.

3. This likewise would be very edifying and confirming to all that fear God. How much would it contribute to establish them in the practice of holiness, and to quicken them in their diligence in obeying and glorifying God in the days of their health, to hear a dying believer say, "Of all the time which I have lived, I have no comfort now in reflecting upon one hour but what I spent in the service of God.. Were I to begin my life, I would redeem time more carefully than ever. One hour in communion with God is far sweeter than many years spent in worldly pleasures. Come here, then, all ye that fear God, and I will tell you what he hath done for my soul. O taste and see that God is good."

4. Consider the examples of God's children in former ages, how useful and edifying their words have been at such a time to all around them. But this head I intend to treat more fully afterwards.

QUESTION. But how shall I behave so as to glorify God

and edify others when I am sick or dying? I would have some particular directions for it.

ANSWER 1. You may do this by your patience under pain and submission to God's will with respect to the event, whether life or death. It is a stumbling-stone to others to see believers fretful in trouble, and unwilling to leave the world when God calls them. But it is most convincing and confirming to see them frankly resigning themselves to God's disposal, saying, "Let God himself choose for me; he is wise, and knoweth best what is needful and proper for me; I have no will but God's will." For any man to desire to live when God calls him to die, or to desire to die when God calls him to live, is equally a sin of cowardice; for he that desires to live is afraid to look death in the face, and he that desires to die would flee from some calamity and take shelter in death. But he is the most valiant man that can die willingly when God would have him die, and live as willingly when God would have him live. This is true Christian valor.

2. By pious exhortations and warnings to those that are about you. It may be the last occasion you may have of glorifying God this way. O do not lose the season which may be usefully improved for the good of souls. For thus a believer may bring more honor to God, and more advantage to precious souls by his sickness and death, than ever he did by all his health and life in the world; for his words have more weight with the people at such a time than at any other. Hence the patriarchs, knowing the prevalency of such words, urged Joseph with Jacob's dying charge: "And they sent a messenger unto Joseph, saying, Thy father did command before he died, so shall ye say unto Joseph, Forgive, I pray thee now, the trespass of thy brethren." Gen. 50 : 16, 17. And as we ought to be ready to give good counsel to all when we lie on sick-beds, so especially we should be concerned for our children and near relations; they are

more affected than others with our sickness, and so will
they be with our sayings; our admonitions may do them
good when we are rotting in the dust.

QUESTION. What ought to be the subject of our remarks
and exhortations to others at such a time?

ANSWER 1. It is very proper to be much in commending the Master you have served, and the excellency of his
service, to those that are about you. Tell them of the equity
and goodness of the laws which you have obeyed; of the
bounty and faithfulness of that Lord whom you have worshipped, loved, and praised; and of the greatness and eternity of that reward you are going to possess. Let the children of God extol their Father, and his care of them and
kindness to them. Let the ransomed of the Lord magnify
their Redeemer, and his wonderful love and sufferings for
them. Tell others what sweetness and satisfaction you
have found in your own experience in attending God's ordinances, and in secret duties; what comfort you have
found in Christ and the promises of his covenant. And
thus let your last breath be spent in exalting and commending Christ and religion to others.

2. Warn others of the vanity of the world and all its
wealth and pleasures. Tell them that they may see by
your case that those things which people are bewitched
with in the day of their health, can signify nothing to a sick
or dying man; they cannot ease us in our pains, they can
afford no peace to a troubled soul; they cannot lengthen
our life one hour, and far less can they save from the wrath
of an angry God. "Oh," may you say, "what a miserable
case had I been in at this time, if I had no better portion
than this world, and nothing else to look to but to its riches
and pleasures. Wherefore, sirs, set not your hearts upon it,
but forsake it before you be forsaken by it, and make choice
of that which will support you in the evil day."

3. Warn them of the evil of sin, and what mischief and

deceitfulness you have found in it. Tell them that "though the devil and the flesh would tempt you to look on sin as a harmless thing, yet the pleasure will soon be gone, and a sharp sting will be left behind. Sin will appear no light matter when the soul is going hence into the awful presence of a holy God. You would give a thousand worlds then for Christ and the blood of atonement to answer for your sins."

4. Tell them the great difference between the godly and the wicked man's choice. The godly man chooseth the good part that cannot be taken from him; he lays up his treasure in heaven where none can reach it, so that it yields him rich supplies when sickness and death come upon him. But O how foolish is the wicked man's choice, that for a moment's fleshly pleasure, doth lose his immortal soul and everlasting happiness. Warn them to mind the one thing needful in time, and not pamper their body for the worms, but to set themselves immediately to close with the offers of Christ, and make sure an interest in his righteousness to cover them in the evil day.

5. Tell them of the evil of sloth and negligence in the work of their salvation; and exhort them to mind it, and to do it with all their might. For however some may censure and deride God's people now for their strictness, diligence, and zeal in the matter of religion, yet when they come to die, they will be ready to wish that they had been more diligent in the work of salvation; that they had loved God, fled to Christ, and sought and served him with all their hearts and souls; and to cry, "O for a little more time; O if God would recover and try us once with health, how diligent would we be." Tell them also, that those who have been most serious and self-denying in the work of salvation, yet when they come to die, do much lament their sloth and negligence; yea, those that have been most reproached by the world for their diligence and fervency, do often wish at

that time, "O that we had been a thousand times more diligent and laborious in God's service."

6. Labor to persuade others of the preciousness of time,
the wisdom of improving the season of youth and of health,
and the great folly of delaying repentance and of putting it
off to a sick-bed. Say to them, "I find now by experience,
that a time of sickness is a most unfit season to do any thing
to purpose for the soul; my mind is so diverted and indis-
posed for spiritual work by sickness and pain, that I cannot
attain to any suitable composure for it. And how miserable
were I, if I had all my work to begin at this time. O take
warning, and improve precious time; and especially the day
of the gospel, the time of the Spirit's striving, and the time
of youth, which is the most usual season of the conversion of
souls, and of bringing sinners into acquaintance with Jesus
Christ."

DIRECTION 6. Let God's children, when sick or dying, feel and
manifest a great concern for the advancement of the kingdom
of Christ, and of true religion among the rising generation.

Zeal for Christ's interests is very becoming his people in
all the periods of their life, but more especially at this time.
When Christ is ready to take you to his kingdom in heaven,
O be not unmindful of his kingdom on earth. It would be
acceptable to God, and pleasant in the sight of men, to see
you expressing a warm concern for the rising age, and for
promoting the welfare of the souls of your children and others
that survive you; and seeing you can be no longer useful to
those you leave behind, by your counsels, examples, or prayers as formerly, do your utmost for them now. And this
concern the children of God in time of sickness may evidence
several ways.

1. By earnest prayers to God, both for the prosperity of
his church, and the flourishing of religion in general, and
also for your children and relations in particular, that they
may be a holy seed and a generation to serve God, and

show forth his praise in the world, when you are gone off the stage.

2. By intrusting the care of your children's education to such tutors and guardians as will be concerned for their souls and will set before them godly examples and instructions in their young and tender years.

3. By filling your wills with pious advices and solemn charges to your children and relations, with respect to their serving God and worshipping him in their families and in secret; so that they can never look into your testaments, and the legacies left to them, but they will see something that may be affecting, arousing, and edifying to their souls.

4. By honoring the Lord with your substance, and leaving something of what God hath blessed you with to pious uses; particularly for the religious education of the children of the poor, for buying Bibles and other good books for them, and for propagating Christian knowledge in ignorant places. For by fatal experience we may observe that the most godly parents do not know how their children will employ the estate they leave them, whether as fuel for their lusts, or as oil to feed the lamps in God's sanctuary. It is proper for themselves then, before they go off the stage, to dispose of some part of their substance for the glory and service of that God who gave it unto them.

5. It might contribute to promote piety, and make deeper impressions upon the minds of your children and friends, if, under the warnings of death, you should imitate the example of the prophet Elijah, who in his lifetime made a writing, which he procured to be delivered to king Jehoram after his death. 2 Chron. 21 : 12. So in like manner you might write letters and leave them in the hands of your friends and executors, full of advices, charges, admonitions, consolations, or threatenings, to be delivered to your children or friends upon occasion either of their good or bad conversation after your death; which probably would be more re-

garded by them than the counsels you gave them in the
time of your life; for, in some respect, they would be received and read by them as if they were letters from heaven.

DIRECTION 7. Let the children of God labor to fortify themselves
against all Satan's temptations and assaults, which they may
expect to meet with in time of sickness and affliction.

A time of affliction is commonly a time of temptation,
for the old serpent knows the fittest seasons for assaulting
the children of God; and he will not be wanting to improve
this opportunity of advantage for falling upon the poor soul.
When Pharaoh heard that the people were entangled in the
wilderness, he pursued them; so when Satan sees a soul
entangled with distress and trouble, he thinks it high time
to make an attack. He seeks to winnow and sift away the
believer's grace, and therefore he comes when the corn is
under a threshing by the rod. When Job was smitten in
his estate, health, and all other comforts, then this coward
falls upon him, and tempts him to impatience, murmuring,
and wrong thoughts of God.

At this time, O believer, you have special need to be on
your guard, and look out. Reckon always, when sickness
or trouble cometh, the prince of this world cometh also.
Stand then to your defence, and put on your armor, especially the shield of faith, that you may be able to quench the
fiery darts of the devil. You have need at this time to put
in practice our Lord's direction, "Watch and pray, that ye
enter not into temptation." Pray for wisdom and skill to
counteract the evil one, and that you may not be ignorant of
his devices, and pray particularly for grace to make you
proof against all his false representations of God and his
providence to you; for he that durst represent Job falsely to
an all-seeing and all-knowing God, will with much boldness
represent God falsely to you, who see and know so little.
He will be ready to tempt you to think that God is angry
with you, and dealing with you as an enemy. Thus was

Job tempted : " Behold, he findeth occasions against me, he counteth me for his enemy : he putteth my feet in the stocks, he marketh all my paths." Job 33 : 10, 11. But observe what Elihu answers : " In this thou art not just ; God is greater than man. Why dost thou strive against him ? for he giveth not account of any of his matters." But seeing I have spoken before of the wrong thoughts of God which we are apt to harbor in time of affliction, Chapter II., Direction 3, I shall proceed to speak of some other temptations wherewith Satan doth assault God's people when in distress, and furnish some answers thereto.

TEMPTATION 1. Saith the tempter, " Thou art nothing but a hypocrite : all thy religious performances have been done in hypocrisy, to be seen of men : thou never hast repented or believed sincerely in the sight of God."

ANSWER. I acknowledge there hath been much hypocrisy in me, but I hope it is not allowed and reigning hypocrisy ; I always wrestled against it : wherefore I am not a hypocrite. I regarded the esteem of men too much, but I hope I value the esteem of God much more. My faith and repentance are weak, but I hope they are sincere. And whatever defects and shortcomings have formerly cleaved to these graces in me, I do now unfeignedly repent of all my sins, I look to Him whom I have pierced, and mourn. I am heartily willing to be justified by the righteousness of Christ alone, and to be cleansed and sanctified by his Spirit ; and here I give up myself to Christ as my only Saviour. And this I hope is, through grace, true repenting and believing, which God will accept, for Christ's sake, whatever my former defects have been.

TEMPTATION 2. But saith the tempter, " Thy repentance cannot be true ; for thy heart is not broken, and thine eyes do not shed tears for sin."

ANSWER. It is my very great burden and constant complaint to God, that I cannot attain to a greater measure of sorrow and contrition for sin; but yet it is my comfort, that repentance is not to be confined to such degrees and symptoms of sorrow as some do win at. I hope I can say through grace, that my heart is set against all sin, great and small; and I would give up all I have in the world to be wholly delivered from sin.

TEMPTATION 3. Saith the tempter, "But thy day of grace is past, it is too late for thee to think of repenting or believing: God will not accept of thee now."

ANSWER. Nay, I hope it is not so with me, seeing God gives me a heart that pants after him and Christ in the way of commanded duty. The offers of salvation through Christ are made to all who believe and repent; and late penitents are not excluded from the benefits of these gracious offers more than others.

TEMPTATION 4. But saith the tempter, "Thou art none of God's elect, and if thou be not chosen to salvation, thou canst not be saved."

ANSWER. Secret things belong to God, and it were presumption in me to pry into his secret decrees; but one thing I am sure of, that every soul that is chosen to faith and repentance, is also chosen to salvation: I trust God hath chosen me to the former, and therefore to the latter.

TEMPTATION 5. But saith the tempter, "You overvalue your graces and duties, and so they cannot be true and real."

ANSWER. Nay, I count them all but loss and dung in comparison with Christ. I desire always to be deeply humbled under a sense of my sinfulness and unworthiness, and to abhor every motion that would carry me away from Christ and his righteousness, and would tempt me to rely on my grace and duties, or put them in the least in Christ's room.

TEMPTATION 6. "The issue of thy sickness may be death; and thou art not ready, for thou hast no assurance of thy salvation."

ANSWER. A perfect certainty is not to be expected here;

there will be still some questions, some doubts and fears; but these I resolve not to indulge now, but to break through all, that I may embrace Christ and be found in him. The desires of my soul are to Christ and the remembrance of his name; and such I believe he will not suffer to perish. "I believe; Lord, help my unbelief."

TEMPTATION 7. "But thou art a stranger to the invisible world; how wilt thou adventure into that world of spirits with which thou hast so little acquaintance?"

ANSWER. Christ, who is my head and best friend, is no stranger to it; he is the Lord of that land, and provides mansions for all his people there; and he will receive every one of them home, and lodge them safely. "The spirits of just men made perfect," were once what my spirit now is; they were strangers to that world before they came to it, as well as I; but their Head being there, encouraged them to go to it; and now they rejoice in it as the kindly dwelling-place of all the saints.

TEMPTATION 8. "But thou art vile, and God is infinitely pure and glorious; how canst thou think of approaching so near to him?"

ANSWER. Though a weak eye be not able to look upon the sun, yet I hope to be fitted and strengthened for that glorious sight. Besides, God doth now appear to us in his Son Jesus Christ, where his infinite glory is pleasantly veiled so that saints may behold him. Those glorified souls above were once vile as well as others; but their Saviour did cleanse them, and present them to the Father without spot or wrinkle. And whatever be my unworthiness, I am relieved by considering my union with Christ, and looking on the glory and dignity of my Head. Surely God will not despise the members of his dear Son, nor trample on any that are his flesh and bones.

TEMPTATION 9. "But what will become of thy wife and children when thou art taken from them?"

ANSWER. If I trust God so willingly with my soul and my eternal concerns, why may I not trust him with my relations also? Have I not seen how wonderfully he hath provided for others? Doth not every thing in the world depend on his will and pleasure? How easy is it then for God to supply his own?

TEMPTATION 10. "But still, death is terrible to nature; he is even the king of terrors."

ANSWER. My Redeemer hath tasted death for me, and taken out its fearful sting; he hath conquered death, and keeps the keys of death and hell. Wherefore, through him will I sing, "O death, where is thy sting? O grave, where is thy victory?"

TEMPTATION 11. "But it is terrible to think of appearing before God's tribunal to be tried and judged."

ANSWER. My friend and intercessor will be the Judge there. Will Christ condemn the members of his own body whom he hath so often comforted?

Besides these, a holy God may sometimes suffer the tempter to assault his own people in time of their affliction with his fiery darts and his fiercest battering engines, such as temptations to atheism, blasphemy, and despair, whereby their souls may be terribly shaken and sore amazed.

Your relief in this case is to look to your Head, and remember how he was himself buffetted by this enemy, and assaulted with the most odious temptations, that he might thereby get an experimental touch and feeling of your condition, in order to his sympathizing with you, and relieving you from this enemy whom he hath already conquered in your name. But for these things he will be inquired of by the house of Israel. You must exercise faith in your exalted Head.

CHAPTER IV.

SPECIAL DIRECTIONS TO UNREGENERATE PERSONS, WHEN AFFLICTED BY SICKNESS OR OTHERWISE.

DIRECTION 1. Take a serious view of the miserable condition of a Christless person under sickness or heavy affliction.

CONSIDER the vast difference between your case and that of a true believer: he hath ground of consolation in the greatest distress, but you have none. However sharp the rod of correction be to him, yet it is in the hand of a Father: but you have to do with an angry and sin-avenging God; and who may stand in his sight, if once he be angry? for he commands both the first and second death, and he can cast you both into the grave and hell at once: "Hell followed the pale horse." Rev. 6:8. Death is the king of terrors, but hell is a thousand times more terrible. When God afflicts his children, he stands to them in the relation of a loving Father; but he deals with you as an incensed Judge. Though he sees it necessary for their good to chastise them, yet he doth it with a relenting hand; yea, every stroke goeth as it were to his heart. "In all their affliction he was af-flicted." Isa. 63:9. But when he ariseth to punish his incorrigible enemies, though they cry he hath no pity. "I will. laugh at your calamity, and mock when your fear cometh." Prov. 1:26.

2. If your sickness threaten you with death, what a dark and melancholy prospect must you have of your ap-proaching change. Why, O Christless soul, it is what you are wholly unprepared for. The old house falls down about your ears before you have another lodging provided. When death casts you to the door, you have nowhere to lay your head, unless it be on a bed of fire and brimstone. O how surprising and fearful will the change be that death will

make with you. A change from earth to hell, from light to darkness, from comforts to terrors, from hope to despair, from the offers of grace to the revelation of wrath ; a change from the society of saints on earth, to the company of the damned in hell. Whatever fond hopes of salvation you have now, your hopes shall lead you no further than to the king of terrors, and then "your hope shall be cut off, and your trust shall be a spider's web." Job 8 : 14. Though it costs you much pains to weave and support this web now, it will prove a weak and slender defence to your soul, when death comes with his besom of destruction and sweeps both you and it away to hell. You will then be taken from all the means of grace you have abused, and be for ever deprived of an opportunity of buying the oil of grace : your lamp shall go out at death, and never be lighted any more.

3. In this extremity you have no quarter to look to for comfort. O Christless sinner, what will you do in the day of visitation ? To whom will you flee for help ? Your houses, your lands, your money, your honors, your companions, your relations will all be miserable comforters to you. Every thing will look black and dismal round about you. If you look without you for help, you may see your friends weeping and lamenting your case ; but this will do nothing but increase your vexation and misery. If you look within you for relief, conscience, that before you would not suffer to speak, will meet you with bitter stings and upbraidings. It will bring to your view the sins you had forgotten, the time you have misspent, the health you have misimproved, the offers of grace you have refused, the great salvation you have neglected. What folly was it for you to provoke God and slight Christ for a little worldly profit, or a little brutish pleasure ' Can these relieve you when the arrows of the Almighty stick within you, and the terrors of God do set themselves in array against thy soul ? In the mean time the devil, that tempted you to your soul-ruining course, will

step in and represent your sins in their blackest colors and aggravations, to render you altogether hopeless and desperate.   O sinner, thou that refusest rest from Christ in the day of health and grace, shalt find no ease from created things in the day of sickness and death.   Your sickness will allow no rest to your body, and your sin will permit no ease to your soul.   You may expect the fulfilling of the threatening in Deut. 28 : 65–67 : "The Lord shall give thee a trembling heart, and failing of eyes, and sorrow of mind.   And thy life shall hang in doubt before thee, and thou shalt fear day and night.   In the morning thou shalt say, Would God it were even ; and at even thou shalt say, Would God it were morning," because of the pain of thy body and anguish of thy spirit.

DIRECTION 2. Let unregenerate persons carefully improve their sickness and affliction as means to further their conversion, and pray that God may bless it for that end.

Many have begun their acquaintance with God and with themselves in the time of affliction ; the furnace is frequently the Spirit's laboratory, where he forms his vessels of praise. There are many who, while health and strength continue, mind nothing but vain pleasures.   One day they go to their games and sports, another day to their cups and lascivious company, another day to visiting their friends ; and thus they spend the whole time of their health and prosperity in sin and vanity.   All the warnings, counsels, and exhortations of parents, friends, and ministers, do them no good ; they cannot endure to entertain a serious thought of God or of Christ, of death, of heaven, or of hell, or judgment to come.   But when God doth cast them into sickness or some great affliction, they, through the blessing of God, begin to come to themselves like the prodigal, and think of returning again to their Father.   Several instances to this purpose might be given.   The earl of Rochester is a late one, whose life was notoriously lewd, profane, and atheistical, and who had wickedly employed his wit and talents to ridicule all religion ; yet when he was afflicted with pain and sickness, and brought to the gates of death, he began to entertain quite other apprehensions than he had done before ; he professed he had serious and reverend thoughts of religion and holiness, which before he laughed at; he most earnestly and affectionately warned others to abandon their evil courses, and to live religiously and soberly, and to look upon religion as the greatest reality in the world ; he retracted all his impious and profane language wherewith he used to reflect on the ways of godliness, and willingly attested all this under his hand.

Pray then for the divine blessing on your sickness, that it may contribute to the conversion of your soul, which it doth in several ways :

1. By opening men's eyes to get a true sight of things, to behold religion in its true shape, and sin in its proper colors ; hence the rod is said to give wisdom. Prov. 29 : 15. They who have mocked at religion, and made light of sin all their days, have been taught by bodily sickness to change their tune. Then they begin to have an esteem of the Bible, and to value and send for pious ministers, and to desire the prayers of the people of God. Now they perceive sin to be bitter as gall and wormwood, they loathe and abhor that which they liked before ; now the word of God makes a deep impression on them, and particularly such a word as that in Jeremiah 2 : 19 : "Know therefore and see that it is an evil thing and bitter, that thou hast forsaken the Lord thy God."

2. Sickness helps to set the word preached home upon the heart. When God speaks to us in the day of health and prosperity, we often give him a deaf ear, Jer. 22 : 21 ; but when distress comes, it brings the words of God and of his ministers to our remembrance, as it brought Joseph to the remembrance of his brethren. Gen. 42 : 21.

3. Sickness contributes to loosen a man's heart from the world, and to cool his love thereto; whereby a great hinderance of conversion is removed out of the way, and the man is made to say, "How vain and helpless are the world's comforts to me now. Those things I delighted in formerly are tasteless to me at this time. There is no portion can suit my soul's needs but God himself."

4. It spurs a man on to prayer that formerly neglected it. When the prodigal is brought to distress, he says, "I will arise and go to my father." He forgot his father before, but now he will address him. "In their affliction they will seek me early." Hosea 5 : 15. Thus the Lord frequently begins and promotes the conversion of souls to himself. And O sinner, if this be the fruit of thy sickness, it will not be unto death, but to the glory of God.

DIRECTION 3. Be careful to obey God's voice in the rod, and beware of slighting it.

Every sickness hath a message from God, and his voice you ought to hearken to with reverence and attention. Micah 6 : 9. What saith he to you at this time? O sinner, he saith, "Retire from the world, think on death and eternity, abhor those lusts and idols which God is smiting you for, flee speedily to the stronghold; repent and be converted, that your sins may be blotted out." This is God's voice to you; and consider how provoking it will be to him if you slight it.

1. You will provoke God to slight your voice when you cry to him, and stop his ear against the voice of your supplications. Zech. 7 : 13.

2. You will provoke God to cease from being a reprover to you, so that he will speak to you no more.

3. You will provoke him to bring heavier judgments on you, yea, so to draw his sword of justice against you, that he will sheathe it no more, as he threatens, Ezek 21 : 5.

4. God may break off all intercourse and correspond-

ence with you, as with those addressed in Ezek. 20 : 31 :
"As I live, saith the Lord God, I will not be inquired of
by you."

5. He may seal you up for ever under your sins, hardness, and pollution, and say to you as to some we read of,
"Because I have purged thee, and thou wast not purged,
thou shalt not be purged from thy filthiness any more, till I
have caused my fury to rest upon thee."   Ezek. 24 : 13
"Ephraim is joined to his idols; let him alone." Hos. 4 : 17.
"He that is filthy, let him be filthy still."   Rev. 22 : 11.
He that is hardened against the voice of my rods, let him be
hardened still.   Well then, O sinner, while God is speaking
with you, hearken to his voice, and obey it; say, "Lord,
what wilt thou have me to do?"

DIRECTION 4. Cast back your eyes upon the sins of your past
    life, and labor to be deeply humbled for them before the
    Lord.

Seeing you are summoned to prepare for going to the
judgment-seat of God, where your soul is to receive its final
sentence, labor to prevent the terror of that appearance by
your judging yourself beforehand.   And this you must do,
by summoning yourself before the bar of conscience, examining carefully into your state, accusing and condemning
yourself for your sins.   And see that you be impartial in
this work, willing to know the truth, and discover the worst
of your case.   You must see and be duly sensible of your
danger; otherwise you cannot think to escape.   Take a
close view of your sins, in their nature, aggravations, and
deservings.   And in order to this, if you have any measure
of strength for it, let the exposition of the ten commandments in the catechism be distinctly read to you.   Make a
pause upon every question, and say within thyself, "Have
I not omitted what is here required by God; and have I
not committed what is here forbidden by God?   How oft
have I repeated those sins; how long have I lived in the

practice of them.   Oh, do not so many years' sins need a
very serious repentance, a very deep humiliation ?   Oh, doth
not such a vile sinner as I stand greatly in need of Christ to
be my ransom for such a vast number of sins ; will not their
weight press me eternally down to the lowest hell, if they
remain unpardoned, and be laid upon my head ?"   Wherefore view them closely, and confess them particularly before
God.

1. Bewail thy original sin, the fountain of all thy actual transgressions, as did David : "Behold, I was shapen
in iniquity, and in sin did my mother conceive me."   Psalm
51 : 5.

2. Acknowledge and mourn over the sinful outbreakings
of thy life, whereby thou hast dishonored God and grieved
his Holy Spirit ; and especially sins against light.

3. Be humbled for thy sins of omission, for neglect of
commanded duties ; particularly for the neglect of prayer in
secret and of family religion.

4. Mourn for the loss of precious time.   Alas, for the
time of youth misspent, the many Sabbath-days trifled
away.

5. Lament thy long slighting of Christ and salvation
through his righteousness, which hath been so pressingly
offered to thee in the gospel.

6. Bewail thy stifling the convictions and quenching
the motions of the Spirit, and thereby provoking him to
depart from you.

7. Mourn for thy unthankfulness to God for mercies and
deliverances, which might have allured you to repentance
and newness of life.

8. Confess thy stubbornness under former afflictions,
which hath provoked God to send new trials upon you.

9. Be humbled for thy earthly-mindedness, in that thou
hast all thy days been careful and cumbered about many
things, and hast neglected the one thing needful.

10. Mourn for the lateness of thy repentance, and thy amazing folly in delaying so long to bethink thyself and turn to the Lord. "O how unwisely have I acted, to misspend the time of health, and delay so great a work till now that I am laid on a sick-bed; and now, if I die before I am converted, I am lost for ever. O Lord, I am ashamed and confounded at my madness and folly, and have no excuse to plead for myself, but must stand afar off with the poor publican, and smite upon my breast and cry, 'God be merciful to me a sinner.'"

DIRECTION 5. Flee immediately to Jesus Christ by a true faith, and close with him as offered to you in the gospel.

Art thou sensible, O sinner, of thy grievous guilt and ill-deservings before God? Then do not despair; for Jesus Christ, who hath offered to divine justice an all-sufficient sacrifice for sin, is offering himself to thee, saying, " O distressed sinner, look unto me and be saved. Turn unto me; why will you die? Come unto me, heavy-laden soul, and I will give you rest. Him that cometh to me, I will in nowise cast out." Will not such gracious words, such moving calls, melt thy heart within thee, and make thee cry to him, "Lord Jesus, I flee to thee as my refuge for deliverance from sin and protection from the wrath to come. I look to thy wounds, I trust in thy righteousness, I depend on thy merit, I lie at thy feet: and this I am resolved to do as long as I have breath to draw in the world."

DIRECTION 6. Call for the elders of the church, that they may pray over you in your sickness.

This is the apostle James' direction to the sick, James 5:14; he doth not say, if any be sick let him send for the physicians, but for the elders or ministers.

It is true, physicians are to be called, but not in the first place. It was Asa's fault that in his disease he sought not to the Lord, but to the physicians; and, alas, how many follow his example. Ministers are only called for in the last place, and very often when the time is past, the sick being at the point of death and scarcely able to speak or hear. But if you desire to reap benefit by the instructions and prayers of ministers, call for them early, and open your case to them; seek their counsel and beg for their prayers. It is their office to teach and pray for you, and they have authority to offer salvation to you through Christ, and to minister comfort to them that are cast down; wherefore a blessing may be expected on their ministrations and performances more than others. Hence God said to Abimelech of Abraham, "He is a prophet, and he shall pray for thee." Gen. 20 : 7. And to Job's friends concerning Job, "Go to my servant Job, and he shall pray for you; for him will I accept; lest I deal with you after your folly." Job 42 : 8.

And lastly, remember that as the apostle James enjoins the sick to call for the elders to pray over them, so at the same time he directs you to confess your faults one to another, Christian to Christian, one friend to another, the people to their minister. James 5 : 16. Not that this gives any warrant to the papists for auricular confession to their priests, which they force upon all men as a satisfaction for sin, and whereby they rack their consciences, when they feel no distress, to confess their most secret sins, to enumerate them all under pain of damnation, and which they use as a device to dive into the secrets of princes, states, and all private persons. But, as Luther, Calvin, Beza, and many orthodox divines do teach, it is very profitable and necessary for those that are inwardly troubled with a sense of their sins, to ease and disburden their consciences by confession to the faithful ministers of Christ, in order to receive from them suitable counsels and consolations, such as Christ hath left in his word for contrite-hearted penitents.

Thus let every man in sickness use all appointed means for preparing his soul for a future state. Thy preparation will by no means hasten death, but sweeten it to you. Death must surely have a most formidable aspect to an unprepared sinner: he may salute it as Ahab did Elijah, "Hast thou found me, O mine enemy?" Why? it brings heavy and doleful tidings to him. But a prepared soul may salute death, Welcome, O my friend, thou bringest me tidings of great joy; everlasting deliverance from sin and all the bitter fruits of it. I shall never complain of these any more.

CHAPTER V.

DIRECTIONS TO THE PEOPLE OF GOD WHEN THE LORD IS PLEASED TO RECOVER THEM FROM SICKNESS AND DISTRESS.

DIRECTION 1. It is very proper, both under sickness and after it, to examine if the affliction be sanctified to you, and hath come from the love of God.

IT would be very comforting for us to know that the afflictions which God visits us with, are not the punishment of a judge, but the chastisement of a father—that they do not proceed from wrath, but from love—that they are not curses, but blessings to us. Now the best way of knowing this, is by the effects which they produce in us, through the blessing of God.

1. Canst thou say that thy affliction hath humbled thee in the sight of God, and made thee confess and bewail thy sins and strayings from God as the procuring cause thereof? Hath it been like Moses' rod that smote the rock and drew out much water? Did you water your couch with tears, and mourn humbly before God for all thy God-provoking sins? Then it is a good sign that sickness is sanctified.

2. Doth thy affliction drive thee nearer God, and cause thee to aim at closer communion with God in duty than formerly, saying, " However careless and formal I have been in duty in time past, it is surely good for me now to draw near to God ?" Then thy sickness is a blessing to thee.

3. Affliction is sanctified when the corruption and deceitfulness of the heart is the more discovered and laid open to the view of the soul, so that the man is made to abhor himself in dust and ashes, and cry out like the leper, "'Unclean, unclean !' I never could have thought my heart was so wicked as now I see it."

4. It is a sanctified sickness, that purgeth the heart and

changeth the life, and gives a death-stroke to thy sins and idols, and makes thee to loathe and abhor them more than ever, saying with Ephraim, "What have I to do any more with idols ?"

5. It is a blessed rod when graces are more quickened and stirred up thereby, and the man turns more fruitful in holy duties and good works ; then it is a budding and blossoming rod like to Aaron's. Numbers 17. It is recorded there of Aaron's rod, that it brought forth buds, blooming blossoms, and yielding almonds. So it is happy with us when our rods and sickness not only produce in us the buds of a profession, and the blossoms of some beginnings of a reformation, but even cause us to yield fruits savory to God. Is conscience become more tender with respect to sin ? Are we more jealous over our hearts ? Are we more fervent in prayer, more lively in praise, more mortified to the world, more desirous of communion with God ? Then may we say with David, " It is good for us that we have been afflicted ;" and with Hezekiah, "Thou hast, in love to my soul, delivered it from the pit of corruption."

DIRECTION 2. Make conscience of offering to God the sacrifice of thanksgiving, upon his recovering thee from sickness or any distress.

The psalmist gives us this direction from God, Psalm 50 : 14, 15 ; and he shows us that it was his own practice in such a case, Psalm 116 : 17, and 103 : 1, 2, 3. The command is just, let us obey it ; the example is excellent, let us imitate it. Praise is comely for the upright. Here I shall give some MOTIVES to thanksgiving.

1. God, who is the author of all thy mercies and deliverances, gives you tongues for this very end, that you may bless and praise him for these mercies. James 3 : 9. Hence man's tongue is called his glory above the rest of the creatures. Psalm 57 : 8. There is none in the earth so endued and qualified for praising God as man is. Beasts have

tongues, but without speech or reason to use them ; but man hath both reason and speech, that he may both admire God's goodness, and with his tongue sound forth God's praise. See then, O believer, that you use your tongue to answer the end of your creation. God expects his due revenue of praise from his children, whom he hath formed for this end, and on whom he hath bestowed many distinguishing favors.

2. The sacrifice of thanksgiving is most pleasing and acceptable to God. He loves your tears and prayers, O believer, but much more your praises. How well pleased was our Lord with the poor Samaritan leper that returned and gave him thanks for curing his bodily distemper. Luke 17 : 19. He dismissed him with a special blessing, and cured him of his soul's diseases as well as of his body's. And therefore,

3. Consider that thankfulness for thy mercies received is a most profitable course for yourself; for it is the way to get more and better blessings bestowed upon you, according to Psalm 67 : 5, 6 : "Let the people praise thee, O God ; let all the people praise thee. Then shall the earth yield her increase ; and God, even our own God, shall bless us." Thanksgiving for former mercies is a kindly way of petitioning for new favors, and God will understand it in this sense.

4. God is so well pleased with the duty of thanksgiving, that he honors it to be the eternal work of heaven; whereas other graces, such as faith, hope, and repentance, will then be melted into love and joy for ever ; so other duties of worship, such as reading, hearing, and prayer, will then be changed into that of praise and thanksgiving. The glorified company above will never be weary of this work ; and shall not we delight in it now, when God is calling us to it by so many new mercies ?

And that thou mayest offer the sacrifice of thanksgiving to God for thy recovery with gracious acceptance, I shall lay before you the following ADVICES :

1. See that your heart be touched with a sense of the greatness of the mercy, and of the goodness of God manifested therein. We must put a due value upon our mercies, and have our hearts affected with God's kind dealing towards us in them, if we would be rightly thankful to God the author of them. Hence it was that David called upon his heart, and all within him, to bless the Lord for his benefits, Psalm 103 : 1 ; and in Psalm 138 : 1, he saith, " I will praise thee with my whole heart." As an instrument of music is the sweeter the more full and rich its volume of sound, so our praise is the more acceptable to God when the heart is full of gracious affections.

2. Let your praise be the result of genuine faith and love in your soul, otherwise it will be an empty sound. Faith is necessary to draw the veil, and show us the perfections of the invisible God, who is the spring and author of all our mercies ; love gives a deep sense of his goodness, enlarges the heart towards God, and opens the lips to show forth his praise.

3. Study to have a deep sense of your own unworthiness and ill desert at the Lord's hand on account of your sins, and ill improvement of former deliverances, saying with Jacob, " I am not worthy of the least of all thy mercies." Gen. 32 : 10.

4. Look above instruments and second causes, and do not ascribe your recovery to physicians or outward means, but to the Lord, the prime author of it, whose blessing alone it is that gives efficacy and success to the appointed means, and by whose mercy only we are spared, and brought back from the gates of the grave. To this the apostle attributes Epaphroditus' recovery : " Indeed, he was sick nigh unto death, but God had mercy on him." Phil. 2 : 27. Hence we are told, "The Lord bringeth down to the grave, and bringeth up." 1 Sam. 2 : 6.

5. Observe closely the remarkable circumstances of the Lord's goodness, and the sweet ingredients of thy mercies.

As, for instance, how discernible the Lord's hand was in thy deliverance, which obligeth thee to say, Surely this is the finger of God; this is the Lord's doing, and it is marvellous in mine eyes: how thy deliverance came to thee as the return of prayer, that makes thee say, Surely he is a prayer-hearing God: how deliverance came when there was but little ground to hope for it. See how Hezekiah observed this ingredient in his recovery from sickness: "I said, in the cutting off of my days, I shall go to the gates of the grave; I am deprived of the residue of my years. I said, I shall not see the Lord, even the Lord, in the land of the living; I shall behold man no more with the inhabitants of the world." Isa. 38 : 10, 11. "What shall I say? he hath both spoken unto me, and himself hath done it." Verse 15. Sometimes God sends deliverances to his people when they are most hopeless, and saying, with the captives of Babylon, "Behold, our bones are dried, and our hope is lost; we are cut off for our parts." Ezek. 37 : 11. Remember, also, how the extremity of thy distress was God's opportunity of sending relief. Abraham never forgot the seasonableness of God's appearing for him in his extreme need upon mount Moriah, when he called the name of the place *Jehovah-jireh*, for preserving the memorial of it: "In the mount of the Lord it will be seen." So doth David, "I was brought low, and he helped me." Psalm 116 : 6.

6. Let the present deliverance bring all former mercies to thy remembrance, that so thou mayest praise God for them all, whether they be national or personal mercies, public or private, spiritual or temporal. New mercies should revive the memory of the old, and all of them should be remembered at such a time; so doth the psalmist direct, "Sing unto the Lord; talk ye of all his wondrous works." Psalm 105 : 2. And what he directs others to, he himself practises: "What shall I render unto the Lord for all his benefits towards me?" Psalm 116 : 12.

7. Be ready to communicate to others an account of the Lord's kind dealings towards you, and the sweet ingredients of his mercies; and particularly of his sending spiritual deliverance to your soul, as well as outward deliverance to your body, when he is pleased to do so. And do this in order to recommend the service of God to others, and to invite and engage them to assist you in blessing and praising the Lord. We see how David observed his soul deliverances, Psalm 116 : 7, 8, and declares his experience to others: "I will declare thy name unto my brethren; in the midst of the congregation will I praise thee." Psalm 22 : 22. "Come and hear, all ye that fear God, and I will declare what he hath done for my soul." Psalm 66 : 16.

8. Remember always to give thanks for mercies to the Father, in the name of our Lord Jesus Christ, as directed in Eph. 5 : 20. Your spiritual sacrifices are only acceptable to God when you offer them up by Jesus Christ. 1 Peter, 2 : 5. As we must seek all our mercies in Christ's name, so we must give thanks for them also in his name. He is the Mediator of our praises, as well as our prayers: believers have not one mercy but what comes swimming to them in Christ's blood, and is the fruit of his death and purchase to them; and therefore he is to be owned and looked to in the receiving of every mercy. And as Christ is the only mediator for conveying blessings and mercies from God to us, so he is the sole mediator for conveying all our services and spiritual sacrifices to God. God accepts of them only as they are perfumed by Christ's meritorious sacrifice and potent intercession.

DIRECTION 3. When the Lord is pleased to grant thee any signal mercy or deliverance from trouble, beware of forgetting the Lord's kindness towards thee.

Forgetting of God's remarkable kind providences is an evil we are naturally prone to when we are in a prosperous state. Hence it is that the Spirit of God gives so many cautions against it in his word; and the saints of God do so solemnly charge their own souls to beware of it, as in Psalm 103 : 2 : "Bless the Lord, O my soul, and forget not all his benefits; who healeth all thy diseases, who redeemeth thy life from destruction." Forget not his benefits, but carefully preserve and treasure them up in thy memory. It was usual for saints under the Old Testament to set up some visible monument to remind them of God's singular favors to them; they erected stones and built altars to be memorials of the mercies they received, and put names on the places for this end. Let all this teach you to guard against this evil of forgetting the Lord's kind providence in recovering you from sickness.

You are guilty of this evil when you do not duly value the mercy, but let it pass as a turn of common providence. When you let the impression of the mercy soon wear off from your hearts; when you make a bad use of it, or do not rightly improve it to God's glory and your own soul's good; when you do not put on new resolutions to walk more exactly, live more fruitfully, and serve God more holily and humbly, then are you guilty of forgetting his benefits.

This is an evil most grievous and provoking to a good and gracious God, as is evident from the many complaints he makes of his people for it, as in Judges 8 : 34; Psalm 78 : 11; 106 : 13. Wherefore watch and pray against it.

DIRECTION 4. Inquire after those fruits of righteousness which are the genuine effects of affliction in the children of God, who are duly exercised thereby.

The apostle speaks of these fruits as naturally following upon sanctified afflictions, and a kindly exercise of spirit under them. Heb. 12 : 11. And therefore it is your duty to inquire if they be produced in you.

1. The increase of true repentance is one of these fruits which is the product of sanctified trials. Job found it in

himself on the back of his affliction: "Wherefore I abhor myself, and repent in dust and ashes." Job 42 : 6. It would be happy if we could find our hearts more soft and melting on the view of sin, after we have been in the furnace of affliction.

2. Another fruit is the improvement of faith. The afflicted believer is taught to look to, and depend more upon God for help in time of need, and less upon the creature. He now sees that vain is the help of man in the day of calamity, and that God in Christ is the only proper object of the soul's trust. This was the fruit of the apostle's affliction: "We were pressed out of measure, above strength, insomuch that we despaired even of life. But we had the sentence of death in ourselves, that we should not trust in ourselves, but in God that raiseth the dead; who delivered us from so great a death, and doth deliver; in whom we trust that he will yet deliver." 2 Cor. 1 : 8–10.

3. Humility and low thoughts of ourselves is another of the fruits of righteousness which sanctified affliction doth yield. How proud and lofty was Nebuchadnezzar before he was afflicted. Dan. 4 : 29, 30. But afterwards he is made to own God, and humbly submit to him as his supreme and almighty Sovereign, and to acknowledge that those who walk in pride he is able to abase. Verse 37. This was God's design in the various trials of his people Israel in the wilderness: "That he might humble thee, that he might prove thee, to do thee good at thy latter end." Deut. 8 : 16. See then, O believer, if this fruit be produced in thee.

4. Another fruit is the spirit of prayer and supplication. This was visible in the psalmist's case, after God had delivered him from the sorrows of death, and heard his voice: "Therefore," says he, "will I call upon him as long as I live" Psalm 116 : 2. O, saith the true believer, God's mercy to me in trouble, and his sending me relief when I cried to him, will make me love prayer the better, and en-

gage me to be more diligent in it all my days; for I still see I have daily need of his helping hand.

5. Heavenly-mindedness is also a fruit of sanctified affliction. Before, the man was inclined to say, It is good for us to be here; let us build tabernacles in this lower world. But now he changeth his language and his thoughts, and saith, It is good for me to draw nigh to God. Arise, let us depart; this is not our rest. This world is nothing but the house of our pilgrimage; heaven only is our home.

6. Another fruit of sanctified trials is greater love to God than formerly. How much was David's heart warmed with love and gratitude to God after his affliction, so that he wants words to express the affections of his soul. "I will love the Lord because he hath heard my voice. I was brought low, and he helped me. Thou hast delivered my soul from death, mine eyes from tears, and my feet from falling. What shall I render unto the Lord for all his benefits towards me?" Psalm 116 : 1, 6, 8, 12.

7. Learning and keeping of God's word is likewise a fruit of sanctified affliction. Psalm 119 : 67, 71. Let us inquire if this fruit be produced in us after sickness. Do we attend to the word more closely; do we believe it more firmly; do we embrace its offers more earnestly; and do we live more in the expectation of that glory which the word doth reveal to us? Then it is good for us that we have been afflicted; for we have learned more of God's word.

8. Tenderness of conscience is a happy fruit of sanctified trouble; when the believer, after it, becomes exceedingly afraid of sin, and of making new wounds in his conscience. He cannot think of adventuring again upon any known sin; for the smart of former wounds, and the pain they occasioned in his soul, when distress lay upon him, makes a deep and lasting impression on his mind, as it did on the afflicted church : "Remembering mine affliction and my misery,

the wormwood and the gall: my soul hath them still in remembrance, and is humbled in me." Lam. 3:19, 20. Now
such fruits of righteousness are an evidence that we have
been suitably exercised under affliction. O to find them pro
duced in us after sickness is over.

DIRECTION 5. Be careful to perform those resolutions, engage-
    ments, or vows you have come under in the time of sickness,
    and walk suitably to them.

As a time of sickness and affliction is a proper season for
making vows to God, and binding our souls with resolutions
to mortify sin in the heart, and purge it away from the life,
to be diligent in duty, and to walk more humbly with God;
so a time of recovery from sickness is a proper season for paying and performing these vows. This was the royal psalm
ist's practice in such a case. "I was brought low, and he
helped me. Truly I am thy servant, I am thy servant. I
will offer to thee the sacrifice of thanksgiving. I will pay
my vows unto the Lord now in the presence of all his people." Psalm 116:6, 16–18. Now, for your assistance in
this matter, I offer you these few ADVICES:

1. Defer not to pay your vows, but be speedy, and take
the first opportunity to pay them. Delays in this case are
most dangerous. Solomon, that wise man, was sensible of
this, which made him give thee this advice: "When thou
vowest a vow unto God, defer not to pay it." Eccles. 5:4.

2. Be still jealous of thy heart, which is prone to deal
treacherously with God after affliction is over. The Israelites' practice is a sad instance of this truth: "When he slew
them, then they sought him; and they returned and inquired early after God. Nevertheless, they did flatter him with
their mouth, and they lied unto him with their tongues; for
their heart was not right with him, neither were they steadfast in his covenant." Psalm 78:34–37. The purposes of
many in affliction are like the vows of mariners in a storm:
they are the first things which they forget and break when

once they win safe to the shore. However patient some may seem to be in sickness, yet when they recover from it, they soon return to their old sins again. They are like metals in a furnace, that melt and turn liquid while in it, but when out soon return to their old hardness. There is good reason for that caution the Lord gives us in Mal. 2 : 16 : " Therefore take heed to your spirit, that ye deal not treacherously."

3. Cry continually for strength from above to enable you to perform your vows. The psalmist took this course, and found it successful : " In the day when I cried, thou answeredst me, and strengthenedst me with strength in my soul." Psalm 138 : 3. And forget not, O believer, that God has treasured up strength for thee in thy head and surety Christ Jesus ; wherefore be still receiving from him, for the performing of all thy engagements. " My son, be strong in the grace that is in Christ Jesus." 2 Tim. 2 : 1. Put thy treacherous heart in thy Surety's hand ; for though thou art weak, yet thy Redeemer is strong. Whenever therefore you perceive your heart begin to start aside from God, be sure to check it, and look up to God in Christ for strength to secure you against its treachery and perfidious dealing : cry with the psalmist, " Be surety for thy servant for good."

4. Guard diligently against thy predominant sin, the sin that hath most easily beset thee, the sin that was most bitter and uneasy to thee in the day of distress. Keep a narrow eye upon it now ; for if once that sin be vanquished, the rest will the more easily be put to flight.

5. Be frequently meditating on thy vows, and on the condition thou wast in when they were made ; and study to keep alive in thy heart the same apprehension of things after sickness, which thou hadst in the time of it. How vain and comfortless did the world and its vanities then appear to thee ; how awful were the truths of God on thy spirits ; how far preferable was the loving-kindness of God to thee than

life ; how precious was Christ then in thy eyes. O that your judgment, thoughts, and impressions of these things may continue still the same.

6. Keep vivid your impressions of the preciousness of time, that you may diligently improve it; and shake off sloth and idleness. Remember what a view you got in the time of sickness of long-lasting eternity ; and what a trouble it was to you to look back and see how much time you had lost in sin and vanity. When sometimes we are brought to the brink of eternity, the near views we then get of its vastness and unchangeableness are frequently so awful and amazing to us, that we are ready to think, though we had Methuselah's years to live, it would be unreasonable wilfully to misspend one hour of them all. Well, then, is sickness over, our time so short, and so little of it remaining behind : will we be so foolish as to be lavish of it still, and trifle it away as before ?

7. Set a special mark upon all those sins, whether of omission or commission, that made death look grim and ghastly upon you in the time of sickness, and against which you resolved ; and see to get every one of them amended and removed. Remember and consider how sad it will be for you, if sickness find you again in the very same sins which formerly stung you. What will you say to conscience, when it shall challenge you ? How will you look death in the face, if it should find you living in the very same sins you formerly mourned for, and promised against ? Death would then be the king of terrors to thy soul indeed.

O then mind thy vows, and say with the psalmist, "Thy vows are upon me, O God ; I will render praises unto thee. For thou hast delivered my soul from death : wilt not thou deliver my feet from falling, that I may walk before God in the light of the living ?" Psalm 56 : 12, 13.

CHAPTER VI.

DIRECTIONS TO THE UNREGENERATE WHEN RECOVERED
FROM SICKNESS AND RESTORED TO HEALTH.

DIRECTION 1. Seeing the afflictions of the wicked are unsanctified, it is necessary you examine what sort of affliction yours
hath been, and what fruits it hath produced in you.

I HAVE in the preceding chapter showed that the afflictions of believers are fatherly chastisements, proceeding from
love ; that they are sanctified, and yield the peaceable fruits
of righteousness : I have given the marks of sanctified afflictions, and mentioned the happy fruits which they produce in
the children of God.

On the other hand, it is necessary to let Christless persons know, that their afflictions are of a different kind : they
are even punishments from God as a judge, proceeding from
wrath ; they are unsanctified to them, and produce no fruits
but what are bitter and unwholesome.

Well then, O Christless soul, hast thou reason' to suspect
the worst concerning thy sickness ; that it hath not been
sanctified, and its fruits are not good ?   O then labor to know
the truth of the matter, that thou mayest be humble under
a sense of thy misery, and flee to Jesus Christ for relief.
And for thy assistance in this inquiry, I will give some MARKS
OF UNSANCTIFIED AFFLICTIONS.

1. If sickness hath not humbled thee under a sense of
thy sins, the procuring cause thereof, nor any wise weakened
sin in thee, nor reclaimed thee from it, but it remaineth in
thee as strong as ever, it is a sign thy affliction is unsanctified.   This was the case of those of whom God complaineth
in Jer. 2 : 30 : " In vain have I smitten your children ; they
received no correction."   As if he had said, The medicine I
gave them did not purge out sin, nor weaken corruption in
the least.   They have been stricken, but have not grieved

for sin ; the fire hath burnt round about them, but they have not laid to heart the sin that kindled the flame.

2. It is a mark of unsanctified affliction when it hath no influence upon a sinner to bring him to serious communing with his own heart concerning the state of his soul, and to inquire in what terms he stands with God that afflicts him. God's voice by affliction is that in Hag. 1 : 7, " Consider your ways." In the day of adversity consider where you are, what you are, what you have done, and what is the meaning of the rod, and what will be the issue of it through eternity, in case it hath a commission to cut the thread of life. Now when a man remains stupid and careless about these important matters, and never noticeth the voice of affliction, so as to inquire seriously about his soul's condition : " Am I under a covenant of works, or a covenant of grace ? Am I a child of God ? Have I fled to the city of refuge, or am I still in a shelterless state ? Am I still under a cloud of wrath, or am I brought under the banner of love ?"—I say, where there are no such inquiries, the affliction is unsanctified.

3. It is a certain sign of unsanctified affliction when a person grows worse by it, and revolts the more the longer he is stricken, like those in Isa. 1 : 5.

QUESTION. When may it be said that a person grows worse by affliction ?

ANSWER. 1. When the sinner's heart turns harder than it was before : so every plague on Egypt increased the plague of hardness in Pharaoh's heart. It fares with many hearts as with iron that is often heated in the fire and quenched in the water, it still increaseth in hardness. 2. When a person giveth way to impatience and murmuring against God while he afflicts him. 3. When the lusts of the heart grow strong and impetuous, and afterwards rage the more for having been stopped in their course by affliction. In such cases a person grows worse by the rod.

DIRECTION 2. Consider the great danger of not being made better, by sickness, and of not complying with the voice of God's rod.

God's voice by his rod doth loudly call sinners to repent and flee to the Lord Jesus Christ for refuge from wrath. Now, when this voice is not hearkened to, but men go on in their reckless and sinful course as before, God is highly provoked, and the issue will be terrible.   For,

1. Though sickness be removed, and the furnace of affliction be cooled for the time, yet the wrath that kindled it continues still to burn.   And you have ground to fear lest you be ranked among those who are the generation of God's wrath, against whom he will have indignation for ever.

2. If lesser rods do not awaken you, you may expect greater and sorer judgments are coming on you.   Yea, God may cause them to come rolling thick upon you, as waves and billows in a storm, one upon the neck of another.   The great depths, both above and below, may be opened together; the displeasure of God, and wrath of men, may conspire and meet to pour themselves as water-spouts upon you at once; and to whom then will you look for help?

3. The Lord may give over dealing with you, or using any further means to reclaim you; he may refuse to correct you any more, or to bestow a rod upon you for your good, and may say of you, as of Ephraim, "Ephraim is joined to idols; let him alone."   Hos. 4 : 17.

4. The Lord may give you up to spiritual plagues and judgments; and indeed this commonly is the result of obstinacy and incorrigibleness under outward rods.   When Israel would not hearken to God's voice, he gave them up to their own hearts' lusts.   Psalm 81 : 11, 12.   Now, these plagues are the severest of all.   External judgments are God's rods, but spiritual judgments are his swords, which pierce the very soul.   Blindness of mind, hardness of heart, searedness of conscience, vile affections, and a reprobate sense, are the

very forerunners of hell and damnation. Those who are impenitent and unfruitful under outward afflictions, have cause to tremble lest God be provoked to inflict these spiritual judgments.

5. Be assured, though God spare you long, yet the glass of his forbearance will at length run out. God's patience towards sinners hath a term and bound which it will not pass. The time will come when a long-suffering God will at last say, "My Spirit shall no longer strive;" and the angel will cry, as in Rev. 14 : 7, "The hour of God's judgment is come." You that abuse God's patience and presume upon it, his treaty of peace will end with you in a little, and the master of the house will rise up and shut to the door. Then patience will come down, and justice will ascend the stage and trample upon and triumph over all that abuse divine patience. Sodom was a wonder of God's patience for a long time; but now it is a lasting monument of his anger.

6. If you be not made better by God's rods or sparing mercies, then your preservation at present will be nothing but a reservation for the day of God's wrath. And the longer your cup of sin is in filling, the fuller shall the cup of God's wrath be for you : by your impenitence and abuse of God's patience, you treasure up wrath for yourself against the day of wrath, Rom. 2 : 4 ; and though you be delivered from some judgments, you are reserved for worse, yea, seven times worse, according to Lev. 26 : 23, 24. Nay, there is a fatal blow designed against you, both soul and body, as soon as your cup is full; and the axe is already laid at the root of the tree. Matt. 3 : 10. One blow of God's axe will cut you off for ever.

Remember this, O sinner; though God's hand be lifted off you at present, and his messenger death be for a little recalled, yet he will quickly return and knock so loud at your door as not to be refused. And what will you do in the day of visitation? How ghastly must the pale horse be, when hell follows him at the heels; and how hot and fiery must that hell be, which is inflamed and blown up by so long impenitence and abuse of patience.

DIRECTION 3. Wonder at the patience of God in sparing such hell-deserving sinners as you are, and be thankful for it.

Hath a long-suffering God preserved the thread of your life, when it was almost snapt asunder by the violence of sickness? Hath he freed you from racking pains, under which you were groaning; nay, saved you from the grave and hell, into which you were falling? And have you not cause of wondering and thanksgiving? To move you to it, consider these few things:

1. How miserable had you been through all eternity, if your sickness had carried you off to another world in your sins. You had been howling with damned spirits, under endless and easeless torments, and for ever cut off from those hopes and offers of mercy you now have. Then the master of the house would have had the door so barred against you that it could never have been opened again to you, knock as you would. Luke 13 : 25.

2. Consider how heavily you have burdened his patience with your heinous sins, and frequent relapses thereinto; and that after convictions, calls, and various rods, sent to reclaim you; so that he was put to say, as in Amos 2 : 13, "Behold, I am pressed under you, as a cart is pressed that is full of sheaves." He was overburdened with your sins, so that the axle-tree of patience was ready to break and let you fall into hell, and yet, behold, he bears with you still.

3. Consider how soon he could have eased himself of the load, and shaken you off into the pit of destruction. In a moment he could have done it, and yet he bears many years with your sins that are so grievous to him. Yea, it is with a sort of reluctance that he eases himself of sinners

after he gets the utmost provocation. "Ah, I will ease me of mine adversaries." Isa. 1 : 24.

4. How ready he is to turn away his anger, and reprieve sinners from destruction, when in their distress they make even a show of repentance and turning unto God, as we see in Psalm 78 : 36, 38. He, like a tender-hearted prince, calls back the warrant for their execution, after it had gone forth.

5. Consider how much many Christless sinners are indebted to Jesus Christ for sparing mercy. He is represented by the vine-dresser interceding that the fruitless fig-tree might be spared and tried yet longer, after orders given to cut it down. Luke 13. Were it not for Jesus Christ, O sinner, however much you forget and slight him, you had surely been in hell long ere now. How oft doth he obtain another year, and after that another, for the unfruitful sinner and unthankful abuser of divine patience.

6. Consider how sparing mercy hath distinguished you from many others, who lived not so long, nor sinned so much as you have done. God hath wounded the hairy scalp of many and taken them away in their youth, when he hath continued you to manhood, and perhaps to old-age, though your sins and ill-deservings be greater than those of many on whom he hath long since taken vengeance.

God hath left many also tossing and groaning on beds of pain, when he hath eased and raised you up. O then return like the thankful leper, and magnify the God of your health. Hath God distinguished you from others by his goodness? It becomes you to distinguish yourselves from others by your thankfulness. O that men would praise the Lord for his goodness—undeserved and distinguishing goodness.

To move you to this, let me set the example of Hezekiah before you. See how thankfully and affectionately he remembered the Lord's mercies in recovering and delivering him from the bitter affliction he had been under : "I said, I am deprived of the residue of my years ; I shall behold man no more with the inhabitants of the world. Like a crane or a swallow, so did I chatter ; I did mourn as a dove. Behold, for peace I had great bitterness ; but thou hast in love to my soul delivered it from the pit of corruption. The living shall praise thee, as I do this day." Yea, he was so overcome with a sense of the Lord's patience and mercy towards him, that he is at a loss how to express it. "What shall I say ? He hath both spoken unto me, and himself hath done it." Isa. 38 : 9–20.

Let all who are recovered from sickness study to imitate that good king in holy admiration and thankfulness to the God of their life.

DIRECTION 4. Study to improve the sparing mercy and goodness of God to you in a right and suitable manner.

O sinner, hath God brought you back from the gates of death and brink of hell, restored you to health, and given you a new offer of mercy and salvation through Christ in a preached gospel, which you formerly despised? Strive now to improve the Lord's patience and kind dealings towards you with the utmost care, and abuse his patience no longer And in order thereto, take the following COUNSELS :

1. Be deeply humbled for your former obstinacy and impenitence, notwithstanding God's gracious and patient dealing. O let the sparing mercy and goodness of God towards thee lead thee to repentance, which is the chief design of it, according to Rom. 2 : 4 : "Despisest thou the riches of his goodness, forbearance, and long-suffering, not knowing that the goodness of God leadeth thee to repentance ?" As if he had said, "Dost thou not see, O man, the kind providence of God in sparing and recovering thee from sickness, taking thee by the hand, and pointing out to thee to go to thy closet to mourn and weep for all thy past sins, and particularly for thy misspending the time of health, and abusing

the Lord's patience?" The consideration of David's goou-
ness and forbearance towards Saul melted Saul's heart, hard
and rugged as it was, and made him lift up his voice and
weep, and say to David, "Thou art more righteous than I;
for thou hast rewarded me good, whereas I have rewarded
thee evil. And thou hast showed this day how that thou
hast dealt well with me; forasmuch as when the Lord had
delivered me into thine hand, thou killedst me not. For
if a man find his enemy, will he let him go well away?"
1 Sam. 24 : 17–19. Oh, far more reason hast thou, O man,
to weep and cry, "God hath found me his enemy, yea, in
my enmity and sins, fighting against himself; he had me
on a sick-bed, and on the very brink of hell, and the least
touch of his hand would have thrust me in; but yet he hath
spared his enemy, and let me go well away. Oh, shall not
these cords of love draw me, and this matchless goodness
invite and hire me to repent? Can any consideration in
the world be more powerful than this to melt my hard heart
into tears of holy shame and sorrow for my stiffneckedness
and rebellion against a gracious and long-suffering God?
Away with these cursed, God-provoking sins of mine. Down
with these weapons of rebellion. Let me never lift them
more against such a merciful sovereign."

2. Zealously improve the time which God in his long-
suffering hath lengthened out to you, in working out the
salvation of thy soul. Have you so long been loading the
patience of God with your sins; have you many a day been
grieving his Holy Spirit, by trifling away your time, slighting his motions, and venturing on sins against light? Oh
then beware of burdening his patience any more; but diligently hearken to every motion of God's Spirit and of your
own conscience for the time to come. You have much
work to do, and but little time to do it in; therefore lay
hold on every opportunity for carrying it on. The consideration of the time you have already lost and misspent should

make you the more diligent in what remaineth. How much of it have you lost in youth; how much in ignorance; how much more in negligence; how much in worldliness; how much in pastimes; how much in idle words; how much in actual sins and provocations against God. And now it may be near the evening of your day; and will you not spend the evening which God is mercifully lengthening out, with extraordinary care and diligence? If a traveller lose the beginning of the day, he must travel the faster in the evening, otherwise he may fall short of his journey, and have his lodging to seek for when night comes. Paul had misspent much of the beginning of his life; and this consideration, when his eyes were opened, stirred him up to be the more diligent in the service of God, so that he was more zealous than any of the rest of the apostles. O man, follow his example, and trifle no longer in the work of God. Art thou not convinced thou hast squandered away enough of this precious treasure of time already? And wilt thou also misspend and throw away the little that remains? Oh, be not so foolish.

3. Be careful to raze all false foundations, and build your hopes of salvation upon the only sure rock Jesus Christ. Let it not discourage thee from digging to the foundation, that so much of thy day is lost; for it is better to do it late than never. Remember, how miserable is the condition of that house which is built upon the sand. Matt. 7 : 27. For when the flood comes, and the storm arises and beats upon it, great and dismal will the fall of that house be. Do not build your hopes of heaven upon God's absolute mercy, upon your convictions, upon your freedom from gross sins, upon your prayers or tears, upon your morality and just dealings with men. Though these be necessary and excellent in themselves, yet they are false foundations to build the hopes of your justification and salvation upon, seeing they are wholly insufficient to bear such a weight. However much

these things have been esteemed and valued by you formerly
in the matter of justification, yet, if you resolve to be a wise
builder you will let them all go, yea, count them all but
loss and dung, that you may win Christ our only hope,
build on him alone, and be found in him, not having on your
own righteousness, which is but filthy rags.

Well, then, raze and tear up every false foundation; dig
deep, till you win to the rock Christ. Dig deep into the
holy law and nature of God; dig till you see the infinite
strictness of divine justice, the unspeakable evil that is in
sin, the hidden vileness and abominations of the heart, your
own inability to do any thing for your help and relief. Dig
yet further, till you see the infinite fulness and freeness of
God's grace in Jesus Christ—that suitable remedy that answers all a poor sinner needs. Dig deep, and dig on till you
win to this Rock; let your cry to God still be, Lord, lead
me to the rock Christ, and his all-sufficient righteousness
only. Act faith upon this rock, rely on it, build all your
hopes on it, and say, "This is my rest for ever; here will I
dwell, for I have desired it. Lord, the desire of my soul is
only to Christ, and to the remembrance of his name."

4. If you would rightly improve the sparing mercy and
goodness of God, let it lead you to repentance and reformation of life. Turn from all these sins, whether of omission
or commission, now in the day of health, which conscience
challenged you for in the time of sickness. Mind Christ's
caution and warning to healed sinners: "Behold, thou art
made whole; sin no more, lest a worse thing come unto
thee." John 5 : 14. Oh let thy sin die with thy sickness,
and do not relapse into thy former security and sinful ways.
Beware of returning with the dog to thy vomit, and like the
sow that is washed, to the wallowing again in the mire of
thy former sins and uncleannesses, lest being entangled and
overcome again with the filthiness which thou now hast
escaped, thy latter end prove worse than thy beginning.

5. And to sum up all I shall say in this chapter, be careful to redeem time, and active in providing for an eternal state. O prize and value the mercy of health and strength more than ever. Sympathize with those who are still lying on sick-beds, and under languishing distempers; neglect not to pity and pray for them. Remember the distressed case you were in yourself when you had no rest in your bones, when wearisome nights were appointed to you, and you were full of tossings to the dawning of the day. Consider how slippery is your standing. Though the late storm of trouble be over, yet the clouds will return after rain.

CHAPTER VII.

DIRECTIONS TO THE SICK WHO ARE APPARENTLY IN A
DYING CONDITION, AND DRAWING NEAR TO ANOTHER
WORLD.

I HAVE already in the first, third, and fourth chapters,
given several directions concerning our submission to the
will of God, making preparation for death, calling for ministers, edifying others by our discourses, settling our worldly
affairs, etc., and therefore I shall not repeat them, but proceed to speak of other things.   Only let me add this word,
if you have hitherto neglected to make your wills, settle
your worldly affairs, send for ministers to discourse with and
pray over you ; delay it no longer, but do it speedily, while
you have the use of your reason and understanding.   And
what I have more to say, take it in the following directions.

DIRECTION 1. Consider, when death stares you in the face, that
now is the time, if ever, to exert the utmost activity in preparing to meet it.

Alas, it is to be regretted that the greater part of men
neglect their souls, misspend their lives, misimprove their
health, and leave undone the work for which they were created, preserved, and favored with the gospel.   Surely a near
prospect of death and judgment cannot but be distressing to
such persons.   What a melancholy thought must it be for a
dying man, " Oh, I had all my time given me to make preparation for endless eternity ; and alas, I never minded it
till now that I must leave this world.   Is there any hope
for such a careless and miserable sinner ?"   I acknowledge
the case is sad, but yet it is not remediless nor desperate ;
seeing there is a sacrifice provided for your sins, and an all-
sufficient Saviour who never cast out any humbled soul that
came to him for mercy.   You have great reason indeed to

abhor and condemn yourself before God for your sin and
folly; yet despair not, but believe, whatever be your sins,
your dangers, your fears, and temptations, that Jesus Christ
is both able and willing to save to the uttermost all that
come to God by him; and that his grace aboundeth more
than your sin aboundeth. O how glad would devils and
damned souls in hell be, if they were but in your case, and
had your offers and hopes; how diligently would they improve the time of mercy. O be persuaded then to spend the
little time that now remains with the utmost care, in making
penitent confession of sin to God and applying to the blood
of Christ for pardon. Nay, even the best of God's people
have need to be diligent at this time, in making actual preparation for dying. God is now saying to you, as Joshua
did to the Israelites, "Prepare your victuals, for within three
days ye shall pass over this Jordan, to go in to possess the
land which the Lord your God giveth you." Joshua 1 : 11.
Lay in provision for your passing over this Jordan of death;
you know not how rough the passage may be.

I shall give some MOTIVES to press this diligent and active
preparation; and therefore consider,

1. The short time of your life that remains is all the
time you have for working out your salvation. What you
do for attaining heaven and avoiding hell must be done now
or never; for there is no work nor device in the grave
whither thou goest, nor is there any coming back to this
world to amend what hath been amiss. Dying is a thing
you cannot get a trial of; it is what you can only do once,
and no more. Heb. 9 : 27.

2. Be diligent now, for as soon as death gets a commission to cut you off, it will execute it; it will not spare you,
nor allow you one minute more time to prepare for eternity.
The most merciless enemies have sometimes been overcome
by the prayers and tears of such as on their knees did beg a
little more time to prepare for another world, and have listen-

ed to their requests; but this enemy, death, will not grant one moment's respite.

3. Consider that your eternal state and condition will be according to the state in which you die. Death will open the doors either of heaven or hell to you, in one of which you shall take up your eternal abode. As the tree falls at death, so will it lie through eternity.

4. Consider what a serious and awful matter it is to die and go into another world, for then you will have immediately to do with God your judge; there will be no veil then between him and your soul. You will then enter into a world of spirits, wherewith you are so little acquainted, not knowing but devils must be your companions for ever. Surely then it is your interest to give all diligence now, to make your acquaintance with the Lord of that world, before you enter into it.

5. Put forth thy utmost activity for thy soul now; for be sure Satan will put forth his utmost against it. If thou be in a Christless state at this time, he will use all his efforts and stratagems to keep thee from Christ, either by flattering thee that thy state is good, thereby to lull thee asleep in sin and security, or by telling thee it is too late to help matters with thee, thereby to drive you into despair. The devil will leave no method unattempted to ruin thy soul when death is near: for he knows his time is short; and if he catch not the soul then, he will never get it: and neither can he hurt it hereafter; for if once it enter heaven, he can trouble it no more.

If thou art a believer in Christ, Satan thy malicious enemy will not fail to attack thee at this time with all his might; for though he may know he cannot keep thee out of heaven, yet he will labor to render thy passage towards it as dark, tempestuous, and uncomfortable as possibly he can. But it is the believer's happiness that this cruel enemy is under a strong chain, and cannot do all he would; for Jesus

Christ is the good shepherd that hath undertaken for all his sheep. Nevertheless, by his wise permission, this adversary may sometimes give great disturbance to a dying saint; which calls thee to the greatest diligence and watchfulness at this time. It is the observation of one, that as the devil is most busy at the conclusion of a duty, as of prayer, that the Christian may be most disturbed and distracted when he is to close up all in the name of Christ, and so all his desires be frustrated; so he is most busy in the conclusion of our days and when death is at hand, seeking by temptations, distractions, and false imaginations to do us all the mischief he can, and all because he knoweth his time is short. "The devil is come down, having great wrath, because he knoweth that he hath but a short time." Rev. 12:12. He may fitly be called *the wolf of the evening*, mentioned in Jer. 5:6, because he comes forth most fiercely in the evening of men's lives, to assault their precious souls. Yea, so busy is he sometimes with believers under dangerous sickness, seeking to overthrow their faith and assurance, that it is the observation of a good man, that he seldom seeth a sick saint, followed close by temptations, recover of that sickness; for Satan, knowing he hath but little time, proves as troublesome to him as he can. Hence that great man of God Mr. Knox, said, when he came to die, "In my lifetime the devil tempted me to despair, casting my sins in my teeth; but now in my sickness he tells me I have been faithful in the ministry, and so have merited heaven; but blessed be God, who brought these texts into my mind: Not I, but the grace of God in me. What hast thou, that thou hast not received?" The children of Israel had never such hot work from their enemies, as when they just came to enter into the promised land.

What need then hast thou, O believer, to be diligent in thy preparations on a dying bed to quicken grace: put forth thy utmost strength; bring all the assistance thou canst from the Captain of thy salvation, when thou hast such a cruel enemy to encounter with. Now is the time for action, though indeed it were wisdom to leave as little to be done at this time as possible.

DIRECTION 2. Continue to the last in the exercise of true repentance and humiliation for sin.

Possidonius, who wrote the life of Augustine, saith, that he heard him often say in his health, that repentance was the fittest disposition both for dying Christians and ministers; and for himself, that he died with tears in his eyes, weeping for sin. When death approacheth nearest, we should thus stir up ourselves to give sin the most deadly blow of any we have given it all our life. As it is most laudable to die forgiving sinners that have wronged us, so also taking revenge upon sin that hath injured a gracious God. The apostle tells us, that indignation and revenge attend true repentance. 2 Cor. 7 : 11. Wherefore, as Samuel took vengeance on Agag a little before his death, and Moses at God's command avenged the children of Israel of the Midianites just before he was gathered to his people, Numbers 31 : 2, and dying Samson gave a more fatal blow to the Philistines than any he had given them before; so a dying Christian should at the last take the severest revenge upon sin, which hath so oft through his life dishonored God, pierced Christ, and grieved his Holy Spirit. It is the last opportunity you will have to show your indignation at it, and therefore do it effectually.

Again, consider it is old sins unmourned for, that many times keep believers so much in the dark when they come to die. These do raise so many thick clouds about their evening sun, and hinder them from going off the stage with such comfortable assurance of God's love as they might otherwise attain to. These did very much hinder Job's peace in the day of affliction, as he complains, "Thou makest me to possess the iniquities of my youth." Job 13 : 26. It is a sad thing when young sins and old bones meet together. Oh that young people would mind this in time; you are doing that now which will abide with you to old-age, if not to eternity. Sin must be bitter some time or other, for God calls it a root that bears gall and wormwood. Deut. 29 : 18. Israel could not have peace nor success while there was an Achan in the camp; so neither can you have consolation or assurance while any sin lies unreckoned for in the conscience. Make a thorough search then into old sins, and mourn over them. We find Paul frequently calling over the sins of his life, and even those he was guilty of before conversion : " I was injurious, a blasphemer," etc. ; whereby he maintained much inward peace and consolation. Be oft looking back to old sins with inward sorrow and faith in Christ's blood, if you would have a death-bed easy and soft to you.

DIRECTION 3. Be mindful of all acts of justice and charity which may be incumbent upon you at this time.

It is great wisdom in men to settle their worldly affairs in the time of health, that so their minds may be free for spiritual exercises, and not disturbed with earthly cares and business when they come to a dying bed ; but if this hath been neglected hitherto, it must not be omitted now. I have given directions about it, Chapter I., Direction 6, so that I shall say little here : only be careful to do justice to every man, as much as in you lieth ; and particularly, by making a just and rational provision for your wife and children ; by ordering payment of all your just debts, without defrauding any of your lawful creditors; and by making restitution in case you have wronged any man. If justice be not done in these matters, how can your souls be disburdened of guilt ?

In the next place, forget not the acts of charity which God requires of all the professors of the gospel.

1. Seek reconciliation with your neighbors, where any

difference or mistakes have taken place, that so you may die in peace and charity with all about you.

2. Be ready from the heart to forgive those that have done you any wrong. If the natural sun should not go down upon our wrath, much less should the sun of our lives. If you carry an unforgiving spirit with you into another world, how can you expect to meet with a forgiving God there, when he hath expressly declared, "If ye forgive not men their trespasses, neither will your Father forgive your trespasses?" Matt. 6 : 15. Oh, then, imitate your glorious Saviour and his martyr Stephen, who at their death begged mercy from God for those that mortally hated them Luke 23 : 34 ; Acts 7 : 60.

3. If the Lord hath given you substance, honor the Lord with it by leaving some part of it to the poor, and to pious uses. I have pressed this once and again before, but I mention it frequently, because it is much forgotten by dying persons in our age. Remember, it is not left arbitrary to you to give or not, as you please ; no, for God doth charge it upon you as a duty, yea, a debt that you owe him : "Charge them that are rich in this world, that they do good; be rich in good works, ready to distribute." 1 Tim. 6 : 17, 18. And he pronounceth them blessed who consider the poor. Psalm 41 : 1. I grant that people are not to leave all their works of charity to a death-bed. These should also be minded in our lifetime, so as to make our own hands our executors, and our own eyes the overseers of our charitable projects ; but surely it is a proper season for showing charity to God's poor when we are leaving them, and cannot have opportunity for showing it more. Remember what is recorded of Dorcas after her death, Acts 9 : 36, that she was a woman full of good works and alms-deeds ; and her friends showed the effects of her charity to Peter after her death : all which was written for our example and admonition, that we may be rich in such good works, that our friends may

have them to show after our death. Surely it is a sign of the degeneracy of this age, and that religion is on the declining hand, when people generally fall so short of the zeal and piety of their fathers in this matter.

4. It would be a commendable work of charity in dying persons, to be giving many good counsels to their relations and children, and to be putting up many fervent prayers to God for them. So Christ, when near to death, committed his spiritual children to his Father, and earnestly begged his protection and care of them : "I am no more in the world, but these are in the world : keep them through thy name; keep them from the evil." John 17 : 11. In like manner cry to God for your children : "Lord, thou hast graciously given them to me ; I now restore them back to thee. They were born to me once; O that they may be born to thee a second time. I am leaving them in the midst of snares and temptations; O that it may be their happiness to be preserved in Christ Jesus. Keep them by thy power through faith unto salvation. Oh take them within the bond of thy covenant, and be thou their father, to protect, direct, and provide for them ; give them a name in thy house better than of sons and daughters, that I may meet with them at thy right hand with everlasting joy."

5. Be suitably concerned also for the whole church of Christ, and especially for those that are in affliction, that God may loose their bonds, and send them liberty and prosperity in his due time. "Do good in thy good pleasure unto Zion ; build up the walls of thy Jerusalem. Peace be within her walls, and prosperity within her palaces."

DIRECTION 4. Labor to overcome the love of life and the fear of death, that you may attain to willingness to die and leave the world when God calleth you to it.

It is no wonder that a wicked man, or one that hath no interest in Christ, should be unwilling to die : for, he is affrighted with the guilt of past sins, and the fears of future torments; and it is impossible to be rid of these till he become a true believer in Christ. No man hath ground to welcome death but the believer; yet it is to be regretted, that so many of them should appear unwilling to leave this world, which is nothing to them but a wilderness and weary land. Lot's soul was vexed and troubled in Sodom, and yet he was loath to leave it; so some believers, when called to leave a vexing world, do show much hankering towards it, and linger behind. This proceeds partly from nature, which dreads a dissolution, and partly from the weakness of grace. But Oh let all God's children labor to overcome this aversion, and go forth to meet death half-way and bid it welcome. And for their help in this matter, I will lay before them the following ARGUMENTS.

1. Consider how little reason a believer hath to be much in love with this present life. It is a sinful life; sin dwells in your nature, breaks out in your life, and pollutes all your duties. How often have you groaned under this burden; and should you not be glad to be eternally delivered from it? It is a life of diseases and infirmities; and should you not be willing to be cured of them all at once? It is a life of temptation: Satan is still harassing thee, and should you not be desirous to be out of his reach? It is a life of persecutions from the wicked: they hate, reproach, and injure you many ways; and is it not desirable to be "where the wicked cease from troubling, and the weary be at rest?" It is a life of clouds and darkness; your sun is often veiled, and your evidences obscured, which occasions many bitter complaints; and should you not desire that time when the day shall break and all shadows fly away? It is a life of calamities and fears; it is like a stormy sea, where one wave rolls upon the back of another; and when one calamity is past, we many times fear a greater is coming; and sometimes the heavens turn so black and gloomy, that we fear a hurricane of judgments is ready to blow; and should you not bless God,

when he comes by death to house your souls, and set you out of harm's way? It is in mercy that God takes away the righteous from the evil to come. Isa. 57 : 1. So dealt he with Josiah : "I will gather thee unto thy fathers, and thou shalt be gathered into thy grave in peace ; and thine eyes shall not see all the evil which I will bring upon this place." 2 Kings, 22 : 20. So is it observable that Methuselah died the very year of the flood, Augustine a little before the sacking of Hippo, Pareus just before the taking of Heidelberg. Luther observes that all the apostles died before the destruction of Jerusalem ; and Luther himself died before the bloody wars broke out in Germany. Thus God frequently hides his people from the temptations and troubles that are coming on the earth. Why? he sees many of them not in case to endure them ; and therefore he in mercy takes them away from a tempting and sinning world, to a land of holiness and rest. While we are here, we live in a world that lies in wickedness ; every sense of the body betrays the soul into sin : the poor soul can scarce look out at the eye, and not be affected ; nor hear by the ear, and not be distracted ; nor smell at the nostrils, and not be tainted ; nor taste at the tongue, and not be allured ; nor touch by the hand, and not be defiled.

O believer, what is this life that thou art so fond of? it is but a living death, or dying life. It is full of grief for things past, full of labor for things present, and full of fears for things future. The first part of our life is spent in folly ; the middle part is overwhelmed with cares, and the latter part is burdened with infirmities and age. And what gain we by prolonging this life? nothing but to suffer more evil. And should a Christian be unwilling to be rid of those grievances?

2. Consider that dying is appointed as the way, and the only way to glory ; there is no way to enter the promised land, but by crossing the Jordan of death. And should not

a stranger desire to be at home with his friends, though he
hath a rough way and stormy sea to pass? Is there any
home like heaven, where your incomparable friend Christ is?
O what a happiness is it to be with Christ, and to see him
as he is. How happy do you think Peter, James, and John
were, in being taken up to mount Tabor, to be eye-witnesses
of their Saviour's transfiguration; but, O believer, death
procures a greater happiness to you: it ushers you to mount
Zion, where you shall not only see your Saviour whiter than
the snow, and brighter than the sun, but yourself transfig-
ured with him, made like him, and eternally secure of his
presence. The three apostles saw but two prophets; but
you shall see all the prophets, all the apostles, all the patriarchs, all the martyrs, all the holy persons you ever conversed with on earth, and, in fine, all the saints in heaven,
each of them shining as the sun; and how sweet will their
company be! O how soon will the trifles of the world vanish, and all its pleasures be forgotten, when once the believer
gets a view of that captivating glory above. When the
shepherds heard but some few notes of the angels' song who
praised God at the nativity of our Saviour, they presently
left their flocks, and ran to Bethlehem to behold the child
Jesus lying in the manger; how much more cause hath a
believer to leave all the pleasures of the world, and run to
behold an exalted Jesus sitting on the throne of his glory,
with all his saints and angels singing praises around him?

If Cato and Cleombrotus, two heathens, after reading
Plato's book of the immortality of the soul, did voluntarily,
the one fall on his sword, the other break his neck from a
precipice, that they might the sooner come, as they fancied,
to partake of those joys; what a shame is it for Christians,
who have a surer and clearer discovery of those things from
God's own book, to be found unwilling to enter into those
heavenly joys, when their Redeemer calls for them thither?

3. Consider how willing Christ was to come from heaven

to earth for you; and should you be unwilling to remove from earth to heaven for him, yea, for yourselves? for the gain is yours. O did Christ assume your nature, become obedient to death, and purchase an inheritance for you with his blood; and will you be backward to go and take possession of it? O for a Christlike obedience.

4. Consider what a reproach is cast on Christianity by a believer's unwillingness to die. For Christians to pray and speak much of Christ, of heaven and glory, and yet be unwilling to enter into that glory, what is it but a mistrusting of God, and a tempting of strangers to think there is no reality in religion?

And since death is not easy to grapple with, receive the following COUNSELS how to attain to this blessed disposition, a willingness to die.

1. Be frequently putting forth the acts of faith upon the righteousness of Christ; and believe that Christ died to bring in a perfect righteousness for believers, that they all might be complete in him. Now why should a believer be afraid to appear before God in Christ's righteousness, which is so pleasing and acceptable to him? They are said to be "without fault before the throne of God." Rev. 14:5. If a believer were to appear before God in his own righteousness, clothed with his own duties and performances, it would be dreadful to think of dying; but to have the white garment of our elder Brother to put on, gives another view of death. Alas, it is our neglecting the daily exercise of faith in the righteousness of Christ, that makes the thoughts of death so unwelcome.

2. When you attain to peace and reconciliation with God, labor to preserve it. State and clear your accounts with God every day; and watch against those sins that wound conscience, waste comfort, and grieve the Spirit of adoption. When we think God is displeased with us, we are afraid of going to him.

3. Study to be more denied to the enjoyments of this life, and to use them with a holy indifference; otherwise there will be an unwillingness to leave them.

4. Labor to be deeply sensible of the burden of indwelling sin and corruption, and the workings thereof in your heart; and this will make the thoughts of death welcome, because it eternally delivers you from it.

5. Seek further discoveries of the loveliness of Christ, and the daily exercise and increase of your soul's love to him; for it is the nature of love to long after communion with the person that we love.

6. Make death familiar to you by frequent forethoughts of it. Retire oft from the world to think of dying, even when you are in your best health.

7. Be much taken up in the sweet employment of praising God, and exalting the worthy Lamb that was slain; and this will incline you to be there where this is the continued work.

8. Be oft thinking of those warnings and forerunners of death, which God sends to wean your heart from the love of life, and dispose you to a willingness to die. For this end, God sends manifold diseases, pains, infirmities, wants, straits, losses, crosses, and disappointments. And in a special manner, let old people view the forerunners and harbingers of death which God sends to prepare his way; such as the decays and infirmities of old-age, which we have elegantly described in figurative expressions, Eccles. 12 : 2–7 : "Then the light of sun, moon, and stars shall be darkened;" that is, in old persons, the intellectual powers and faculties, which are as lights in the soul, shall be weakened. And then "the clouds return after rain;" that is, their distempers are frequent, like a continual dropping in a rainy day, and the ending of one is but the beginning of another. Verse 3. "Then the keepers of the house do tremble;" that is, the head and hands which were employed for the preservation of the body

do shake. "The strong men bow themselves;" that is, the legs and thighs, which are the pillars of the house, become weak and feeble. "The grinders cease because they are few;" that is, the teeth, which, like the upper and nether millstone do grind out meat and prepare it for digestion, then cease to do their part. "Those that look out of the windows are darkened;" that is, the eyes wax dim, whereby God calls us to turn them away from beholding vanity, to look after the things that are not seen. Verse 4. "The daughters of music are brought low;" that is, they have neither voice nor ears: they can neither sing themselves, nor take pleasure in the voice of singing men or women. Then death pulls us as it were by the ear, to think of the music above. Verse 5. "The almond-tree flourisheth;" that is, the hair grows white, like the almond-tree in blossom. And as the out-parts of the body do weaken and decay, so also do the inward parts thereof; therefore it is said, verse 6, "The silver cord shall be loosed, the golden bowl broken, the pitcher broken at the fountain, and the wheel broken at the cistern;" that is, the silver cord of the sinews is loosed, which carries the faculty of sense and motion from the head, through the body; the head, which like a golden bowl or box, contains the brain, that is, the fountain of sense and motion, through age is broken and turns crazy; the pitchers and wheels of the arteries, which carry the nourishing blood and vital spirits from the well of the heart unto each part of the body, become like broken vessels. All these things do warn old persons to take their affections off from the things of time and set them upon things above, that they may be helped to say, we "desire to depart and to be with Christ."

But after all, some believers will have objections against willingness to die; some of which I shall consider.

OBJECTION 1. I am about to be cut off in the flower of my age.

ANSWER. Instead of fretting on this account, you ought

rather to adore and praise a gracious God, that is willing to
bestow the reward of the whole day upon thee, who hast
only labored some hours of it. Praise him that is willing
to take you so soon home; whereby you will prevent much
sin and sorrow in the world.

OBJECTION 2. I have houses and lands, and a comfortable dwelling on the earth.

ANSWER. These are only needful in your passage through
the world; above, there is no use for these comforts. There
God provideth mansions for his people a thousand times more
comfortable. John 14:2; 2 Cor. 5:1. Surely houses of
God's building and of Christ's furnishing are preferable to
the cottages built by men's hands.

OBJECTION 3. But I am loath to leave God's ordinances,
and the sweet communion I have had with him therein.

ANSWER. Above, there will be no need of ordinances, sacraments, bibles, or ministers; for the lamb will be the light
of the heavenly temple, and all hid things in religion will
be discovered in Christ's face. There you will celebrate an
eternal Sabbath, drink the fruit of the vine new with Christ,
be ever with the Lord, without any cloud or interruption of
your communion with him. Is it any loss to be taken from
the shallow streams, and set by the fountain that is ever full
and running over?

OBJECTION 4. I am loath to leave the company of godly
friends and relations.

ANSWER. Death will take you to your friend Christ,
which is far better than them all. And for one friend you
lose on earth, you shall find a hundred in heaven; and those
godly relations you leave here, you shall meet again there,
where you will have far sweeter communion than you can
possibly have upon earth with them, or the best of men,
who, while here, have several infirmities and passions, that
many times make their converse less pleasant.

OBJECTION 5. But I would fain see the glory of Zion

upon earth, when God's promises to her shall be accomplished.

ANSWER. So Moses would fain have seen Israel's happiness in the promised land; but his dying in the firm belief of God's fulfilling all his promises to them there, was more acceptable to God than his beholding the performance. And the glory of the church militant is a sight nothing comparable to that of the church triumphant above.

OBJECTION 6. But I would gladly stay to do God more service in his church below, whose necessities are so great.

ANSWER. You will not want opportunity for serving and glorifying God above, where you will be in far better case for it. Here, our hearts are often out of tune for God's work, and we are forced to hang our harps upon the willows; but above, there are no willows to hang them on; no saint there will ever complain of any indisposition of heart or tongue

Moreover, God knows the necessities of his church, and is more concerned for them than thou canst be; and it is easy for him to raise up instruments to carry on his work when thou art gone.

OBJECTION 7. I am afraid of the pain and pangs of death. The thoughts of these make me shrink back.

ANSWER. Many die without much seeming sense of pain, and it is probable have less pain at the hour of death, than they have felt under previous diseases. Or if the pains be sharp, they are soon over; and each pang of death will set sin a step nearer the door, and thy soul a step nearer home; and therefore it becometh a Christian to die cheerfully, and to be glad when he can find the grave.

Now, what I have said in this chapter is to the believing soul; for it is no wonder that the souls of the ungodly at death shrink back into the body and tremble to go forth, when they can have no prospect of any better lodging than utter darkness.

DIRECTION 5. Study to imitate the ancient worthies, by dying in faith.

This was the character and epitaph of the Old Testament saints: "These all died in faith." Heb. 11 : 13. As they had lived by faith, so they died in faith. They not only continued true believers to the last, dying in the state of faith, but they died in the exercise of faith also. Now the exercise of faith in dying includes SEVERAL PARTICULARS worthy to be imitated by all dying believers.

1. An open and professed adherence to the doctrine of faith and truths of Christianity. This faith all Christians should zealously own in the view of death, and persevere in it to the last without wavering. This would be to die like martyrs, though we die in our beds. How steadfastly did old Polycarp adhere to Christ and his truths to the last, and so died in faith. When he was urged by the proconsul to deny Christ, he answered, " These fourscore and six years have I served him, and he never once offended me; and how shall I now deny him ?"

2. Dying in faith imports an inward, hearty, and firm belief in the fundamental articles of the Christian faith, and improving them so as to make them the foundation of our comfort and hope at the hour of death. For instance, we must yield our departing souls, in the firm belief of their living and existing in a separate condition after this life, and of that future state of blessedness and rest which God hath prepared for all believers. Again, we must dismiss this body to the grave, in a firm belief and hope of a joyful resurrection at the last day. Thus that holy man Job both lived and died in faith. " I know that my Redeemer liveth, and that he shall stand at the latter day upon the earth. And though after my skin, worms destroy this body, yet in my flesh I shall see God." Job 19 : 25, 26. A Christian dies in faith, when he so believes these truths as cheerfully to obey God's call, and venture into the invisible world upon

the testimony which God has given concerning it; as Abraham did in going out to an unknown land. "By faith Abraham, when he was called to go out into a place which he should after receive for an inheritance, obeyed; and he went out not knowing whither he went." Heb. 11 : 8.

3. The believer dies in faith, when he makes fresh application to Christ as his only hope and Saviour, takes him in his arms of faith, as old Simeon did before his death, saying, "In the Lord Christ I have righteousness and strength;" though I have neither righteousness nor strength in myself, yet I have both in him, my blessed surety and Redeemer. We have many uses for faith in Christ at the hour of death. By faith we must depend upon Christ's blood for making atonement, and washing away the guilt of all our past sins. By faith we must put on the righteousness of Christ for covering our naked souls, when they are to appear and stand before God. By faith we must rely on Christ for strength to suffer pain, resist temptations, and conquer death and all our enemies. By faith we must look to Christ as our leader, and trust him for our safe conduct through the dark valley of death, and for our safe landing on the shore of glory.

4. The believer dies in faith, when he trusts his departing soul with confidence in his Redeemer's hand, saying with Paul, "I know in whom I have believed, and am persuaded that he is able to keep that which I have committed to him against that day." 2 Tim. 1 : 12. This was the psalmist's practice: "Into thy hand I commit my spirit; for thou hast redeemed me, O Lord God of truth." Psalm 31 : 5. So the man that dies in faith commits the jewel of his soul to his Redeemer's keeping, and confides in his care of it. Why? he made it, he hath redeemed it, he loves it, it is his own, a member of his body, and he will not hate his own flesh. He loves his dying saints much better than we love an eye, a hand, or any other member of our body, which, most certainly, we will not lose, if it be in our power to save it.

5. Dying in faith imports that the dying saint confides in God's faithfulness and truth for making good all those promises to his church and people after his death, which are not yet accomplished. We should go off the stage of life in the firm belief of God's fulfilling all his promises concerning the prosperity of his church, the calling of the Jews, the destruction of antichrist, and the second coming of our Lord; and likewise concerning our families, that God will be as good as his word, and be a father to the fatherless, and a husband to the widow.

Would you then be so happy as to die in faith, take these ADVICES:

1. Be careful to get faith beforehand; for death is a time to use faith, not to get it. They were foolish virgins who had their oil to buy when the bridegroom was close at hand.

2. Study to live every day in the exercise of faith; and be still improving and making use of Christ in all his offices, and for all those ends and uses for which God hath given him to believers.

3. Frequently clear up your evidences for heaven, and beware of letting sin blot them to you.

4. Record and lay up the experiences of God's kind dealings with you, and be often reflecting upon them, that you may have them ready at hand in the hour of death.

5. Meditate much on those promises which have been sweet and comfortable to you in the time of trial, and beg that the Lord may bring them to your remembrance when you come to die.

DIRECTION 6. Place the examples of other dying saints before you, and study in like manner to shine in grace, and be exemplary in piety and heavenly discourse, for the glory of God and good of souls, when you are going off the stage.

·This is the last opportunity you can have of doing service to God and the interests of religion; wherefore strive to improve it diligently for the honor of God, and to the edifica-

tion of those that survive you. How pleasant is it to see
God's people leaving the world commending Christ and his
service, and perfuming the place they lie in with their last
breath.   I have, Chapter III., Direction 5 and 6, adduced
several motives to press this point, and given directions concerning the discourse and behavior of the children of God
when on sick-beds, which I shall not repeat.

That which I design here is, to set before you the examples of some eminent saints, and their pious and holy
sayings when they were dying ; and this in order to confirm
and establish others in religion, and also to excite them to
imitate those shining worthies when they also come to die.
Surely it is for this very end that God hath ordered us to be
compassed about with so great a cloud of witnesses.   Heb.
12 : 1.   Thus doth the apostle improve their example.
Heb. 11.   And how earnest is he in this matter : "And
we desire that every one of you do show the same diligence,
to the full assurance of hope unto the end ; that ye be not
slothful, but followers of them who through faith and patience
inherit the promises."   Heb. 6 : 11, 12.

I shall begin with some examples from THE SACRED
HISTORY ; and,

1. With the King of saints, our Lord Jesus Christ.   O
how sweet and comforting were his discourses unto his disciples when his death drew nigh ; and what a heavenly
prayer did he make for them, and all his elect ones at that
time !   These we have recorded in the 14th, 15th, 16th, and
17th chapters of John : which are most seasonable at all
times for us to read and meditate upon, but especially when
death is approaching.   And likewise let us read the history
of our Lord's crucifixion, in which we may observe the wonderful expressions of his faith in God, his patience under sufferings, his pity to his enemies, his love to his mother and
his disciples, his concern for his Father's glory, his obedience
in his death, and his willingness to be offered up.   Thus the

blessed Sun of righteousness did shine forth most gloriously at his setting, with the radiant beams of heavenly graces and virtues; and herein he hath set a pattern to all dying saints to the end of the world.

2. Jacob, when he was on his death-bed, called his sons together, and gave them many special charges and blessings; we have his excellent words recorded in Genesis 48 and 49. And in particular, how sweetly doth he speak of the coming of the Messiah to them. Genesis 49 : 10, 18. And how affectionately doth he commend God's goodness and kind providence towards him through his life: "The God which fed me all my life long unto this day, the Angel which redeemed me from all evil, bless the lads." Gen. 48 : 15, 16.

3. Joseph, when he was dying, spoke lovingly to his brethren, who had dealt cruelly with him, and assured them of the Lord's faithfulness in keeping his promise to their fathers: "I die, and God will surely visit you, and bring you out of this land." Gen. 50 : 24.

4. Moses, when he was to go up to mount Nebo to die there, left many blessings, and gave many weighty charges to the children of Israel; we have his holy and ravishing words recorded in Deut. 32 and 33. And particularly, how pleasantly doth he commend God and his ways to the people: "He is the Rock, his work is perfect; for all his ways are judgment; a God of truth and without iniquity, just and right is he." Deut. 32 : 4.

5. Joshua, when he was near his end, gave many solemn charges and exhortations to the people, which we have narrated in Joshua 23 and 24. There we may see the remarkable methods he takes to rivet impressions and convictions upon them, now when he can instruct them no longer. And particularly, he appeals to their consciences concerning the faithfulness of God in keeping his word to them, that so he might engage them to fidelity to him. "And behold, this

day I am going the way of all the earth; and ye know in all your hearts and in all your souls, that not one thing hath failed of all the good things which the Lord your God spake concerning you." Josh. 23 : 14.

6. David, when his end was near, assembled the people, and solemnly charged them, as in the audience of God, to keep his commandments. 1 Chron. 28 : 8, 9. And particularly, he charged his son and successor, Solomon, to know the God of his father, and to serve him with a perfect heart and with a willing mind.

7. The apostle Paul, when taking his last farewell of the elders of Ephesus, most solemnly charges them to take heed to themselves and the flocks over which the Holy Ghost hath made them overseers. Acts 20 : 28. And how sweetly doth he sing in the view of approaching death : " I am now ready to be offered, and the time of my departure is at hand. I have fought a good fight, I have finished my course, I have kept the faith. Henceforth there is laid up for me a crown of righteousness, which the Lord, the righteous Judge, shall give me at that day ; and not to me only, but unto all them also that love his appearing." 2 Tim. 4 : 6–8.

In imitation of these scripture saints, the people of God in all ages have studied to glorify God and edify men at their death, by commending God and godliness to their friends and families. These we ought to teach by our example, both how to live and how to die, as others have done before us. Thus said once a dying saint to his family, " I have formerly taught you how to live, and now I teach you how to die."

Now, because in all ages the words of dying Christians have been much observed, and God hath remarkably blessed them to the establishment and confirmation, quickening and exciting of others to imitate them, I shall bring examples from HUMAN HISTORIES and writings, and mostly from Clark's

Lives, of sundry eminent saints whose graces have shone brightest, and their sayings been most heavenly, when the sun of their life was at the setting.

1. That old disciple Polycarp, when he came to the stake at which he was burnt, desired to stand untied, saying, "Let me alone; for He that gave me strength to come to the fire, will give me patience to endure the flame without your tying."

2. So holy Cyprian triumphed over death, saying, "Let him only fear death, who must pass from this death to the second death." When he heard the sentence of death pronounced against him, he said, "I thank God for freeing me from the prison of this body."

3. Basil, when the emperor Valens sent his officers to tempt him with great preferments to turn from the faith, rejected them with scorn, saying, "You may offer these things to children." And when they threatened him with sufferings, he said, "Threaten your purple gallants with these things, that give themselves to their pleasures."

When Modestus the prefect threatened Basil to confiscate his goods, to torment him, to banish him, or kill him, he answered, "He need not fear confiscation, that hath nothing to lose; nor banishment, to whom heaven only is a country; nor torments, when his body would be dashed with one blow; nor death, which is the only way to set him at liberty." The prefect telling him he was mad, he said, "I wish I may for ever be thus mad."

4. Ignatius being led from Syria to Rome to be torn in pieces of wild beasts, expressed his fear lest it should happen to him as to some others, that the lions out of a kind of reverence, would not dare to touch him. And therefore he often wished that "their appetites might be whetted to dispatch him. For," said he, "the lions' teeth are but like a mill, which though it bruiseth, yet wasteth not the good wheat, only prepares and fits it to be made pure bread. Let

me be broken by them, so I may be made pure manchet for heaven."

5. The great Mr. Knox, our reformer, when he lay dying was much in prayer, ever crying, "Come, Lord Jesus; sweet Jesus, into thy hands I commend my spirit." Being asked by those that attended him if his pain was great, he answered that "he did not esteem that a pain which would be to him the end of all trouble and the beginning of eternal joys." Ofttimes, after some deep meditations, he said, "O serve the Lord in fear, and death shall not be terrible to you; blessed is the death of those that have part in the death of Jesus."

After a sore temptation from Satan formerly mentioned, over which he triumphed at length, he said, "Now the enemy is gone away ashamed, and shall no more return. I am sure now my battle is at an end, and that without pain of body or trouble of spirit, I shall shortly change this mortal and miserable life for that happy, immortal life which shall never have an end." After one had prayed for him, he was asked whether he heard the prayer; he answered, "Would to God you had heard it with such an ear and heart as I have done;" adding, "Lord Jesus, receive my spirit." With which words, without any motion of hands or feet, as one falling asleep rather than dying, he ended his life.

6. Dr. Gouge, when he was old and dying, was sore afflicted with the stone and other painful maladies; yet, though by reason of his pains he was oft heard to groan, he never once murmured against the dispensations of God. He never cried out, *a great sufferer*, but oft, *a great sinner;* yet still comforted himself that there is a great Saviour. In his greatest torments he would say, "Well, yet in all these there is nothing of hell, or of God's wrath. Oh, my soul, be silent, be patient: it is thy God and Father that thus orders thine estate. Thou art his clay; he may tread

and trample upon thee as he pleaseth; thou hast deserved much more. It is enough that thou art kept out of hell; though thy pains be grievous, yet they are not intolerable, thy God affords some intermissions; he will turn it to thy good, and at length put an end to all; and none of these comforts can be expected in hell." In his greatest pains he often used holy Job's words, "Shall we receive good from the hands of the Lord, and not evil also?" When any of his friends would have comforted him by telling him of his eminent gifts and service in the ministry, he would answer, "I dare not think of any such thing for comfort; only Jesus Christ, and what he hath done and endured, is the ground of my sure comfort." The thoughts of death were pleasant to him, and he often termed death his best friend, next to Jesus Christ; and he would bless God that he had nothing to do but to die.

7. I have read of another minister peaceful under the like extreme pains. When he was asked how he did, his frequent answer was, "The bush always burning, but not consumed; though my pains are above the strength of nature, yet they are not above the supports of grace." He would pray, "Lord, drop comfort into these bitter waters of Marah. Let the blood of sprinkling, which extinguisheth the fire of thine anger, allay my burning pain. Oh, if my patience were greater, my pains would be less. Lord, give me patience, and inflict what thou wilt. This is a fiery chariot, but it will carry me to heaven. O my God, break open the prison door, and set my poor captive soul free; I desire to be dissolved, but enable me willingly to wait thy time." He would again cry, "When shall the time come, that I shall neither sin more, nor sorrow more? Lord, keep me from dishonoring thy name by impatience. Oh, who would not, even in burnings, have honorable thoughts of God? Lord, thou givest me no occasion to have hard thoughts of thee. Blessed be God, for the peace of mine

inward man, when my outward man is so full of trouble. This is a bitter cup, but it is of my Father's mixing; and shall I not then drink it?"

8. Mrs. Jean Askew, who was a martyr in king Henry's reign, thus subscribed to her confession in Newgate: "Written by me Jean Askew, that neither wisheth death, nor feareth its might, and as merry as one bound towards heaven." When the chancellor sent her letters at the stake, offering her the king's pardon if she would recant, she refused to look upon them, giving this answer: that "she came not hither to deny her Lord and Master."

9. Mr. James Bainham, when he was at the stake in the midst of the burning fire, which had consumed his legs and arms, spoke these words: "O, ye papists, behold, ye look for miracles, and here now ye may see a miracle; for in this fire I feel no more pain than if I were on a bed of down; it is to me as a bed of roses."

10. John Lambert, as he was burning in Smithfield, and his legs were quite consumed with the fire, lifted up his hands, his fingers flaming like torches, but his heart abounding with comfort, and cried out, "None but Christ, none but Christ."

11. Mr. Robert Glover, a little before his death, had lost the sense of God's favor, for which he was in great heaviness and sorrow; but when he came within sight of the stake at which he was to suffer, he was on a sudden so filled with divine comfort, that clapping his hands together, he cried out to his servant, "He is come, he is come;" and so died most cheerfully.

12. It was a saying of Augustine, "Boughs fall off trees, and stones out of buildings; and why should it seem strange that mortal men die?"

13. Mr. John Dodd had so violent a fever, that there was but little hope of his life; yet at length his physician coming to him, said, "Now I have hope of your recovery."

To whom Mr. Dodd answered, "You think to comfort me with this, but you make my heart sad. It is as if you should tell one who had been sore weather-beaten at sea, but thought he had now arrived at the haven where his soul longed to be, that he must go back again to be tossed with new winds and waves."

He would often say in his last sickness, "I am not afraid to look death in the face. I can say, Death, where is thy sting? Death cannot hurt me."

He used to say, "The knowledge of two things would make one willing to die; namely, What heaven is, and that it is mine." "Yes," said one, "if a man were sure of that." To whom he answered, "Truly, assurance is to be had; and what have we been doing all this while?"

Some others of the sayings of this holy man were so pithy and remarkable, I cannot pass them here.

Mr. Dodd once visited a godly minister on his death-bed who was much oppressed with melancholy, and complained to him, "Oh, Mr. Dodd, what will you say of him who is going out of the world, and can find no comfort?" To whom Mr. Dodd answered, "What will you say of our Saviour Christ, who when he was going out of the world, found no comfort, but cried out, My God, my God, why hast thou forsaken me?" He said of afflictions, "They are God's potions, which we may sweeten by faith and faithful prayer; but we, for the most part, make them bitter, putting into God's cup the evil ingredients of our impatience and unbelief." He called death, "the friend of grace, though it be the enemy of nature; for whereas the word, sacraments, and prayer do but awaken sin, death kills it." He used to say, "A man is never in a hard condition unless he have a hard heart and cannot pray." He instructed Christians how they should never have a great nor lasting affliction, and that was by looking unto the things that are not seen, which are eternal. 2 Cor. 4 : 17, 18. For what can be great to him that counts the world nothing; and what can be long to him that counts his life but a span long? When he saw a Christian look sad, he would say as Jonadab did to Ammon, "Art thou a king's son, and lookest so ill?" And when such complained to him of their losses and crosses, he would use the words of Eliphaz to Job: "'Do the consolations of God seem small unto you?' God hath taken from you your children or your goods, but he hath not taken from you himself, his Christ, nor his Spirit, nor heaven, nor eternal life."

To a friend of his that rose from a mean to a great estate, he sent word, that "this was but as if he should go out of a boat into a barge or ship; but he ought seriously to remember, that while he was in this world, he was but floating upon a sea."

He often said, that if it were lawful to envy any, he would envy those that turn to God in their youth; whereby they escape much sin and sorrow, and are like Jacob that stole the blessing betimes. He used to compare reproofs given in a passion to scalding potions, which the patient could not take down; in reproofs, we should labor for meekness of wisdom, using soft words and hard arguments.

He was a most popular minister, but much persecuted. Once he took a journey to see his father-in-law Mr. Greenham, and to bemoan himself to him on account of his crosses and hard usage. Mr. Greenham having heard all he could say, answered him thus: "Son, son, when affliction lieth heavy, sin lieth light." Mr. Dodd used oft to bless God for this speech, saying, "If Mr. Greenham had bemoaned him as he expected, he had done him much hurt." He forgot not this saying in his old age, but made excellent use of it for himself and others.

14. Œcolampadius, that famous divine of Switzerland, when lying on his death-bed, and being asked whether the light did not offend him, answered, pointing to his breast,

Hic sat lucis, "Here is abundance of light;" meaning of comfort and joy. He asked one of his friends, "What news?" His friend answered, "None." "Then," saith he, "I will tell you some news; I shall presently be with my Lord Christ."

15. A certain godly man passing through his last sickness with extraordinary calmness of conscience, being asked by some of his friends about it, answered, that "he had steadfastly fixed his heart upon that sweet promise, 'Thou wilt keep him in perfect peace whose mind is stayed on thee; because he trusteth in thee.'" Isa. 26 : 3. "And my God," said he, "hath graciously made it fully good unto my soul."

16. Mr. Robert Bolton, minister at Broughton, well known by his writings, in the time of his last sickness, which was long and sharp, often breathed out these words: "Oh, when will this good hour come; when shall I be dissolved; when shall I be with Christ?" Being told, that to be dissolved was indeed better for him, yet it would be better for the church that he would stay here; he answered, "If I shall find favor in the eyes of the Lord, he will bring me again, and show me both it and his habitation; but if otherwise, lo, here I am, let him do what seemeth him good." Being asked by another, if he could not be content to live, if it pleased God, he answered, "I grant that life is a great blessing of God, neither will I neglect any means that may preserve it; and do heartily submit to God's will: but of the two, I infinitely desire more to be dissolved and to be with Christ." He bade all that came to see him make sure of Christ before they came to die; and look upon the world now as a lump of vanity. He encouraged the ministers that came to him to be diligent and courageous in the work of the Lord, and not to faint nor droop for any affliction that should meet them in it.

When he found himself very weak, he called for his wife and children. He desired her to bear his dissolution, which was near at hand, with a Christian fortitude; a thing he had been preparing her for by the space of twenty years; and bade her make no doubt but she should meet him again in heaven. He exhorted his children to remember those things he had frequently told them before; adding, that "he hoped and believed that none of them durst think of meeting him at that dread tribunal in an unregenerate state."

Some of his parishioners coming to watch with him, it was requested, that as by his instructions he had taught them the exceeding comforts that were in Christ, so he would now tell them what he felt in his own soul. "Alas," said he, "do you look for that of me now, that want breath and strength to speak? I have told you enough in my ministry: but yet, to satisfy you, I am by the wonderful mercies of God, as full of comfort as my heart can hold; and I feel nothing in my soul but Christ, with whom I heartily desire to be." And observing some weeping, he looked to them and said, "Oh, what an ado there is before one can die."

When the pangs of death were upon him, being told that some of his dear friends were about him to take their last farewell, he caused himself to be raised up in his bed, and after a few gaspings for breath, he said, "I am now drawing on apace to my dissolution: hold out, faith and patience; your work will speedily be at an end." And then shaking them all by the hand, he prayed heartily and particularly for them, and desired them to make sure of heaven, and to bear in mind what he had formerly told them in his ministry, protesting to them that the doctrine he had preached to them for the space of twenty years was the truth of God, as he should answer it at the tribunal of Christ, before whom he should shortly appear.

When he was struggling with death, a very dear friend taking him by the hand, asked him if he felt not much pain. "Truly, no," said he, "the greatest I feel is your cold hand."

17. Mr. John Holland, a godly minister, continued his

usual practice of expounding the Scriptures in his family to
the last; and the day before his death he called for a Bible,
and causing some one to read the eighth chapter of Romans,
he discoursed upon it verse by verse; but on a sudden he
said, "O stay your reading; what brightness is this I see;
have you lighted up any candles?" A bystander said, "No,
it is the sunshine;" for it was about five o'clock in a clear
summer's evening. "Sunshine," said he, "nay, it is my
Saviour's sunshine. Now, farewell world; welcome heaven;
the day-star from on high hath visited my heart: O speak
it when I am gone, and preach it at my funeral; God deal-
eth familiarly with man: I feel his mercy, I see his majesty,
whether in the body or out of the body I cannot tell, God
knoweth; but I see things that are unutterable." And in
this rapture he continued till he died.

18. I knew, not long ago, an eminently godly man,
G—— M——, that fell into extraordinary raptures some-
time before his death, such as his bodily strength and spirit
were not able to support, though he had no sickness. Sometimes he was so swallowed up and overcome by the manifestations of God's love to his soul, that his words could not
be well understood; his natural color, heat, and strength,
would so go off, that all about him would conclude him to
be dying; but when he was able to get words uttered, they
were so heavenly and ravishing concerning the love of Christ
and freeness of grace, that bystanders could not hear him
without weeping. Sometimes ministers, when they came to
visit him, and found him in these raptures, were forced to
turn all their prayers in his behalf into praises; except that
they would put up some petitions to God, that "He might
graciously spare and be tender of his weak body, and enable
him to bear that load of loving-kindness God was pleased
to let out to him, and which his present bodily strength was
not sufficient for." Yea, they would be put to cry, "Lord,
if it be thy will, hold thy hand, for he is but a clay vessel;

this new wine will burst the old bottle; preserve him in life as a monument of the rich grace of God, for the conviction of atheists and carnal people, and for the confirmation of the faith of the children of God." Sometimes he would cry in abrupt expressions, "O, angels, help me to praise him; O, saints, admire his love, and wonder at him." Again, "O flames of love; my soul seeth Christ; the heavens open; I see a throne, and the Lamb in the midst of the throne. O what think ye of Christ? my soul breathes, breathes towards him; my spirit is exhaled out of me by the manifestations of God." He used frequently to say with a heavenly air to his friends, "O what think ye of Christ?" When his ecstasy did somewhat abate, so that he attained a pleasant calmness of thought and freedom of speech, he would discourse of the mysteries of religion, the electing love of God, the freedom of grace, the unsearchable riches of Christ, and the glorious contrivance of redemption through his death and sacrifice. I say, he would talk of these things more like an angel than a man; for such was his heavenly eloquence, fluency of words, and facility of speaking upon these subjects, which otherwise was not natural to him, that those who came to see him were exceedingly surprised and astonished to hear him. His body gradually weakened under these raptures of spirit, and he longed much to leave the world, because he thought he could be so little useful in it for advancing God's honor. He reckoned himself bound to improve the short time he was like to have here, in commending Christ and religion to all he had access to, and also to admonish them of any thing he knew amiss in them, which he did most convincingly. And having occasion to see some who disparaged the established church, and the ordinances dispensed in it, he highly commended the ordinances, and told them that from his own sweet experience he could say, that God was to be found in them. He seemed to have sin wonderfully mortified; for he complained of no other heart-plague but self, and it was his great exercise to get self wholly subdued; he pursued it through many of its windings and lurking places, and after all he would regret his little success against it. "For," said he, "when I am in my most elevated frames, and admitted to the nearest access to my Redeemer, the subtle enemy self will enter in with me, and offer to pull the crown off his head before my face."

Once, after hearing a sermon on Psalm 85 : 8, "I will hear what God the Lord will speak," he broke out in a rapturous discourse to one that came to see him, blessing God that he had spoken to him in that sermon. "And O," said he, "what am I, that the Rock of Israel should have spoken to me these three sermon-days bygone, assuring me that all my sins are forgiven? What am I, a vile worm, that he should be so kind and condescending as to discover Christ and heaven in such a manner to me, and assure me that I shall shortly be with him? Oh, I thought that I had sinned him away from me, but I see he will not bide away. O admirable grace! O help me to praise him."

When death drew near, there was some alteration in his case, yet he never questioned his interest in Christ, but still asserted, "I know he is my God and my Redeemer, and I will shortly be with him." And once, when he was ready to complain for want of God's wonted manifestations, he said, "The Lord knew his body was now weak, and could not bear what formerly he had met with; yet," said he, "glory to his name, he hath given me three blinks since my last illness began."

19. Dr. Harris, head of Trinity college in Oxford, in his last sickness used to exhort all about him to get faith above all things. "It is your victory, your peace, your life, your crown, and your chief piece of spiritual armor. Howbeit, get on all the other pieces, and go forth in the Lord's might. Stand to the fight, and the issue shall be glorious. Only forget not to call in the help of your General. Do all from

him, and under him." On the Lord's-day he would not have any kept from the ordinances upon his account; and when they returned from the sermons, he would say to them, "Come, what have you for me?" And when any gave him account of what they had heard, he would resume the heads thereof, and say, "O what excellent truths are these. Lay them up carefully, for you will have need of them." When friends came to visit him, he would say, "I cannot speak but I can hear." Being asked where his comfort lay, he answered, "In Christ, and in the free grace of God."

One telling him that he might take much comfort in his labors, and the good he had done, his answer was, "All is nothing without a Saviour; without him my best works would condemn me. Oh, I am ashamed of them, they are mixed with sin. I have done nothing for God as I ought. Oh, loss of time sits very heavy upon my spirits. Work, work apace; assure yourselves nothing will more trouble you when you come to die, than that you have done no more for God, who hath done so much for you."

Sometimes he used thus to breathe out himself: "I never in all my life saw the worth of a Christ, nor tasted the sweetness of God's love as now I do." Being asked by ministers what they should chiefly request for him, he answered, "Do not only pray for me, but praise God that he supports me, and keeps off Satan from me in my weakness; beg that I may hold out. I am now a good way home, near the shore; I leave you tossing on the sea. O it is a good time to die in."

In all his wills which he made, he took care this legacy should be inserted, "Item, I bequeath to all my children, and to their children's children, to each of them a Bible, with this inscription, None but Christ." He used to say, "It is a hard thing for a saint to forgive himself some faults, when God hath forgiven them."

20. David Chitræus, when he lay dying, lifted up his

head from the pillow to hear the discourse of his friends that
sat by him, and said, that "he should die with the greater
comfort, if he might die learning something."

21. Mr. Cooper, when dying, said, "I saw not my children when they were in the womb, yet there the Lord fed
them without my care or knowledge. I shall not see them
when I go out of the body, yet shall they not want a father."
Again, "Death is somewhat dreary, and the streams of that
Jordan between us and our Canaan run furiously; but they
stand still when the Ark comes."

22. The reverend Mr. Halyburton, that shining light in
St. Andrews, when dying, commended Christ and godliness
with great earnestness to all that came to see him. He exhorted his brethren to diligence in the ministry. "It was
the delight of my heart," said he, "to preach the gospel. I
desired to decrease, that the Bridegroom might increase; and
to be nothing, that he might be all. I repent that I did not
more for him. O that I had the tongues of men and angels,
to praise him." When he was advised to lie quiet, he said,
"Whereupon should a man bestow his last breath, but in
commending the Lord Jesus Christ, God clothed in our
nature, dying for our sins?"

He caused to be read one of Mr. Rutherford's letters, that
to Mr. John Mein, and then said, "That is a book I would
commend to you all; there is more practical religion in that
letter, than in a book of a larger volume."

He exhorted some ministers that came to see him to
faithfulness. "As for the work of the ministry," said he,
"it was my deliberate choice; were my days lengthened out
much more, and as troublesome as they are likely to be, I
would rather be a contemned minister of God than the greatest prince on earth." He said, when taking farewell of his
wife, children, and servants, "Here is a demonstration of the
reality of religion, that I, a poor, weak, timorous man, as
much afraid of death as any, am now enabled, by the power

of grace, composedly and with joy to look death in the face. I dare look it in the face in its most ghastly shape, and hope within a little while to have the victory. I cannot but commend the Lord Jesus. As far as my words will go, I must proclaim it, he is the best master that ever I saw." To his son he said, "If I had as many sons as there are hairs on your head, I would bestow them all on God." To some present, he said, "Sirs, I have great fears that a rational sort of religion is coming among us : I mean by that, a religion that consists in a bare attendance on outward duties and ordinances, without the power of godliness ; and thence people shall fall into a way of serving God which is mere deism, having no relation to Christ Jesus and the Spirit of God." He expressed his fears of a storm coming on the church of Scotland ; but he said, "The day would break, and the Lord would arise, and he hoped the church would be made a wonder, and the Lord say, Lo, this people have I formed for myself. He can make a nation to be born at once." He often cried with the spouse in the song, "When shall the day break, and the shadows flee away ? Turn, my beloved, and be thou as a roe, or a young hart on the mountains of Bether."

He said, "Shall I forget Zion ? Nay, let my right hand forget her cunning, if I prefer not Jerusalem to my chiefest joy. O, to have God returning to this church, and his work going on in the world : if every drop of my blood, every bit of my body, every hair of my head, were all men, they should all go to the fire to have this work going on." He said, "If I should say that I would speak no more in the name of the Lord, it would be like a fire within me. I am calling you to see a miracle : God is melting me down into corruption and dust, and he is keeping me in a calm. I could not believe that I could have borne, and borne cheerfully, this rod so long ; this is a miracle, pain without pain ; and this is not a fancy of a man disordered in his brain, but of one lying in full composure. O blessed be God, that ever I was born. I have a father and mother and ten brethren and sisters in heaven, and I shall be the eleventh. I shall shortly be at that glory that I have been long expecting. Worthy is the Lamb to receive glory."

23. Mr. Hugh Mackaill, in his speech before his death, said, "I have esteemed the solemn engagements of this nation to the Lord pregnant performances of that promise, Isa. 44 : 5, where it is evident that where church reformations come to any maturity, they arrive at this degree of saying, I am the Lord's, and subscribing with the hand unto the Lord. So was it in the days of the reforming kings of Judah, and after the restoration from the captivity of Babylon, in the days of Nehemiah. This same promise did the Lord Jesus make yea and amen to us, when he redeemed us from spiritual Babylon. I glorify him, that he hath called me forth to suffer for his name and ordinances, and the solemn engagements of the land to him. Hereafter I will not talk with flesh and blood, nor think on the world's consolations. Farewell, all my friends, whose company hath been refreshing to me in my pilgrimage ; I have done with the light of the sun and moon. Welcome eternal life, everlasting glory. Praise to Him that sits upon the throne, and to the Lamb for ever."

24. The famous Mr. Durham, in his last sickness, which was long and lingering, was visited by a minister, who said to him, "Sir, I hope you have so set all in order, that you have nothing else to do but to die." "I bless God," said Mr. Durham, "I have not had that to do these many years."

25. The dying prayer of Mr. Rowland Nevant for his children was, that the Mediator's blessing might be the portion of every one of them ; adding to them, I charge you all, see to it that you meet me on the right hand of Christ at the great day. When he was sometimes much spent with his labors, he would appeal to God, that though he

might be wearied in his service, He would never be weary of it. Being often distressed in his body, he would say he was never better than in the pulpit, and that it was the best place that he could wish to die in.

26. When Mr. Philip Henry was dying, his pains were very sharp. He said to his neighbors who came to see him, " Oh make sure work for your souls by getting an interest in Christ while you are in health; for if I had that work to do now, what would become of me ?" A little before his last illness, he wrote to a reverend brother, " Methinks it is strange that it should be your lot and mine to abide so long on earth by the stuff, when so many of our friends are dividing the spoil above; but God will have it so; and to be willing to live in obedience to his holy will, is as true an act of grace as to be willing to die when he calls." One asking him how he did, he answered, "I find the chips fly off apace, the tree will be down shortly." He was sometimes taken with fainting-fits, which when he recovered from, he would say, "Dying is but a little more." Once he said, after recovery, " Well, I thought I had been putting into the harbor, but I find I must go to sea again."

27. Mr. Matthew Henry's death was somewhat sudden. A little before he died, he said to some about him, " You have been used to take notice of the sayings of dying men : this is mine, That a life spent in the service of God and communion with him, is the most comfortable and pleasant life that any one can live in this world."

28. Holy and learned Mr. Rutherford, a little before his death, left a written testimony to our covenanted work of reformation ; and therein he proves the warrantableness of nations entering into covenant with God under the New Testament times, and shows that this practice is the accomplishment of several Old Testament prophecies, such as Jer. 50 : 4, 5 ; Isa. 2 : 3 ; Zech. 8 : 2 ; Isa. 19 : 23, 24, 25, which relate to gospel times ; and when he was dying, sent several

messages to the presbytery of St. Andrews, desiring them to
adhere to God's cause and covenant. In his sickness he
often broke out in sacred raptures, extolling and commending the Lord Jesus, whom he often called his blessed Master,
his kingly King. When his death drew near, he said, "I
shall shine, I shall see him as he is, I shall see him reign,
and all his fair company with him, and I shall have my
large share; my eyes shall see my Redeemer, these very
eyes of mine, and no other for me." When exhorting one
to be diligent in seeking God, he said, "It is no easy thing
to be a Christian; but for me, I have gotten the victory,
and Christ is holding out both his arms to embrace me."
He was wonderfully strengthened against the fears of death;
"For," said he, "I said to the Lord, if he should slay me
five thousand times, I would trust in him; and I spoke it
with much trembling, fearing I should not make my boast
good. But as really as ever he spoke to me by his Spirit;
he witnessed unto my heart that his grace should be sufficient for me." He said to some ministers that came to see
him, "My Lord and Master is the chief of ten thousand of
thousands; none is comparable to him in heaven or in earth.
Dear brethren, do all for him: pray for Christ, preach for
Christ, feed the flock committed to your charge for Christ;
visit and catechize for Christ; do all for Christ, and beware
of man-pleasing. Feed the flock out of love, the chief Shepherd will appear shortly." Once when he recovered from
a fainting-fit, he said, "I feel, I feel, I believe, I enjoy, I
rejoice, I feed on manna." As he took a little wine in a
spoon, Mr. Robert Blair said to him, "You feed on the dainties of heaven, and think nothing of our cordials on earth."
He answered, "They are all but dung; yet they are Christ's
creatures, and in obedience to his command, I take them."
After some discourse, Mr. Blair said to him, "What think
ye of Christ?" to which he replied, "I shall live and adore
him. Glory, glory to my Creator, and to my Redeemer for

ever. Glory shines in Emmanuel's land." Afterwards he said, "O that my brethren did know what a Master I have served, and what peace I have this day. I shall sleep in Christ; and when I awake, I shall be satisfied with his likeness." Then he said, "This night shall close the door, and put my anchor within the veil; I shall go away in a sleep by five o'clock in the morning;" which exactly took place. That night, though he was very weak, he often had this expression, "Oh for arms to embrace him! Oh for a well-tuned harp."

When some spoke to him of his former carefulness and faithfulness in the work of God, he said, "I disclaim all that; the gate I would go in at is 'redemption and forgiveness of sins through his blood.'" His last words were, 'Glory, glory dwelleth in Emmanuel's land."

29. When Hugh Kennedy, provost of Ayr, was dying, a minister said to him, "You have cause, sir, to be assured that the angels of God are now waiting at the side of this bed to convey your soul to Abraham's bosom;" to whom his answer was, "I am sure thereof; and if the walls of this house could speak, they could tell how many sweet days I have had in fellowship with God, and how familiar he hath been with my soul." He was one of the greatest wrestlers with God there was in the age wherein he lived, and had most remarkable returns of prayer. The great Mr. Welsh, in a letter from France, said of him, "Happy is that city, yea, happy is that nation that hath a Hugh Kennedy in it; I have myself certainly found the answers of his prayers from the Lord in my behalf."

30. The great Mr. Robert Bruce, minister of Edinburgh, when dying through weakness and old-age, being asked by one of his friends how matters stood now between God and his soul, answered, "When I was young, I was diligent, and lived by faith on the Son of God; but now I am old, and not able to do so much, yet he condescends to feed me

with lumps of sense." The morning before he died, he came to breakfast at table, and having eaten, as usual, one single egg, he said to his daughter, "I think I am yet hungry; you may bring another." But presently he fell into a deep meditation; and having mused a while, he said, "Hold, daughter, hold; my Master calls me." With these words his sight failed him, whereupon he called for the Bible; but finding his sight gone, he said, "Turn to the eighth chapter of the epistle to the Romans, and set my finger on these words, 'I am persuaded that neither death nor life shall be able to separate me from the love of God which is in Christ Jesus my Lord.' Now," saith he, "is my finger upon them?" They told him it was. Then without any more, he said, "God be with you, my children; I have breakfasted with you, and shall sup with my Lord Jesus Christ this night;" and so gave up the ghost.

31. John Stewart, provost of Ayr, was a singularly pious man; yet when he lay dying, he said to some about him, "I go the way of all flesh, and it may be some of you doubt nothing of my well-being; yea, I testify, that except when I slept or was on business, I have not these ten years been without thoughts of God so long as I should be in going from my house to the Cross: and yet I doubt myself, and am in great agony, yea, at the brink of despair." But a day or two before he died, he turned his face to the wall from company for two hours. Then Mr. Ferguson the minister coming in, asked what he was doing; upon which he turned himself with these words: "I have been fighting and working out my salvation with fear and trembling; and now, I bless God, it is perfected, sealed, confirmed, and all fears are gone."

32. Luther, when he fell sick, made his will, in which he bequeathed his detestation of popery to his friend and to the pastor of the church, and said, "O Lord God, I thank thee that thou wouldst have me live a poor and indigent

person upon earth. I have neither houses nor lands, nor possessions, nor money, to leave. Thou, Lord, hast given me wife and children; them, Lord, I give back unto thee; nourish, instruct, and keep them. O thou Father of orphans and judge of the widow, as thou hast done to me, so do to them."

In his last prayer, Feb. 18, 1546, he hath these words: "I pray God to preserve his gospel among us; for the pope and the council of Trent have grievous things in hand. O, heavenly Father, I give thee thanks that thou hast revealed to me thy Son Jesus Christ, whom I believe, whom I profess, whom I glorify, and whom the pope and the rout of the wicked persecute and dishonor." Mr. Fox saith of Luther, "That a poor friar should be able to stand against the pope was a great miracle; that he should prevail against the pope was a greater; and after all to die in peace, having so many enemies, was the greatest of all."

33. Mr. Joseph Alleine, a most faithful, laborious minister, being deprived of the use of his arms and legs before his death, was asked by a friend, how he could be so well contented to lie so long in that condition. He answered, "What, is God my Father, is Jesus Christ my Saviour, and the Holy Spirit my sanctifier and comforter, and shall I not be content without limbs and health? He is an unreasonable wretch that cannot be content with a God, though he had nothing else."

When his people of Taunton came to Dorchester to see him, he was much revived, and would be set up in the bed and have his curtains drawn aside; he requested them to stand round the bed, and caused his hand to be held out to them, that they might take it, as formerly when he had been absent from them. And though very weak, he spoke to them thus: "O how it rejoiceth my heart to see your faces, and to hear your voices, though I cannot speak as heretofore unto you. Methinks I am now like old Jacob, with all his sons about him. Now you see my weak state; thus I have been for many weeks since I parted with you, but God hath been with me. My friends, life is mine, death is mine; in that covenant of which I preached to you, is all my salvation and all my desire; although my body doth not prosper, I hope through grace my soul doth. I have lived a sweet life by the promises, and hope through grace to die by a promise. It is the promises of God that will stand by us. Nothing but God in them will sustain us in a day of affliction. My dear friends, I feel the power of the doctrines I preached to you, on my heart; the doctrines of faith, of repentance, of self-denial, of the covenant of grace, of contentment, etc. O that you would live them over, now I cannot preach them to you. It is a shame for a believer to be cast down under afflictions, that hath so many glorious privileges, justification, adoption, sanctification, and eternal glory. We shall be as the angels of God in a little while: nay, to say the truth, believers that live in the power of faith, are, as it were, little angels already. O, my friends, live like believers; trample this dirty world under your feet; be not taken up with its comforts, nor disquieted with its crosses; you will be gone out of it shortly."

When they came to take leave of him, he would needs pray with them as well as his weak state did suffer him. Then he said, "Farewell, my dear friends; go home and live over what I have preached to you, and the Lord provide for you when I am gone. Now I cannot preach to you, but let my wasted strength and useless limbs be a sermon to you. There are many professors who can pray well, and talk well, whom we shall find at the left hand of Christ another day. You have your trades, your estates, your relations: be not taken up with these, but with God; O live on him. For the Lord's sake, go home and take heed of the world, worldly cares, worldly comforts, worldly relations. Oh, let not my labors and sufferings, let not my wasted strength and useless limbs, rise up in judgment against you at the great day of the Lord." Then he said, "The Lord having given authority to his ministers to bless his people, accordingly I bless you in his name"—using the words he always used after a sacrament—"The Lord bless you and keep you; the Lord cause his face to shine upon you, and give you peace. And the God of peace, that brought again from the dead our Lord Jesus, that great Shepherd of the sheep, through the blood of the everlasting covenant, make you perfect in every good work to do his will, working in you that which is well-pleasing in his sight, through Jesus Christ: to whom be glory for ever and ever. Amen."

In the morning his first words would be, which he also used in his health, "Now we have one day more, this is one more for God; now let us live well this day, work hard for our souls, lay up much treasure in heaven this day, for we have but a few to live."

Being taken to Bath, where he met with extraordinary kindness from strangers—for many resorted to him, to see him and hear him speak, having heard what a monument of mercy he was—he delighted himself much in the consideration of the Lord's kindness to him, and the tokens of love from strangers, and would often say, "I was a stranger, and mercy took me in; in prison, and it came to me; sick and weak, and it visited me." He had been much persecuted, and put in prison for no other crime but preaching the gospel.

He had a most pious and affectionate wife, who waited closely upon him; to whom he said, "Now, my dear heart, my companion in all my tribulations and afflictions, I thank thee for all thy pains and labors for me at home and abroad, in prison and at liberty, in health and sickness." And he prayed that the Lord would requite her, fill her with all manner of grace and consolation, and support and carry her through all difficulties.

He had some conflicts with Satan a little before his

death. Once he uttered these words: "Away, thou vile fiend, thou enemy of all mankind, thou subtle sophist: art thou now come to molest me, now that I am just going; now that I am so weak, and death upon me? Trouble me not, for I am none of thine: I am the Lord's; Christ is mine and I am his, his by covenant; I have sworn myself to be the Lord's, and his I will be; therefore be gone." These last words he repeated often, pleading his covenant with God as a means to resist the devil and his temptations. When he looked on his weak and wasted hands, he would say, "These shall be changed: this vile body shall be made like to Christ's glorious body. O what a glorious day will the day of resurrection be! Methinks I see it by faith. How will the saints lift up their heads and rejoice; and how sadly will the wicked world look then. O come, let us make haste, our Lord will come shortly. If we long to be in heaven, let us hasten with our work; for when that is done, away we shall be taken. O this vain, foolish, dirty world. I wonder how reasonable creatures can so doat upon it. What is in it worth looking after? I care not to be in it longer than while my Master hath work for me; either doing or suffering: were that done, farewell to earth."

This eminent saint had this testimony given him by one: "It may be said of him, in as high a degree as of most saints on earth, that each thought was to him a prayer, each prayer a song, each day a Sabbath, each meal a sacrament, and so his life on earth a foretaste of that eternal repast to which he hath now arrived."

34. The noble Marquis of Argyle, being a zealous friend of our covenanted reformation, was put to death May 27, 1661. His friends contrived methods for his escape out of the castle of Edinburgh; but he thanked them, and told them he would not disown the good cause he had so publicly espoused, but resolved to suffer the utmost. When the sentence of death was passed by the parliament, on Satur-

day, May 25, he said, "I had the honor to set the crown upon the king's head, and now he hastens me to a better crown than his own." Then he was sent to the Tolbooth. His excellent lady embracing him when he entered, wept bitterly, saying several times, "The Lord will requite it." No one in the room could refrain from tears; but the marquis himself was perfectly composed, and said, "Forbear, forbear; truly I pity them, they know not what they are doing: they may shut me in where they please, but they cannot shut out God from me. For my part, I am as content to be here as in the castle, and as content in the castle as in the tower of London"—where he was first put—"and as content there as at liberty; and I hope to be as content upon the scaffold as any of them all." He added, that he remembered a scripture cited lately to him by an honest minister in the castle, and endeavored to put it in practice: when Ziklag was taken and burnt, and the people spoke of stoning David, "he encouraged himself in the Lord his God." All his short time, till Monday, he spent with the greatest serenity and cheerfulness, and in the proper exercises of a dying Christian. He said to some ministers, allowed to be with him in the prison, that shortly they would envy him who was going before them; and added, "Mind what I tell you: my skill fails, if you who are ministers will not either suffer much or sin much; for though you go along with these men in part, if you do it not in all things, you are but where you were, and so must suffer: and if you go not at all with them, you shall but suffer."

The marquis was naturally timorous, but he desired those about him to observe, as he could not but do, that the Lord had heard his prayers and removed all fear from him. And indeed his friends' work was to restrain and qualify his fervent longings after his dissolution, and not to support him under the near views of it. The Lord was exceeding kind to him at this time; for on Monday morning, the day he suffered, when he was in the midst of company, and thronged with subscribing papers relating to his estate, he was so overcome with a special manifestation from God, that he broke out in a rapture, and said, " I thought to have concealed the Lord's goodness, but it will not do : I am now ordering my affairs, and God is sealing my charter to a better inheritance, and just now saying to me, 'Son, be of good cheer ; thy sins are forgiven thee.' "   After he had retired some time alone, when he opened the door, Mr. Hutcheson, one of the ministers that attended him, said to him, " What cheer, my lord ?"   He answered, " Good cheer, sir ; the Lord hath again confirmed and said to me, from heaven, ' Son, be of good cheer ; thy sins are forgiven thee.' "   And he gushed out in abundance of tears of joy, so that he retired to the window and wept there.   Afterwards he said in a perfect rapture to Mr. Hutcheson, " I think his kindness overcomes me : but God is good to me, and lets not out too much of it here, for he knows I could not bear it ; get my cloak, and let us go."   But being told that the town-clock was kept back, so that the hour was not yet come, he answered, " They were far in the wrong ;" and presently kneeled down and prayed in a most sweet and heavenly manner, to the refreshment of all that were present.

When he was going out to the scaffold, he said, " I could die like a Roman, but I choose rather to die as a Christian. Come away, gentlemen ; he that goes first, goes cleanliest." When going down, he called Mr. James Guthrie to him, and embracing him in the most endearing way, took his farewell of him.   Mr. Guthrie, at parting, addressed the marquis thus : " My lord, God hath been with you, he is with you, and God will be with you ; and such is my respect for your lordship, that if I were not under the sentence of death myself, I could cheerfully die for your lordship."   So they parted for a short season, in two or three days to meet in a better place.

The marquis, in his speech on the scaffold, hath these words: "God hath laid engagements upon Scotland; we are tied by covenant to religion and reformation. Those that were then unborn are engaged to it, and it passeth the power of any under heaven to absolve a man from the oath of God."

35. Mr. John Welsh was minister of the gospel at Ayr. Mr. Rutherford, in his preface to his Survey of Antinomianism, calls him "that apostolic, heavenly, and prophetical man of God;" and tells us that he heard it from those who were witnesses of his life, that of every twenty-four hours he gave usually eight to prayer, and that he spent many nights in prayer to God, interceding for suffering Protestants abroad, as well as for his mother-church. Mr. Welsh, when prisoner in the castle of Blackness, and in the view of death—being condemned to it for maintaining the liberties of the church, though afterwards the sentence was changed into banishment—hath these words, in a letter to his Christian lady:

"I long to eat of that tree which is planted in the midst of the paradise of God, and to drink of the pure river, clear as crystal, that runs through the street of the new Jerusalem. I long to be refreshed, with the souls of them that are under the altar, who were slain for the word of God and the testimony that they held; and to have those white robes given me, that I may walk in white raiment with those glorious saints who have washed their garments, and made them white in the blood of the Lamb. Why should I think it a strange thing to be removed from this place to that where my hope, my joy, my crown, my elder Brother, my Head, my Father, my Comforter, and all the glorious saints are, and where the song of Moses and the Lamb is sung joyfully; where we shall not be compelled to sit by the waters of Babylon and hang our harps on the willow-trees, but shall take them up and sing the new hallelujah, Blessing, honor,

glory, and power to Him that sits upon the throne, and to
the Lamb, for ever and ever? What is there under the old
vault of the heavens, and in this old, worn earth, which is
groaning under the bondage of corruption, that should make
me desire to remain here? I expect that new heaven and
new earth wherein righteousness dwelleth, wherein I shall
rest for evermore. I look to get an entry to the new Jerusalem at one of the twelve gates, whereupon are written the
names of the twelve tribes of Israel. I know that Jesus
Christ hath prepared them for me. Why may I not then,
with boldness in his blood, step into that glory, where my
Head and Lord hath gone before me? Jesus Christ is the
door and the porter; who then shall hold me out? O thou
fairest among the children of men, the delight of mankind,
the light of the Gentiles, the glory of the Jews, the life of the
dead, the joy of angels and saints, my soul panteth to be
with thee. I refuse not to die with thee, that I may live
with thee; I refuse not to suffer with thee, that I may
rejoice with thee. O when shall I be filled with his love?
Surely if a man knew how precious it is, he would count all
things but dross and dung to gain it. I long for that scaffold, or that axe, or that cord, that might be to me the last
step of this my wearisome journey, to go to thee, my Lord.
Who am I, that he should first have called me, and then
constituted me a minister of the glad tidings of the gospel of
salvation these many years; and now last of all to be a sufferer for his cause and kingdom? These two points, first,
that Christ is the head of the church; secondly, that she is
free in her government from all other jurisdiction, except
Christ; yea, as free as any kingdom under heaven, not only
to convocate, hold, and keep her meetings and assemblies, but
also to judge of all her affairs amongst her members and
subjects: these are the cause of our sufferings. I would be
most glad to be offered up as a sacrifice for these glorious
truths; but, alas, I fear that my sins, and the abuse of such

glorious things as I have found, should deprive me of so fair a crown. Yet my Lord doth know, if he would call me to it, and strengthen me in it, it would be to me the most glorious day and gladest hour I ever saw in my life; but I am in his hands, to do with me whatsoever shall please him."

This eminent saint spent much of his time in the mount of prayer and wrestling with God, was admitted to very intimate nearness with him, and had many secret things revealed to him from God. He used to say, " he wondered how a Christian could lie in bed all night, without rising to spend some of the night in prayer and praise."

In his last illness he had a great weakness in his knees, caused by his continual kneeling at prayer; the flesh became insensible and hard, like a sort of horn; but when in his weakness he was urged to remit somewhat of his former self-denial, his answer was, "he had his life of God, and therefore it should be spent for him." During his sickness he was so filled with the sensible enjoyment of God, that he was sometimes overheard in prayer to use these words: "Lord, hold thy hand, it is enough; thy servant is a clay vessel, and can hold no more."

36. Mr. Christopher Love, minister of Laurence-jury in London, was beheaded on Tower-hill, August 22, 1651, in the time of Cromwell, for suspected plotting against his government. His words on the scaffold were most pathetic and weighty: "Although," said he, "there is but little between me and death, yet this bears up my heart, there is but little between me and heaven. It comforted Dr. Taylor the martyr, when he was going to execution, that there were but two stiles between him and his Father's house; now there is a less distance between me and my Father's house—but two steps between me and glory. It is but lying down upon that block, and I shall ascend upon a throne. I am this day sailing towards the ocean of eternity,

through a rough passage, to my haven of rest—through a Red sea to the promised land. Methinks I hear God say to me as he did to Moses, Go up to mount Nebo and die there; so to me, Go up to Tower-hill and die there. Isaac said to himself that he was old, and yet he knew not the day of his death; but I cannot say so. I am young, and yet I know the day of my death; and I know the kind of my death, and the place of my death also. I am put to such a kind of death as two famous preachers of the gospel were put to before me; John the Baptist and Paul the apostle were both beheaded. I read also in Rev. 20 : 4, 'The saints were beheaded for the word of God, and the testimony of Jesus.' But herein is the disadvantage which I lie under in the thoughts of many; they judge that I suffer not for the word of God or for conscience, but for meddling with affairs of state. To this I shall briefly say, that it is an old trick of Satan to impute the cause of God's people's sufferings to be contrivances against the state, when in truth it is their religion and conscience they are persecuted for. The rulers of Israel would have put Jeremiah to death upon a civil account, though indeed it was only the truth of his prophecy that made the rulers angry with him; and yet, upon a civil account, they pretend he must die, because he fell away to the Chaldeans, and would have brought in foreign forces to invade them. The same thing is laid to my charge, of which I am as innocent as Jeremiah was. So with Paul; though he did but preach Jesus Christ, yet his enemies would have had him put to death under pretence that he was a mover of sedition. Upon a civil account, they pretend, my life is to be taken away; whereas it is because I pursue my covenant, and will not prostitute my principles and conscience to the ambition and lust of men. I had rather die a covenant-keeper, than live a covenant-breaker. Beloved, I am this day making a double exchange: I am changing a pulpit for a scaffold, and a scaffold for a throne;

and I might add a third: I am changing the presence of this numerous multitude on Tower-hill for the innumerable company of saints and angels in heaven—the holy hill of Zion; and I am changing a guard of soldiers for a guard of angels, which will receive me and carry me to Abraham's bosom. This scaffold is the best pulpit that ever I preached in. In my church pulpit, God through his grace made me an instrument to bring others to heaven, but in this pulpit he will bring me to heaven." Afterwards he said, "Though my blood be not the blood of nobles, yet it is Christian blood, minister's blood; yea, more, it is also innocent blood. I magnify the riches of God's mercy and grace towards me, that I, who was born in Wales, an obscure country, and of obscure parents, should be singled out to so honorable sufferings. For the first fourteen years of my life, I never heard a sermon preached; yet in the fifteenth year of my life it pleased God to convert me. Blessed be God, who not only made me a Christian, but also a minister, judging me faithful and putting me into the ministry, which is my glory. I had rather be a preacher in a pulpit than a prince upon a throne; I had rather be an instrument to bring souls to heaven, than that all nations should pay tribute to me. Formerly I have been under a spirit of bondage; yea, sometimes I have had more fear in drawing out a tooth, than now I have for cutting off my head. When fear was upon me, death was not near; now death is near me, my fear is vanished. I am comforted in this: though men kill me, they cannot damn me; though they thrust me out of the world, yet they cannot shut me out of heaven. When I have shed my blood, I expect the full declaration of the remission of sins through the blood of Jesus Christ. I am going to my long home, and ye to your short homes; but I shall be at my home before ye be at yours." He prayed, that seeing "he was called to do the work which he never did, he might have the strength which he never had."

Dr. Wild, in his elegy, hath these lines:

> "Methinks I hear beheaded saints above
> Call to each other, Sirs, make room for Love.
> Who, when he came to tread the fatal stage—
> Which proved his glory, and his enemies' rage—
> His blood ne'er run to's heart; Christ's blood was there,
> Reviving it; his own was all to spare;
> Which, rising in his cheeks, did seem to say,
> Is this the blood you thirst for? Take it, I pray.
> Spectators in his looks such life did see,
> That they appeared more like to die than he.
> Lightning, which filled the air with blazing light,
> Did serve for torches at that dismal night;
> In which, and all next day for many hours,
> Heaven groaned in thunder, and did weep in showers.
> Nor do I wonder that God thundered so;
> His *Boanerges* murdered lay below."

37. Mrs. Joyce Lewis being condemned to be burnt for the Protestant religion in queen Mary's reign, when she heard that the writ for her execution was come, said to her friends, " As for death, I fear it not; for when I behold the amiable countenance of Jesus Christ my dear Saviour, the ugly face of death doth not much trouble me."

38. Bullinger of Zurich, in his sickness, said to his friends, " If the Lord will make any further use of me and my ministry in his church, I willingly obey him; but if he please, as I much desire, to take me out of this miserable life, I shall exceedingly rejoice that he pleaseth to take me out of this corrupt and wretched age to go to my Saviour Christ. For if Socrates was glad when his death approached, because he thought he should go to Homer, Hesiod, and other learned men whom he expected to meet with in the other world; how much more do I joy, who am sure that I shall see my Saviour Jesus Christ, as also the saints, patriarchs, prophets, apostles, and all the holy men who have lived from the beginning of the world? Now, when I am sure to see them, and to partake of their joys, why should I not willingly die, to enjoy their perpetual society and glory?"

39. Mr. Theodore Beza, a famous pastor in Geneva, when he apprehended the approach of death, revised his will; and so, dismissing all worldly thoughts, wholly betook himself to expect the time of his departure, which he had much longed for. He often used the apostle's saying, "We are his workmanship, created in Christ Jesus unto good works;" and that of Augustine: *Domine quod cæpisti perfice, ne in portu naufragum accidat*—"Lord, perfect that which thou hast begun, that I suffer not shipwreck in the haven;" and that saying of Bernard: *Domine, sequemur te, per te, ad te. Te, quia veritas; per te, quia via: ad te, quia vita*—"Lord, we will follow thee, by thee, to thee: thee, because thou art the truth; by thee, because thou art the way; to thee, because thou art the life."

40. Melancthon of Wittemberg, Luther's dear companion, said that "he much longed to be dissolved, and that for two reasons: that he might enjoy the much-desired presence and sight of Christ and of the heavenly church, and that he might be freed from the cruel and implacable discords of divines."

41. Mr. John Bradford, a minister and martyr in queen Mary's reign, when the keeper told him that the next day he was to be burnt in Smithfield, put off his cap, and lifting up his eyes to heaven, said, "I thank God for it; it comes not now to me on a sudden, but as a thing waited for every day and hour; the Lord make me worthy of it." One Cresswell offering to interpose for him, and desiring to know what his request was, he said, "I have no request to make. If the queen give me my life, I will thank her; if she will banish me, I will thank her; if she will burn me, I will thank her; if she will condemn me to perpetual imprisonment, I will thank her." The chancellor pressing him to do as others had done, in hopes of the queen's mercy, he said, "My Lord, I desire mercy with God's mercy; that is, without doing or saying any thing against God and his truth.

But mercy with God's wrath, God keep me from. God's mercy," added he, "I desire, and also would be glad of the queen's favor to live as a subject without clog on conscience; but otherwise, the Lord's mercy is better to me than life. Life in his displeasure is worse than death, and death with his favor is true life."

In his letter to Dr. Cranmer, Dr. Ridley, and Dr. Latimer, he hath these words: "Our dear brother Rogers hath broken the ice valiantly. This day, or to-morrow at the utmost, hearty Hooper, sincere Saunders, and trusty Taylor will end their course and receive their crown. The next am I, who hourly look for the porter to open me the gates after them, to enter into the desired rest. God forgive me my unthankfulness for this exceeding great mercy. Though I suffer justly—for I have been a great hypocrite, unthankful, etc., the Lord pardon me; yea, he hath done it, he hath done it indeed—yet what evil hath he done? Christ, whom the prelates persecute, his truth which they hate in me, had done no evil, nor deserved death. O what am I, Lord, that thou shouldst thus magnify me? Is it thy will to send for such a wretched hypocrite in a fiery chariot, as thou didst send for Elias?"

In one of his meditations, after confession of sin, he said, "O what now may we do; despair? no, for thou art God, and therefore good; thou art merciful, and therefore thou forgivest sin; with thee there is mercy and propitiation, and therefore thou art worshipped. When Adam sinned, thou gavest him mercy before he desired it; and wilt thou deny us mercy, who now desire the same? Adam excused his fault, and accused thee; but we accuse ourselves, and excuse thee; and shall we be sent empty away? How often in the wilderness didst thou spare Israel, and defer thy plagues at the request of Moses, when the people themselves made no petition to thee. Now, not only do we make our petitions to thee, but we also have a Mediator, far above

Moses, to appear for us, even Jesus Christ, thine own Son; and shall we, dear Lord, depart ashamed? O merciful Lord, for thine own glory suffer not the enemy of thy Son Christ, the Romish antichrist, thus wretchedly to delude and draw from thee our poor brethren, for whom thy dear Son once died. Suffer him not to seduce the ignorant with his vain opinion, that his false gods, his blind, mumbling, feigned religion, or his foolish superstition, doth give him such conquests, such victories, and such triumphs over us. But, O Lord, this is thy righteous judgment, to punish us with the tyrannical yoke of blindness, because we have cast away from us the sweet yoke of the wholesome words of thy Son our Saviour."

In his letter to Mrs. Anna Warcup, he said, "My staff standeth at the door. I look continually for the sheriff to come for me; I bless God I am ready for him. Now go I to practise that which I have preached. Now I am climbing up the hill; it will cause me to puff and blow before I come to the cliff. The hill is steep and high, my breath is short, and my strength is feeble. Pray therefore to the Lord for me, that as I have now through his goodness even almost come to the top, I may by his grace be strengthened, not to rest till I arrive where I should be."

He was remarkable for humility and self-abasement, though a most eminent saint. He subscribed some of his letters, The most miserable, hard-hearted, unthankful sinner, John Bradford. A very painted hypocrite, John Bradford. *Miserimus peccator*, John Bradford. The sinful John Bradford.

42. Mr. Edward Deering, a little before his death, said to his friends, "As for my death, I bless God I feel and find so much inward joy and comfort to my soul, that if I were put to my choice whether I would die or live, I would a thousand times rather choose death than life if it may agree with the holy will of God."

43. Mr. Robert Rollock, when dying, prayed, "Lord, I have hitherto seen but darkly in the glass of thy word ; now grant that I may enjoy the eternal fruition of thy counte nance, which I have so much desired and longed for. Haste, Lord, and do not tarry ; I am weary both of nights and days ; come, Lord Jesus, that I may come to thee. Break these eye-strings, and give me others : I desire to be dissolved, and to be with thee ; haste, Lord Jesus, thrust thy hand into my body, and take my soul to thyself. O my sweet Lord, set this soul of mine free, that it may enjoy her husband."

44. Galeacious Carracciolus, marquis of Vico, when dying, took leave of his wife and all his Christian friends, telling them he would lead them the way to heaven. And he cried to Jesus Christ, that "as he had sought Him all his life, so now He would receive and acknowledge him as his own."

45. The famous Lord Duplesis in France, when dying, was much concerned for the church of God in distress, praying earnestly for her deliverance. He particularly blessed such of his grandchildren as were in pursuit of learning, saying, that "he was assured they should be blessed with the blessings both of heaven above, and of the earth beneath." When a minister spoke of the service he had done the church by his writings, he said, "Alas, what was there of mine in that work ? Say not that it was I, but God by me." Then lifting up his hands above his head, he cried three times, "Mercy, mercy, mercy !" adding, that he did it to show that it was alone the mercy of God to which he had recourse. He declared that his faith was altogether founded on the goodness of God in Jesus Christ, who by the Father had been made unto him, as to all others that believed in him, wisdom, righteousness, sanctification, and redemption. "Away," said he, "with all merit : I call for nothing but mercy, free mercy." When one was blessing God for giving him such peace and

comfort at his end, he said, "I feel, I feel what I speak."
As to his faith in the truths of God, he said "he was entirely persuaded thereof by the demonstration of God's Holy
Spirit, which was more powerful, more clear, and more certain than all the demonstrations of Euclid." When secretly
praying, he was overheard saying in broken sentences, "I
fly, I fly to heaven. Let the angels carry me to the bosom
of my Saviour." Afterwards he said, "I know that my
Redeemer liveth, and I shall see him *with these eyes: hisce
oculi;*" which words he repeated four or five times.

46. Jerome of Prague, when he was fastened to the
stake, and the executioner began to kindle the fire behind
him, bade him kindle it before his face; "For," said he, "if
I had been afraid of it, I had not come to this place, having
had so many opportunities offered me to escape it."

47. Mr. Hooker, a minister in New England, when one
that stood weeping at his bedside as he lay dying, said to
him, "Sir, you are going to receive the reward of all your
labors;" replied, "Brother, I am going to receive mercy."

48. Mr. Heron, another minister there, dying and leaving a family of many small children, his poor wife fell a
weeping, and said, "Alas, what will become of all these
children?" He pleasantly replied, "Never fear; He that
feeds the young ravens, will not starve the young Herons."
Which afterwards came to pass accordingly. It was an
ancient observation concerning the English martyrs under
the bloody Marian persecution, that "none of them went
more joyfully to the stake, than those who had the greatest
families to commit unto the Lord."

49. Chrysostom, when the empress Eudoxa, an Arian,
sent a threatening message to him, said, "Go tell her, *Nil
nisi peccatum timeo,* I fear nothing but sin." When he
was sentenced to banishment, he said, "None of these things
trouble me; for I said before within myself, If the empress
will, let her banish me; the earth is the Lord's, and the ful-

ness thereof. If she will, let her saw me asunder; Isaiah was so used. If she will, let her cast me into the sea; I will remember Jonah. If she will, let her cast me into a burning fiery furnace, or to the wild beasts; the three children and Daniel were so served. If she will, let her stone me, or cut off my head; I have St. Stephen and the Baptist for my companions. If she will, let her take away all my substance; naked came I out of my mother's womb, and naked shall I return thither again."

But I must break off, for the time would fail me to enumerate the many instances of the faith, love, patience, hope, courage, and constancy of the saints and martyrs of Jesus, when in the view of death. Some have told the persecutors that "they might pull their hearts out of their bodies, but they could never pluck the truth out of their hearts." Others have said, that "if every hair of their heads were men, they should suffer death for Christ and his truths." "Oh," said one of them, "can I die but once for Christ?"

Let these examples prompt us to seek grace from God, and make it our earnest study to imitate and follow such a cloud of witnesses, that we may die martyrs in resolution; that our graces may be most lively at the last, our evening sun may shine brightest, and we may go off the stage glorifying God, and leaving a sweet savor behind us, as these famous worthies, whose praise is in the churches, have done before us.

DIRECTION 7. Let dying persons be much in prayer and ejaculations to God.

Prayer is the native breath of renewed souls; it is as necessary to their spiritual life, as breath is to the natural life. "Hide not thine ear at my breathing." Lam. 3 : 56. The first thing a child of God doth, when he is new-born, is to breathe by prayer. "Behold, he prayeth." Acts 9 : 11. And it is also his last work in the world to pray. "And they stoned Stephen, calling upon God, and saying, Lord

Jesus, receive my spirit. And he kneeled down, and cried with a loud voice, Lord, lay not this sin to their charge. And when he had said this, he fell asleep." Acts 7 : 59, 60. A dying Christian hath many to pray for : he is to pray for the church of God, for his friends and relations, and also for his enemies, as Stephen did. But especially he must pray for himself, that sin may be forgiven, and that he may have a safe conduct through the dark valley. I have heard of some that have been found dead upon their knees ; a noble posture to die in. How suitable is it to enter praying into the land of praise. So did Stephen; yea, so did our blessed Saviour himself: "Father, forgive them, for they know not what they do. Father, into thy hands I commend my spirit." The last words that holy Usher uttered were, "But, Lord, in a special manner forgive my sins of omission." "Lord," said dying Beza, "perfect that which thou hast begun; that I suffer not shipwreck in the haven." I remember to have read of an old minister who, when he found death approaching, said, "I desire to die like the poor thief, crying to the crucified Jesus for mercy. I am nothing, I can do nothing, except what is unworthy. My eye and hope and faith is to Christ on his cross. I bring an unworthiness like that of the poor dying thief unto him, and have no more to plead than he. Like the poor thief crucified with him, I am waiting to be received by the infinite grace of my Lord, into his kingdom." Let us in like manner die, crying to a crucified Jesus for mercy: "Lord, remember me, now thou art in thy kingdom."

O, dying Christians, remember, the time of prayer is near an end ; after death there will be no more occasion for prayer. O, then, beg that the Spirit of prayer may be so poured down upon you at this time, that you may be enabled to pour out your heart before God, both for yourself and others. O how earnestly should you pray then, when you are taking your leave of prayer. Mind the example which your

9*

Redeemer gave you; it was before his death that he offered up prayers and supplications with strong crying and tears unto God. I acknowledge sick and dying persons are frequently out of case for making prayers of any great length or continuance; which consideration should excite us to the greater diligence in prayer in time of health, and therefore they ought to be the more frequent and fervent, in short and suitable ejaculations to God, as their exigencies do require.

MEDITATIONS AND EJACULATIONS PROPER FOR A SICK AND DYING PERSON, AND ESPECIALLY FOR A DYING BELIEVER.

O Lord, thou art the God of my life, and hast the keys of death in thy hand. Thou hast measured the length of my life, and appointed the hour of my death. The number of my months and days is with thee, and thou hast appointed the bounds over which I cannot pass.

What is my life but a vapor, that appeareth for a little time and then vanisheth away? At the longest, how short is it; and at the strongest, how weak. "What man is it that liveth here, and shall not see death? When a few days are come, I shall go the way whence I shall not return." God hath decreed it, sin hath deserved it, my frailty demonstrates it, death's harbingers proclaim it, and I must expect it.

There is no discharge in this war, no exemption from death's stroke. Death's messengers are come to warn me that my last day and last hour draweth nigh. The sound of their Master's feet is behind them. This clay-house must be dissolved, my soul dislodged, and my place here shall know me no more; I shall soon be as water spilt on the ground, that cannot be gathered up again.

O that I may be suitably exercised in my present weak and dying condition. When my flesh faileth, and my heart fainteth within me, O that God may be the strength of my heart and my portion for ever. When the keepers of the house do tremble, let God watch over it, and be the keeper of my soul. When the grinders cease, because they are few, let my soul be fed with manna from heaven. When the daughters of music are brought low, let my soul be disposed for hearing the song of Moses and the Lamb, in the temple above. When those that look out at the windows are darkened, let the eyes of my soul be enlightened to behold, with the dying martyr Stephen, the heavens opened, and the glorious Jesus standing at the right hand of God, making intercession for me and ready to receive me. Let my hope and desire look out at the windows, and say; "Why is his chariot so long in coming; and why tarry the wheels of his chariot? Make haste, my Beloved, and be thou like a roe or a young hart on the mountains of Bether."

O that I may observe the afflicting hand of God in my present sickness. Surely affliction cometh not out of the dust, nor doth trouble spring out of the ground. O Lord, rebuke me not in thy indignation, nor chasten me in thy hot displeasure. Have mercy on me, O Lord, for I am weak; and heal me, for my bones are vexed. When thou with rebukes dost correct man for iniquity, thou makest his beauty to consume away like a moth; surely every man is vanity. The sorrows of my heart are enlarged; O bring me out of my distresses. Look upon my affliction and my pain, and forgive all my sin. I look for sympathy to my great Highpriest, who is touched with the feeling of my infirmities. My help and strength is in him.

O that when I am afflicted, I may not despise the chastening of the Lord, nor faint when I am rebuked of him. Let me hear the rod, and him that hath appointed it. Let me kiss the rod, and accept of the punishment of mine iniquity. O that in my affliction I may be helped to humble myself greatly before the God of my fathers, and make a true and penitent confession of my sins.

Oh, what shall I say to thee, O thou Preserver of men?

I will say, Lord, be merciful to me: heal my soul, for I have sinned against thee. I acknowledge that through an evil heart of unbelief, I have many a time departed away from the living God. O how vainly and foolishly have I lived in the world. How lavish of my precious time. How unmindful of my latter end. How careless of my immortal soul. How little in preparation for eternity. Oh, my own heart condemns me, my sins testify against me; and thou who knowest them better than I do myself, together with their several aggravations, mightest justly condemn me too. But my comfort is, that with thee the Lord there is mercy, that thou mayest be feared; and with thy Son there is plenteous redemption; wherefore, for his sake be pleased to forgive me all my past transgressions, whether in thought, word, or deed—those that I remember, and those that I have forgotten—and let them never be charged on me to my shame and confusion in this world, nor to my everlasting ruin in that which is to come. Lord, forgive the follies of my childhood, the extravagances of my youth, and all the iniquities of my riper years.

Oh, I am polluted with sin, and dare not appear before God with my own filthy rags upon me. When Adam lost his original righteousness, he fled from God, and dreaded the summons of offended justice. Now, there is no appearing before God with acceptance, but in the garment of his Son my elder brother. None can have boldness to enter into the holiest of all, but by the blood of Jesus. O enable me to disclaim whatever duties I have performed, or graces I have exercised, and to rely on a crucified Christ alone for pardon and life. Though thou slayest me, let me die trusting in and cleaving to a crucified Jesus.

Now the powers of darkness will seek to raise a tempest to shipwreck the vessel of my soul, when it would enter into the eternal haven. O that, like the wise mariner when the storm approacheth, I may endeavor to secure the vessel with the anchors of faith and hope fastened on the Rock Christ.

O that, when the time of combat with my last enemy cometh, I may, above all, take the shield of faith, whereby I may be sheltered from the sting of death, and may quench the fiery darts of the wicked one.

O that the Lord of hosts, the Captain of my salvation, may be with me in my last conflict, and may help me to put on the whole armor of God, and give me skill to use it, that I may be able to stand in the evil day. Teach my hands to war and my fingers to fight, that through thee I may do valiantly, and tread down all my enemies. O that now I may finish my course, and fight the good fight of faith, that at death I may receive the crown of righteousness, which the righteous Judge will give to all that love his appearing. O that my faith may ripen into a full assurance, that I may go off the stage with joy, and an abundant entrance may be administered unto me into the kingdom of my Lord and Saviour Jesus Christ.

O that the night of my death may shine bright with the sparkling stars of heavenly graces. Lord, increase my faith. Let the pilgrim's staff of faith be never out of my hand till I come to my journey's end. O let me get Christ all in my arms, like old Simeon before his death, that I may say, like him, " Now let thy servant depart in peace ; for my eyes have seen thy salvation." Kindle the fire of heavenly love in my soul, and give me a taste of heavenly joys. O for one beam of thy light, to banish away all my doubts and fears. Lord, let in something of heaven to my soul, before itself go into heaven.

Lord, take me not out of this life till thou hast fitted me for a better. May I be fitted for heaven before I leave the earth, and finish my work before I finish my course. Make me ready to meet thee at thy coming, that so thy coming may not be the matter of my terror, but the matter of my hope, desire, and expectation. O that I may be in a longing frame for that blessed time, when he will come and put a period to all my sins, sorrows, troubles, and temptations here; and when I shall exchange my present being in the body, for an everlasting being with the Lord. Lord, strengthen my faith and hope, so that neither the sweetness of life, the pain of death, nor apprehensions about my future state, may make me unwilling to die. Is my Redeemer ascended, and gone before me to prepare a place for me? Why then should I be slothful to go in and possess the good land?

Mercy hath filled up all my life, and brought me near to the end of it. O let it not leave me now, when all the enjoyments of the world are nothing to me, and I am to take an everlasting farewell of them all. Now one smile of thy face, one taste of thy love, would be strength and joy to my departing soul. O remember the word to thy servant, upon which thou hast caused me to hope: hast thou not said, "I will never leave thee, nor forsake thee?" O fulfil this word to me in the time of my need: O let me never go off the stage with a heavy heart, or a guilty conscience; but may I depart in peace, and sleep in Jesus. Let me breathe out my departing soul to thee, and trust it in thy hand and safe-keeping; and let my flesh rest in hopes of rising gloriously at the last day, through him who is the resurrection and the life, the Lord Jesus Christ.

Love and praise is the exercise of saints for ever; may I be acquainted with it here. O shall I not love and praise him, who hath forgiven all mine iniquities, healed all my diseases, redeemed my life from destruction, and crowned me with loving-kindness and tender mercies? He hath caused goodness and mercy to follow me all the days of my life; and shall I not follow him with praises at the end of it?

Now the time of my departure is at hand, and the lamp

of life is ready to be extinguished. O that I may die in faith, that whether the lamp go out of its own accord, or by some sudden blast, it may be lighted again by the immortal beams of the Sun of righteousness. And though I be overtaken by the sleep of death and lie down in the bed of the grave, yet shall I awake again in the morning of the resurrection, that morning which shall never be succeeded by an evening; when I shall behold thy face in righteousness, and be eternally satisfied with thy likeness.

Now I am going the way of all the earth, ready to launch forth into eternity, where I shall be fixed in my everlasting condition. Grant me, Lord, the perfect use of my senses, of my understanding and reason, that I may glorify thy name and edify my neighbors to the last moment of my departure; and now, when I am to conflict with the king of terrors, O support and assist me in my sorest extremities and last agonies. O mercifully mitigate death's pangs, and let my passage be easy and my landing safe. Stand by me in my dying moments, and secure my soul in thy hands from all its deadly enemies; and when I am numbered among the dead, let me also be numbered among the redeemed and blessed of the Lord for ever.

O Lord, thou determinest both the bounds of man's life and the bounds of his habitation. If a hair of my head cannot fall to the ground without thy providence, far less can my whole body fall into the grave without it. Thou hast told me plainly that I must die, but mercifully hast concealed the time, place, and manner, that I might always stand upon my guard, every hour expect thy coming, and have my accounts in my hand, always prepared to give them up to thee my Judge. Justly mightest thou have snatched me away by a surprising call and sudden stroke; but in thy goodness thou givest me warning, and time to set my house and soul in order. O graciously finish what is now wanting of the work of thy grace in my heart and soul, and thoroughly accomplish and furnish me to appear in thy blessed presence. May I now die to sin every hour, that I may not die for sin hereafter. Cause sin wholly to die before me, that it may not rise in judgment against me after death.

O God, be thou my refuge and strength, and a very present help in trouble ; and then I will not fear though the waters of affliction rage and be troubled, and though all the mountains of earthly comforts shake with the swelling thereof. There is a river, the streams whereof shall make glad the city of God. O let my soul dwell beside those living streams, and drink of them for ever. In the valley of the shadow of death, Lord, be thou present as the good Shepherd, with thy guiding rod and supporting staff; and make my departure easy and full of peace and hope. Lord, carry me safe through the dark passage upon which I am entering, and let me find it a gate of glory, a door opened into the everlasting kingdom and joy of the Lord. Lord Jesus, receive my spirit, and let it be presented, justified and spotless, to the Father, that it may come to the spirits of just men made perfect, and join with them in singing the new song, " Worthy is the Lamb that was slain, and hath redeemed us to God by his blood, to receive power, honor, glory, and blessing for ever. Amen."

MEDITATIONS FOR DROOPING BELIEVERS WHEN DEATH IS NEAR

Travellers who have met with many storms, troubles, and dangers in their journeys, rejoice when they come near to their own country ; and shall not I, a stranger and pilgrim, that have been long wandering in a wilderness, be glad when I come near my blessed home, my dear friends, and eternal habitation ?

With what cheerfulness do some women endure the pains of childbearing, being supported by the hope of a child's being born into the world. And what is the joy of a man-child being brought into this sinful and miserable world, to the joy of a sanctified soul's being brought out of it into heaven for ever? It is pleasant when the hard winter goeth over, and the time of the singing of birds, the messengers of spring, doth come; and shall not I rejoice when sickness and forerunners of death do tell me that the winter of my darkness and trouble is past, and the summer of my eternal light and joys is at hand?

What though death be the king of terrors, is not glorious Christ the King of comforts? Have not I met already with this blessed King; and why should I fear to meet with the other? Oh let my strength and support at this time come from Christ, my covenanted Redeemer.

O Lord, deliver my soul from death, mine eyes from tears, and my feet from falling. O bring me out of the miry clay, set my feet upon a rock, and establish my goings, and put a new song in my mouth, even praises to our God.

If Jacob went down so cheerfully into Egypt when God had said unto him, "Fear not to go down, for I will go down with thee, and I will bring thee up again," why should a believer fear to go down to the grave, when God hath undertaken to go down with him thither and to bring him up again? His body may be turned into dust, but God is in covenant with his dust, and will not suffer the least particle of it to be lost.

Are not the righteous taken away from the evil to come? Do they not rest in their beds and enter into peace? Why then should I shrink from dying? When the Lord is to bring heavy wrath and judgments upon a land, he frequently houses many of his people in heaven beforehand; and how happy are those that win the house before the sweeping hail-shower doth fall. A believer needeth not to look for any settled fair weather in this world: it will be nothing but one shower up and another down, till he be housed in heaven. Oh why, then, should I linger in this wilderness?

How highly honored is the believer in being made an heir of God, and a joint-heir with his own Son Jesus Christ; so that Christ and the believer do, as it were, divide heaven between them: they have the same Father, dwell in the same house, sit at the same table, reign on the same throne, and partake of the same glory. Oh what honor is this which is put on a worm of the earth. It is indeed but little that the young heir enjoys of the inheritance while in this world; no more than will serve to bear his charges to heaven, where he shall get all, forget his present straits, and remember his poverty no more. Oh why then should not I, like a young heir, be looking and longing for the expiring of my minority, when I shall arrive at ripe age, and enter upon the full possession of the inheritance? Oh that I could send out faith and hope, those two faithful spies, to survey the promised land, or at least to visit the borders of my elder Brother's country; what an encouraging report would they bring back! My glorious Lord is gone; he hath left the earth, and entered into his glory; my brethren and friends have many of them arrived there also. How great is the difference between my state and theirs. I am groaning out my complaints, but they are singing God's praise. I am in darkness, and cannot see God, but they are in light, and see him face to face. O my Lord, shall I stay behind when they are gone? Should I be satisfied to wander in the wilderness, far distant from my Father and my God, when they are triumphing above, dividing the spoil? No; I will look still after them with a steadfast eye, and cry, O Lord, how long? I will wait now in hope, yea, rejoice in the forethoughts of the day when my minority shall be expired, my pilgrimage finished, my banishment over, that I may get home to my country and friends above.

What though my days be dark and gloomy now, my winter be sharp and stormy: why, it is but short, and nearly over; the eternal summer approacheth; the long day, the high sun, and the fair garden of my well-beloved above these visible heavens, will quickly make amends for all. Let me get up by faith and visit the new land, view the fair city, and behold the white throne, and the Lamb that sits thereon, that I may rejoice in hope of the glory of God.

Shall many of the heirs of wrath go singing and rejoicing to hell; and will an heir of God go drooping and sorrowing to heaven? Oh, let me not, by my behavior on a death-bed, bring up a bad report upon Christ's good way and the land which he hath purchased.

Have I such great and precious promises left me, and shall I not live and feed upon them in time of my need? Shall I not trust the word of Him that is faithful and true? Hath he not said to me, "When thou passest through the waters, I will be with thee; and through the rivers, they shall not overflow thee: when thou walkest through the fire, thou shalt not be burnt, neither shall the flame kindle upon thee?" When the disciples were sore tossed with winds and waves, thou camest to them in the fourth watch of the night, walking on the waters; and when their fears were increased, thou saidst, "It is I; be not afraid." Thou rebukedst the winds, and there presently followed a great calm. My Redeemer's compassions continue; his bowels of mercy still yearn over our sorrows, as in the days of his flesh. "Jesus Christ is the same yesterday, to-day, and for ever."

Ah, I have too little improved my acquaintance with precious Christ in the day of my life; how ready am I to mistake him when he changeth his dispensations towards me. Though I have been long at Christ's school, what small proficiency have I made in the work and mystery of faith. How little have I learned to believe in the dark, and to drop anchor at midnight upon the Rock of ages, and to look out for the dawning of the day.

Surely the day shall break, and the shadows flee away;

my King cometh; my well-beloved is on his way; he hath sent his letter before him to warn me of it, saying, "Behold, I come quickly." Oh that like the cold and wearied night-watchman, I may be looking out for the appearing of the morning-star and the breaking of the eastern sky; and may be ever crying, "Even so, come, Lord Jesus, come quickly."

Thou hast said, "Light is sown for the righteous, and gladness for the upright in heart." Surely God's seed shall not lie always beneath the clods; the time is at hand when it shall spring, and joyful will the crop be at last. Oh that like David in affliction, I could encourage myself in the Lord my God, and say, "The Lord liveth, blessed be my Rock." Why should I droop while my Lord liveth, and my Rock standeth? My hopes may die, my comforts may die, my gifts die, my riches die, my relations die, my body die; but, good news, "The Lord liveth, blessed be my Rock." The disciples had a melancholy tale while Christ was dead and lying in the grave; but that sad time is over: he is now risen, and will die no more. Nay, he hath proclaimed it for my comfort, saying, "Fear not; I am the first and the last. I am he that liveth, and was dead, and behold, I am alive for evermore, Amen; and have the keys of hell and of death."

When my soul is cast down within me, let me remember God from the land of Jordan and the hill Mizar, that I may reason myself out of all my fears and discouragements; for yet "the Lord will command his loving-kindness in the daytime, and in the night his song shall be with me, and my prayer to the God of my life."

"Why then art thou cast down, O my soul; and why art thou disquieted within me? hope thou in God, for I shall yet praise him, who is the health of my countenance and my God."

Now, when death is at hand, let not my Saviour be afar off. He who remembered the dying thief, and spoke comfortably to him, let him now remember me when he is seated in his kingdom, and say to my soul, " This day thou shalt be with me in paradise." When it is absent from the body, let it be present with the Lord. Let the angels now be ready to do their office, to carry my departing soul into Abraham's bosom. Let me now depart, that I may be with Christ; yea, be for ever with the Lord, that I may see his face. Let me dwell there, where they have no night, need no candle, nor light of the sun for ever—where God shall wipe away all tears from their eyes, and there shall be no more death, neither sorrow nor crying.

Father, into thy hands I commit my spirit. By the hands of Him who hath redeemed it, let it be presented to thee without spot or wrinkle, or any such thing.

ADDITIONAL MEDITATIONS PROPER FOR ANY SICK PERSON IN THE VIEW OF DEATH.

The Lord is pleased sometimes to cast men down on beds of sickness, and draw the curtain between the world and them, that they may take a view of their past life and future state. Now it is time for me to look into my soul, and examine my state. Oh, how many do miss salvation, when they think themselves sure of it. They mistake a form of godliness for the power of it, and thereby deceive themselves, thinking themselves something when they are nothing.

Some go so far as to shed tears, as Esau did; profess fair, yea, fight for the Lord, as Saul and Jehu did; wish for the end of the righteous, as Balaam did; desire God's people to pray for them, as Pharaoh and Simon Magus did; walk softly and mourn for fear of judgments, as Ahab did; joy in gospel ordinances and reform in many things, as Herod did; prophesy and speak well of Christ, as Caiaphas and Judas did; be convinced and tremble at hearing a sermon, as Felix did; yea, seemed to taste the good word of God and the powers of the world to come, as apostates have done; and yet for all these attainments, remain strangers to the saving work of the Spirit on the heart.

O that the consideration of hypocrites' attainments might alarm me out of my security, and make me restless till I find the distinguishing marks of true grace and sincere faith in my soul. O that I could say, there is a principle in me that will not suffer me to build on any foundation in the world but Christ and his righteousness; that makes me content with Christ, with all his offices, with all his precepts, and with his very cross for his sake. Doth the love of Christ keep me back from sin more than the law, or fear of hell? Have I aimed at God's honor in all my actions, civil, natural, and religious? Am I humble and self-denying as to my own wisdom, will, credit, ease, and honor, and to all the enjoyments of the world? Am I acquainted with the throne of grace, and desirous to keep up a constant correspondence with it? O let me not rest till I perceive in my soul those things which accompany salvation.

O how comforting would it be to me now, if I could say with good Hezekiah in his sickness, "Remember now, O Lord, how I have walked before thee in truth and with a perfect heart, and have done that which is good in thy sight." O that I could pray, and say, with Jesus my Saviour when in the view of death, "Father, I have glorified thee on the earth; I have finished the work which thou gavest me to do: and now, O Father, glorify thou me with thine own self, with the glory which thou hast ordained for me before the world was."

Alas, Lord, I must confess my iniquities have gone up above mine head; my misspent time, my unfruitfulness under the means of grace and waterings of ordinances, may cause me to cry out, Woe is me, for the leanness of my soul and barrenness of my heart. I have been an empty vine, bringing forth fruit only to myself; I have hid my Lord's money, and therefore deserve the doom of the wicked and slothful servant. But my relief is in my Surety's righteousness. Blessed be the Lord, who hath sent his Son to bless those who by nature lie under the curse, and to intercede for those that cannot speak for themselves. O how suitable is he to my soul's case. I have indeed a multitude of sins, but he hath a multitude of tender mercies; I have deep and heinous guilt, but he hath a deep fountain for washing it out; I am sold under sin, but he hath a ransom to buy me back again; my wound is great, but his balm is excellent. Surely it is my wisdom to go to Christ with all my grievances, and always to lie and cry at my Redeemer's door.

O that now, when the sun of my life is setting, the blessed Sun of righteousness may rise and shine upon my soul. Goodness and mercy have followed me while I lived: O that Christ and glory may meet me when I die. I must acknowledge thy goodness: were this the last hour I had to live, and this the last word I had to speak in the world, I might well say, Lord, thou hast been a merciful and gracious God to me; my whole life hath been a continued course of mercy; Lord, crown the end of it with mercy also. Surely the sea is not so full of water, nor the sun so full of light, as thou art full of grace and mercy. O let not my sins stop the current of thy tender mercies at this time. Lord, drown all my sins in the sea of Christ's blood, that my soul may not be sunk by them in the ocean of divine wrath. Lord Jesus, embrace my perishing soul in thy arms; let thy cross be my security, and thy wounds my refuge.

O thou who hearest the young ravens when they cry, be not silent to me at this time, lest if thou be silent to me, I be like to them that go down to the pit.

Lord, I am now called to the work I never did; give me the strength I never had. Surely it is an important matter to die, and my eternal state dependeth upon dying aright. What I do amiss in my life one day, I may amend in the

next; but not so here—I can die but once: if I mar this
piece of work, I cannot come back to mend it again; if I forget any thing necessary for my journey, I cannot return to
get it. Oh, a wrong step in going out of this life is highly
dangerous. In one respect it is like the sin against the Holy
Ghost, and can never be forgiven; for I cannot come back
to mourn for it. Of all the business I ever undertook, I have
most need to take care of my dying.

Oh, is death coming to take down this earthly tabernacle,
and put the one half of me in the dark grave, and the other
half of me in heaven or in hell; and shall I give sleep to my
eyes and slumber to my eyelids, till I find myself so prepared that I dare look death in the face, and dare hazard my
soul upon eternity?

- O to have right impressions of the certainty of death,
and the uncertainty of life. What is my life but a vapor, a
sand-glass of sixty or seventy years, which will soon run out?
Eternity and a judgment-seat are now hard upon me. The
blast of the last trumpet is at hand. There will shortly be
a proclamation by one standing in the clouds, that time shall
be no more. The world looks big in men's eyes in time of
health; but when the eye closes, when the breath departs,
and the imprisoned soul is ready to leap out into eternity,
can the world give any satisfaction? No, no; a lamp full
of the oil of grace will be valued more than a house full of
gold. The finest things on earth will then appear nothing
but painted dust and gilded clay. How gladly would the
greatest worldling then give all his gold and silver, riches
and honors, for one sight of Christ's fair face, one smile of
his countenance. O wherefore should men in health neglect
the market of grace, and slight the pearl of great price?
Why should they spend their money for that which is not
bread, and their labor for that which satisfieth not?

Lord, save me from the hypocrite's case at death, whose
candle of profession and of hope burns and blazes fair all the

way with him, but goeth out in the dark trance of death; and there he stumbles and falls, and shall rise no more. O that my profession and hope may be of God's creating. If God light my candle, then shall my feet be enlightened through the dark valley, and neither death nor hell shall be able to put it out.

Lord, subdue sin in me, and let it be continually dying now, that it may certainly be dead before me. God forbid that my sins should survive me.

O, that when the stroke of death dissolves my body, my soul may escape as a bird out of the snare of the fowler, and may ascend to the heavenly regions to enjoy God himself.

O let me look through the gates of mortality, and long for the jailer's coming to set me at liberty. Lord, help me to overcome the love of life and the fear of death. If my neighbor lend me any thing, I pay it again with thanks; and shall I not restore my life to God with thanks, who hath been pleased to lend it to me so long? Arise, and let me depart, for this is not my rest; heaven is my home. Lord, bring me to it: the joys of it are too great to enter into me, O make me fit to enter into them.

While I lie on a sick-bed, Lord help me to patience in my sickness without murmuring.

How willingly would the damned in hell endure my pains a thousand years, if they had any hopes of being saved at last. Blessed be God that my sickness is not hell, that my pains are not eternal.

O that I may look on my affliction as coming from the hand of him who is the Lord of health and of sickness, of life and of death; who killeth and maketh alive, bringeth down to the grave, and raiseth up again. The sovereign and wise Lord hath determined the time when my affliction shall end, as well as the time when it began. Thirty-eight years were appointed the sick man at Bethesda pool; eigh-

teen years to the woman that Satan kept bound; twelve
years to the woman with the bloody-issue; ten days' tribulation to those of Smyrna; three days' plague to David.   The
number of the godly man's tears is registered in God's book;
yea, the hairs of his head are numbered.

When David got his choice of his own chastisement, he
chose rather to be corrected by the hand of God, than by
any other means, saying, "Let me fall into the hands of the
Lord, for his mercies are great."   "I was dumb, and opened
not my mouth, because thou didst it."   Glory to God that
I am fallen into his merciful hand.   Hath God appointed
that man's coming into the world shall be attended with
pain and crying, and his going out of it with grief and
trouble; and shall I quarrel at it?   No; I desire humbly to
submit to the correction of mine iniquity, and to bear the
indignation of the Lord, because I have sinned against him.
O that the sickness of my body may be a means of health
to my soul.·   May I be chastened of the Lord, so that I may
not be condemned with the world.

It is good for the believer that he is afflicted; why? it
springs from divine love, and it works for his soul's good.
Affliction is a seal of his adoption, and no sign of reproba-
tion.   The purest gold is the most tried, the sweetest grape
is hardest pressed, and the truest Christian is heaviest crossed.
But O how soon will the Christian forget all his groans when
he comes to heaven.   As soon as Stephen saw Christ, though
at a distance, he forgot all his wounds and bruises: he minded
no more the terror of the stones about his ears, but sweetly
yielded his soul into his Redeemer's hands.

I read of many in the gospel, that by sickness and diseases were driven unto Christ, who, if they had enjoyed
health and prosperity, would have neglected, like many others, to come to him.   O blessed is that cross that draweth a
sinner to Christ, to lay open his own misery and implore
Christ's mercy.   And blessed be that Christ who never re-

fuseth the sinner that cometh to him, though driven by affliction and misery. To whom shall such a distressed creature
as I go, but to Him who is the only physician that can cure
both my soul of sin and my body of sickness?

Lord, thou hast never denied thy mercy to any sinner
that asked it with a penitent heart. There were many
sorts of sick sinners that came to thee in the days of thy
flesh: the blind, the deaf, the lame, the lepers; those that
were sick of palsies, dropsies, fevers, fluxes, and were possessed with devils; and yet never one of them came crying
for mercy, that went away without his errand, were his sin
ever so great or his disease ever so grievous. Nay, so mer
ciful is my Redeemer, that he offered and gave his mercy to
many that never asked it, being moved with the bowels of
his own compassion and the sight of their misery: so dealt
he with the woman of Samaria, the widow of Nain, and the
man that lay thirty-eight years at the pool of Bethesda. Oh,
if he gave his mercy so willingly to them that did not ask it,
and was found of them that sought him not, will he deny
mercy to my soul that is crying for it?

There is but a step between me and death; Lord, seal
my pardon to me, before I go hence and be no more. O
draw nigh to me and save me; for my soul is full of trouble,
and my life draweth nigh unto the grave. Thy loving-
kindness is better than life: O make me sure of that, and I
will willingly part with this mortal life.

O thou who willest not that any should perish, but that
all should come to repentance, be pleased to make use of
the chastisement of my body as a medicine to cure my soul,
and bring me to a true and sincere repentance. One day is
with thee as a thousand years: O work in me on this, which
may be my last day, whatsoever thou seest wanting in me.
Enable me to present unto thee the sacrifice of a broken and
contrite heart, which thou hast promised not to despise.
Give me a true and lively faith in the blessed Jesus, who is

the propitiation for our sins. He was wounded for our transgressions, he was bruised for our iniquities, the chastisement of our peace was upon him; O heal me by his stripes. Let the cry of his blood drown the clamor of my sins. I am indeed a child of wrath, but Christ is the Son of thy love; O pity me for his sake, and let my soul find sanctuary in his wounds.

O Lord, the waters of affliction are come in even upon my soul. O let the Spirit of God move on these waters, that like the pool of Bethesda, they may cure whatever spiritual diseases thou seest in me. O Lord, consider my affliction, accept my tears, assuage my pain, increase my patience, and finish my troubles. Correct me with the chastisement of a Father, and not with the wounds of an enemy; and though thou take not off thy rod, Lord, take away thine anger.

Lord, the prince of this world cometh: O let him have nothing in me; but, as he accuseth, do thou absolve. I have nothing to say for myself, but be thou my advocate, Lord; and do thou answer for me. I am clothed with filthy garments, and Satan stands at my right hand to resist me; O Lord, rebuke him, and pluck me as a brand out of the fire. Cause mine iniquities to pass from me, and clothe me with the righteousness of thy dear Son. I know, O Lord, that no unclean thing can enter into thy kingdom, and thou seest I am nothing but pollution, yea, my very righteousness is filthy rags: O wash thou me, and make me white in the blood of the Lamb, that I may be fit to stand before thy throne. O take me from the tents of Kedar, to the mansions of light and purity. When my earthly house of this tabernacle is dissolved, O let me have a building of God, a house not made with hands, eternal in the heavens. O bring my soul out of prison, that I may eternally give thanks unto thy name. Amen.

CHAPTER VIII.

DIRECTIONS TO THE FRIENDS AND NEIGHBORS OF THE SICK,
WHO ARE THEMSELVES IN HEALTH FOR THE TIME.

When the Lord sends sickness and affliction to our neighbors, we ought not to be idle and unconcerned spectators of his dispensations, but we should hearken to the voice of God's rod upon others, and consider what it is that the Lord is calling for at our hands. These following directions may be useful to those that are in health.

Direction 1. Be very thankful to God for the great mercy of health and strength, and improve it to his glory.

Surely a healthful person hath great cause to be a thankful person. Health is a mercy that doth season and sweeten every other temporal mercy; without it the greatest wealth and honors, nay, a king's crown, can give no satisfaction. It is far more eligible to be a healthy beggar than a sickly king. What comfort could it afford us under tossing sickness and racking pains, to have the greatest heaps of money to look to, or thousands coming to pay us homage? alas, for our unthankfulness to him who is the God of our health. How little do we prize his goodness in continuing with us such a long season of health and strength, together with the use of our reason and senses, when many others are deprived of them. Surely God were righteous, should he teach us to value the worth of these mercies by the want of them.

Let us consider how many miserable persons there are in the world, and who it is that maketh us to differ from them; how many diseased, distracted, deformed, lame, blind, deaf and dumb people there are; and how easy it had been for God to have put us in their condition, and them in ours. The difference is not owing to any thing in us; their sins are not greater than ours. Had we a due sense of our sins and ill-deservings, we should acknowledge ourselves unworthy of the least of all God's mercies; we should reckon every common mercy a special blessing and unmerited favor to us. Again, let us take a view of the fainting sickness. racking pains, and restless nights of others. Let us look upon our sick friends sweating and burning under fevers; let us hear them groaning and moaning under strong pain. "Their soul abhors all manner of meat, and they draw near unto the gates of death." Sometimes we see them panting and fainting, and not able to speak a word to us. And what is the language of all this to us? Is it not, that we should thankfully adore our gracious God, and bless and magnify him for his distinguished goodness to us? O how much are we indebted to the Lord, that it is not so with us as with others. Wearisome nights are appointed to them, and their bones are full of tossing; all the comforts of this life are tasteless to them; their friends are weeping about them, but cannot help them. "It is far otherwise with me," may you say, "my mercies and relations bring comfort to me; I relish my food, my bed gives me ease, my sleep is refreshing; I have freedom to read and to pray, to meditate and attend the public ordinances. Praise the Lord, O my soul; and all that is within me, bless his holy name. Forget not this benefit of health, that is the chief of all my outward blessings; some would part with all their worldly wealth, to have so much bodily health as I have. Long have I undervalued and abused this choice mercy of health; O that I could mourn for my neglect, and resolve in God's strength to improve my remaining health, for the praise and service of that merciful God who is the author and preserver of it. Let me spend and be spent for God, that gives me all my health and strength for his glory. Let me abhor the ingratitude of those who employ the health which God giveth, in the service of his enemies, and make a sacrifice of it to the devil, the world, and the flesh. O what prodigious folly are those guilty of, who, for satisfying their sensual appetite, deprive themselves of health, which is in itself a thousand times of more value than all their brutish pleasure. God help me to prize this mercy, that can never be prized enough."

DIRECTION 2. Make conscience of visiting your sick friends and neighbors, believing it your duty and interest so to do.

Visiting of the sick is not only the duty of the ministers of Christ, but likewise of all the members of Christ; for we are all enjoined to remember them that are in adversity, and to sympathize with the afflicted, as being ourselves also in the body. "To him that is afflicted, pity should be shown by his friends," saith Job; and our Lord gives it as a character of those whom he will own and acquit at the great day, "I was sick, and ye visited me." Matt. 25:36. This is the way to be like him who is the Father of mercies, and whose soul was grieved for the miseries of Israel. Judg. 10:16. We read how tenderly David sympathized with his enemies when they were sick. Psa. 35:13, 14. And much more ought we to visit and sympathize with our sick friends. To visit the prosperous and healthy is an act of courtesy and civility; but to visit the afflicted and sickly is an act of charity and christianity.

And as it is your duty, so it is your interest and advantage to visit the sick. The wise man tells you, "It is better to go to the house of mourning than to the house of feasting." Eccl. 7:2. King Joash went to see Elisha in his sickness, and wept over him; and he lost nothing by so doing, 2 Kings, 13:14, for he obtained thereby three famous victories over the Syrians. Though it be not warrantable to inquire of the dead, Deut. 18:11, yet we may learn many wholesome lessons from the dying, even though they be speechless. For instance, we may hereby be instructed how to prize health, learn our own frailty, and provide for the time of sickness. When we behold their strength languish-

ing, their tongues faltering, their eyes failing, their counte-
nances pale, we should think with ourselves, "This will be
my case ere long; the next arrow that death shoots may be
levelled at me; how much is it my concern to prepare for
it!" Also we may think what a bitter thing sin is, that is
the cause of all these pains and distress, and how mad they
are who love sin and take pleasure in it. We may see
likewise the great folly of courting and trusting the world,
which leaves the sick and dying man in the greatest
extremity. And we may observe how happy the man is
that hath an interest in Christ, the peace of a good conscience, and a well-grounded hope of heaven, to yield him
support and confidence under his strugglings with sickness
and death. When we hear the dying man's complaints of
his sins, and his lamenting his neglect of duty, and misspending of precious time, we may learn repentance and
reformation. When we observe believers' professions of
love to Christ, and their hope in him to the last, it doth
contribute to the quickening and strengthening of our faith.
A right sight of dying persons is a good means to increase
the spirit of grace and supplication in us. We may fitly
allude here to the answer which Elijah gave to Elisha
when he sought a double portion of his spirit: "If thou
seest me when I am taken from thee, it shall be so unto
thee." 2 Kings, 2 : 10. A double portion of the Spirit shall
be the allowance of those who make conscience of this duty.

DIRECTION 3. Let the friends of the sick and those who visit
    them, deal faithfully with them about their souls.

Consider, this may be the last opportunity you may have
of doing any thing for your friend's soul. If he die, he is
fixed in his everlasting state, so that all advices and counsels then will be fruitless. It is now, or never, that you
must exert yourself for your friend's advantage; there is no
wisdom in the grave to which he is going. God's loving-
kindness cannot be declared in the grave, nor his faithful-

ness in destruction. Psa. 88 : 11. Now is the proper time for doing good to your neighbor's soul. When affliction opens the ear to discipline, be careful to drop in wholesome instructions into it; and when the heart is made tender by sickness, it is a fit season for good counsels to make impressions on it. Let the opportunity be improved with faithfulness and prudence; and in order to this, observe the following ADVICES :

1. Labor to know the sick man's spiritual condition, that your application may be suitable for it. The knowledge of the disease is previously requisite unto the cure : as the mistake of a physician about a man's disease may be as dangerous as the disease itself, so here it is highly dangerous to mistake the case of the sick man's soul ; for then lenitives may be applied when corrosives are needful—promises may be administered when threatenings are more proper.

2. Beware of flattering the sick with vain hopes of life when he is more likely to die, lest he be tempted to delay or slacken his preparation for another world. It is fit that plainness be used with respect to his danger, that he may be quickened to his work.

3. The sick is to be admonished and told that sickness comes not by chance, nor by second causes merely, but by the wise direction and special providence of God; that sometimes God smites out of displeasure for sin and for the sinner's correction and amendment, and sometimes for the trial and exercise of his people's graces; that the sharpest afflictions shall work for good to them that love God, and are rightly affected and improved under God's hand ; that it is a great mercy to a sinner, when God by his rod gives him warning and space to repent and flee to the blood of sprinkling, and to cry to God for pardon, and doth not snatch him out of the world by sudden death ; upon which account the voice of the rod should be carefully hearkened to and thankfully obeyed.

4. If the sick person be ignorant, he is to be catechized and instructed in the principles of religion, especially concerning his faith and repentance, and his accepting of the covenant of grace and the method of pardon and salvation through the righteousness of Christ apprehended by faith. And it may be proper to obtain his assent to some of the fundamental truths of Christianity, or his answer to such questions as these :

Do you believe in God the Father, Son, and Holy Ghost, one God in three persons, the Maker and Governor of the world ?

Do you believe that Jesus Christ, who assumed our nature, obeyed the law, died on the cross, rose from the dead, and ascended to heaven, is the eternal Son of God, and the only Saviour of sinners ?

Are you sensible that you are a lost sinner by Adam's fall, and besides that, guilty of innumerable actual sins ; and that you have broken God's holy commandments in thoughts, words, and deeds, and for so doing deserve God's wrath both in this life and that which is to come ?

Are you truly grieved and sorry for breaking God's law, neglecting his worship, misspending your time, and pursuing the vanities of the world ?   And would you live otherwise, if you were to begin your life again ?

How do you think to get your guilt removed, your sins pardoned, and your peace made with God ?   Are you desirous from your heart to be reconciled to God through Jesus Christ the blessed peacemaker ?

Do you heartily approve of the gospel method of reconciliation, by the righteousness and sacrifice offered up by the Lord Jesus Christ as your Surety, in your name and stead ? And is your soul desirous to choose and accept of Christ for your Mediator and Saviour, in all his offices of Prophet, Priest, and King ?

Do you renounce all confidence in any other, all dependence on your own duties and righteousness, and put your whole trust and confidence in Christ and the merits of his blood, saying, " Whom have I in heaven but thee, and there is none on earth that I desire besides thee ?" Do you believe that there is no salvation in any other ; and that there is no name under heaven whereby you can be saved, but Jesus Christ only ?

Do you desire to be wholly renewed and sanctified by virtue of Christ's blood, and to show forth the reality of your faith by good works and a holy life, for the time you have to live in the world ? And, as evidence thereof, are you willing to restore what you have taken wrongfully from any, and to cast out all malice or hatred you have borne to any, and ask forgiveness of any you have injured ?

Do you believe that Christ is coming at the last day to judge all the world, both the quick and the dead, whom he shall then raise from the grave, and that your dead body shall rise with the rest ?

Do you believe the immortality of the soul, and its living in a separate state after death, and that the souls of believers do thence pass into glory, where they shall be ever with the Lord ?

5. In dealing with the sick, you are to separate between the precious and the vile, and make a difference between the converted and the unconverted. And seeing different applications are requisite, you are, according to your knowledge, to study to suit your counsels, admonitions, and prayers to their condition ; not using the same words to the ungodly as to the godly, lest you flatter them with ill-grounded hopes that their state is safe, while they are strangers to a work of regeneration. The great truth is to be declared to all, that "Unless a man be born again, he cannot see the kingdom of God." O it is dangerous to speak peace when God speaks war.

6. If the sick person seem to be secure, or have not a

due sense of his sins, endeavors must be used to convince him of the guilt, pollution, and danger of them, in order to his humiliation. Presumptuous sinners are not to be flattered, lest we betray their souls into eternal ruin, and so their blood be required at our hand. No fond love, no slavish fear, must keep us from telling them the hazard of their present state. Their secure conscience must be awakened to see the demerit of sin, and the terribleness of the justice of a sin-avenging God, before whom no Christless impenitent sinner can stand: this is necessary in order to a sinner's discovering his lost case in himself, and his fleeing to Christ for refuge. It is God's method first to cast down the soul, before he lift it up—to plow the heart by conviction, before he cast in the seed of consolation.

7. If the sick person had studied to walk uprightly, but is at present discouraged on account of the sharpness of the rod, Satan's temptations, the guilt of sin, fear of death, or the like, then suitable counsels, resolutions, and comforts are to be offered, in order to his confirmation and support. Particularly, he may be told that sharp rods are nowise inconsistent with divine love; nay, frequently they are a sign of it: for as standing waters turn corrupt because they have no current, so with those who are not poured from vessel to vessel, their taste remains and their scent is not changed; therefore God, in order to take away the scent of corrupt nature from us, is pleased to change us from state to state by crosses and sickness, in order to our salvation. As Noah's ark, the higher it was tossed with the flood, mounted the nearer towards heaven; so the sanctified soul, the more it is exercised with affliction, is lifted the nearer towards God. Again, it is proper to set before him the freeness and fulness of God's grace, the sufficiency of righteousness in Christ, and his rich and gracious offers in the gospel, by which we are assured that all who repent and believe with all their heart in God's mercy through Christ, renouncing their own

righteousness, shall not perish in their sins, but have life and salvation in him; and that believers in Christ are assured of victory over Satan, death, and all their enemies, because Christ their head hath by his cross conquered the devil, unstinged death, triumphed over the grave, and obtained victory for all his members. So that neither life nor death, principalities nor powers, shall be able to separate them from God's love in Christ.

8. If a sick man be so tempted and troubled in conscience that he is in hazard of despairing of God's mercy, it is necessary to inform him of the greatness and infiniteness of God's mercy—that the most notorious sinners have been pardoned and saved by it, and that it is offered in the gospel to the vilest of sinners. Though God foresaw all the sins which the world would commit, yet these did not hinder him from loving the world so that he gave his only begotten Son to death, to save as many as would believe and repent; so that the sins of one man can never hinder God from loving his soul and forgiving his sins, when he sincerely desires to repent and believe. The cry of the most grievous sins that are recorded, such as those of Sodom, could never reach higher than unto heaven. Gen. 19 : 13. But David assures us that his mercy is great, and reacheth higher than the heavens, Psalm 108 : 4, so that it overtoppeth the greatest of all our sins. If the mercy of God be greater than all his works, it must surely be greater than all our sins. Again, lay before him the infinite virtue of Christ's blood. Acts 20 : 28. Are there any sins so great, or guilt so heinous, but the blood of Christ can wash them away? This was godly Cranmer's support the day he suffered martyrdom, when his sin of renouncing the Protestant doctrine stared him in the face: "Surely," said he, "God was made flesh, and shed his blood, not for lesser sins only, but for greater sins also." He was sadly discouraged, and wept abundantly, till he looked to this meritorious blood; and then he took

heart and died with courage. O this price was so great that it could have merited pardon for the sins of all the devils in hell, as well as of all the men on earth, though every one of them had been red as crimson. Yea, the least drop of this blood is of more merit to procure the mercy of God for our salvation, than all our sins can be of force to provoke the wrath of God for our damnation.

Moreover, let him be put in mind of the willingness and readiness of our Redeemer to receive all sinners that came to him in the days of his flesh, though driven to him by sickness and affliction; so that he never sent any of them away without their errand that came crying for mercy. Nay, he many times sought out objects for his mercy that were not thinking of coming to him, as we showed before. Observe the gentleness of our Lord's carriage to Judas himself, in calling him friend, after his most treacherous dealing: "Friend, wherefore art thou come?" Matt. 26 : 50. Had the wretched Judas laid hold of the word friend out of the mouth of Christ, as Benhadad did of the word brother from the mouth of Ahab, doubtless Judas would have found the God of Israel more merciful than Benhadad found the king of Israel. 1 Kings, 20 : 33.

Let him also consider, that to despair of God's mercy casts the greatest dishonor upon the divine majesty, and is a sin more heinous than all the sins which he before committed; because it doth charge the great God as guilty of perjury, who hath solemnly sworn that he desires not the death of a sinner, but rather that he should repent and live. Ezek. 33 : 11. God was more displeased with Cain for despairing of his mercy, than for murdering his brother, and with Judas for hanging himself, than for betraying his Master. Why? because that by their despair they would make the sins of mortal men greater than the infinite mercy of the eternal God.

DIRECTION 4. Be earnest in prayer to God for your friends when sick or dying; pray with them and for them.

Frequently sick persons are so disquieted with pain and trouble that they are little able to pray for themselves, and therefore they have the more need of the prayers of others. David fasted and prayed for his enemies when they were sick, Psa. 19 : 13 ; much more ought we to pray for our friends in that case. Never did they need our prayers so much as when they are called to enter upon an unchangeable condition—to go to their long home, even that place wherein they must abide for ever. Now they are in the land of prayer; and it is now or never that you must pray and beg mercy for them. When their life is gone, they go from the land of prayer, and are fixed in that place whence they shall never remove; then all prayers and cries for them will be in vain. If your friend be a stranger to Christ, he is on the brink of hell, and knows it not; and will you not cry to God to open his eyes, and save him from falling into that devouring pit, out of which there is no redemption? You would be willing to sit up a whole night for the relief of his body; and will you not spend a part of a night for the good of his soul, that is a thousand times more valuable? Now the question is, whether this precious soul shall be Christ's or the devil's for ever. . And when will you wrestle for your friend, if you do it not now? If the sick person be a child of God, you may pray with more comfort and expectation to be heard. You may, in that case, send the same message by prayer to Christ that the sister of sick Lazarus did : "Lord, behold, he whom thou lovest is sick." John 11 : 3. Lord, pity him, comfort him, abate his distemper, and relieve him from it, if it be thy will; if not, grant him thy gracious presence and safe conduct through the Jordan of death, and a happy landing in the Canaan of glory.

We are told that the prayer of the righteous in such

cases doth avail much. James 5 : 16. And this ought to encourage us to pray one for another. Whatever be the sick person's condition, such confessions and petitions as the following may be made use of in prayer for him.

PETITIONS FOR THE SICK.

Lord, thou hast breathed into man the breath of life; and when thou takest away that breath, he dies, and returns again to his dust. May we be duly sensible of our dependence on thee for all that we enjoy. We acknowledge that our great abuse of the many days of health and welfare thou affordest us doth justly deserve the visitation of sickness and diseases. Alas for us, we lie under a burden of sin, both original and actual; we are all the children of wrath by nature, and under the curse of a broken law; and all other miseries, temporal and spiritual, distempers, pains, death, and hell itself, are the issues thereof. Be merciful to the sick person under thy hand; make known to him his sins, and the cause why thou contendest with him. Make him see that he is lost in himself, and wholly unable to satisfy the demands of offended justice; and do thou reveal Christ to his soul for righteousness and life. Oh give him thy Holy Spirit to create and strengthen faith, that he may lay hold on Christ as offered in the gospel. Work in him the grace of true repentance. Enable him to search his heart and try his ways, so that he may discover every accursed thing, every Achan in the camp, that hath provoked the Lord against him. When thou puttest him in the furnace, be pleased to stand by it, and oversee the metal while it is melting in it. Try him as silver is tried, and bring him out purified, and let him lose nothing in the furnace but his dross. Remove his sins from thy presence as far as east is from west, that they may never trouble his conscience nor rise in judgment against his soul. However bitter the cup may be, let it be medicinal to cure all the diseases of his soul. Oh that these afflictions, which are but for a moment, may work for him a far more exceeding and eternal weight of glory, through Jesus Christ the purchaser.

Look down from heaven, the habitation of thy holiness; behold his affliction and his pain, and forgive all his sin. Show such pity to him as a father doth to his child, and lay no more upon him than he is able to bear. Lord, give patience and strength equal to the burden of trouble thou hast laid on him. In time of his weakness, uphold him by thy strength. Relieve his wants out of thy infinite fulness. Lord, thou knowest his frame, and rememberest that he is dust; save him from extremity of trouble; either abate his pain, or increase his patience to endure what thou measurest out to him. Give him the evidences of all the graces of thy Spirit. Arm and defend him against all the suggestions and temptations of Satan. Take his heart wholly off the world, and set his affections on things above. Lord, make use of this chastisement of his body as a medicine to cure his soul, by drawing his soul that is sick of sin to thyself. Oh enable him, in a penitent, believing manner, to come by repentance to Christ his soul-physician, to get it healed of its maladies. Sanctify his sickness, and let the fruit of it be to purge away his sin.

If thou, O Lord, shalt be pleased to add to his days, bless all means of his recovery. Remove the disease; renew his strength both outward and inward; heal his soul as well as his body, and enable him to walk tenderly before thee, and carefully to remember and perform such vows and promises of obedience as men are wont to make in time of sickness.

If thou hast determined to finish his days by the present visitation, let him find such evidence of the pardon of his sins, of his interest in Christ and eternal life, as may cause his inward man to be renewed while his outward man decayeth; that he may meet death without fear, cast himself wholly on Christ without doubting, and desire to be dis solved, that he may be for ever with Jesus Christ. Lord, make his last works better than his first, and the day of his death better than the day of his birth. Make his last words his best words, his last thoughts his best thoughts, his last hour his best hour. Oh let him die the death of the righteous, and let his last end be like his. Let the eyes of his soul be opened to see his sins and his Saviour, before the eyes of his body be shut by death. Take away the sting of death, the guilt of sin, that he may walk through the valley of the shadow of death, and fear no evil. Open thou his lips, that his mouth may show forth thy praise before he go to the place of silence. And when his strength doth fail, and his tongue is not able to utter words, let the blood of Christ speak for him in heaven; and let thy Holy Spirit within him make requests for him with sighs and groans that cannot be uttered. When the sight of his eyes doth fail him, let the eyes of his faith be strengthened, that his soul may behold Jesus Christ in heaven ready to receive him. Lord, stand by him in his last conflict with his enemies Satan and death, that he may overcome both, and be more than a conqueror through Christ that hath loved him. Into thy hands we commend his spirit.

Lord, teach us all to see how frail and uncertain our condition is, and so to number our days that we may seriously apply our hearts to heavenly wisdom, through Jesus Christ. Amen.

DIRECTION 5. Be careful to furnish your friends with suitable company and spiritual converse, when they are sick or dying.

As worldly company and converse are great hinderances, so spiritual company and converse are special helps to the sick and dying. Now, that the friends of the sick may prevent the one and provide for the other, let the following ADVICES be remembered:

1. Remind your friends to make their wills in season, and dispatch the settlement of their worldly affairs, that so they may not be disturbed at the last, nor anywise diverted from their main work by thoughts or conversation about the world.. A mind abstracted from the world is a most suitable disposition for a dying man. You cannot carry the things of this world with you when you go hence, and it is not fit that you should carry the thoughts of them.

2. Keep carnal company from them as much as possible, and all those that would divert them by idle or worldly discourse. It is both impertinent and cruel to throw such impediments in the way of those that are going speedily to their endless state.

3. Do what you can to get faithful ministers and godly Christians to be much about them; persons able to instruct and counsel them about their soul's matters, and also to pray with them and for them.

4. Be often reminding your sick friends of their chief work, and the things which belong to their peace. Whatever be their state, whether gracious or graceless, it is proper to be often reminding them of the vanity and emptiness of the world, that can neither give ease to the body nor comfort to the soul, when either of them is in trouble; of the sinfulness of sin, which is the spring of all diseases and miseries whatever; of the preciousness and usefulness of Christ to a sinner in all cases, and especially at a dying hour; of the inexpressible felicity of believers in Christ after death, and similar truths.

5. If you think yourself not able to instruct or advise your sick friends as they need, then read some good book to them, that may be suitable to the condition of their souls; and if you have not a fitter at hand, read some chapters and directions of this book to them, as you may see most proper for them. But above all books, read to the sick the holy Scriptures, and some particular chapters and psalms

there, such as the last three chapters of Genesis, the last
chapter of Deuteronomy, the 17th chapter of the first book
of Kings, the 2d chapter of the second book of Kings, the
14th and 19th chapters of Job, the Psalms of David, and
particularly the 6th, the 23d, 25th, 30th, 38th, 41st, 42d,
49th, 51st, 71st, 73d, 77th, 88th, 89th, 90th, 103d, 116th,
118th, 130th, 142d, and 143d Psalms; the 12th chapter
of Ecclesiastes; the 38th, 53d, 54th, and 55th chapters of
Isaiah; the last three chapters of Luke; the 14th to 17th
and 20th chapters of John; the 8th chapter of Romans; the
15th chapter of first Corinthians; the 5th of second Corinthians; the 4th of first Thessalonians; the 11th and 12th of
Hebrews; the last three chapters of Revelation, and the like.

DIRECTION 6. Be likewise suitably concerned for the bodies of
your friends, when they are sick.

If you would evidence a suitable concern for them, then
you must deal tenderly and compassionately with them in
their sickness, bear with their impatience and fretting, weary
not of them, nor grudge at the trouble they put you to; for
shortly you yourselves may be put in the like case, when
you shall be as great a trouble to others as your friends are
now to you.

It is also necessary to employ physicians, and use the
best means for the recovery of your friend's health. The
means indeed must not be trusted to instead of God, but
used in subserviency to him, who hath appointed them, and
who only can give success to them. We must beware of
Asa's sin, that sought to the physicians and not to the Lord.
Let us neither take food nor medicine without prayer to God
for his blessing thereon.

DIRECTION 7. When the sickness of your relations or neighbors
doth issue in death, study a Christian and suitable behavior
under such a dispensation.

When a parent loseth a promising child, or a child
loseth a loving parent, or when death deprives us of any

near relation, it is a speaking and trying providence; and we have much need of grace and counsel from God to conduct aright under it. Let us observe these ADVICES:

1. It is necessary in such a case that we have a tender sense and feeling of God's afflicting hand. There are two extremes which we must equally avoid, namely, to make light of the death of relations, and to be excessively grieved on that account. God will have us neither to despise his rod nor to faint under it. Heb. 12:5. God is displeased with those who are stupid and insensible under such afflictions. Hence he complains of such: "I have smitten them, but they have not grieved." Jer. 5:3. God will have us feel his hand, inquire into the meaning of the rod, and search for those sins that have provoked God to smite us. It is a sign of a selfish and unchristian spirit to be unconcerned for the death of friends, and much more is it so in those children who have a secret satisfaction in the death of parents, because of the worldly riches or liberty which they get thereby. God often follows this wicked temper with his heavy judgments even in this life.

2. Consider that God is calling you by the death of others, to keep up lively and lasting impressions of death and eternity upon your own spirits. God knoweth how advantageous it would be for men so to do, and therefore he sets frequent spectacles of mortality before their eyes for this end. But such is the corruption and earthliness of our minds, that we soon forget the thoughts of death. When we see our friends in the pangs of death, or laid in the grave, it strikes us with some fear and concern, to think that this will one day be our own case; but no sooner is the dead interred, and the grave filled up again, than all these serious thoughts begin to vanish, and men return to their sins and pleasures as before. Ah, what folly is this! Should not men always keep alive the serious thoughts of death and a future state? Are we not always alike mortal? Are we not as liable to

death's arrest at other times, as when examples are before our eyes?

3. When God takes away your children or relations, let it draw your hearts and affections more towards God and things above. As when a shepherd taketh up in his arms a lamb of the flock, the ewe followeth him of her own accord and will not leave him; so when the great Shepherd of the sheep taketh a child or friend from you, it should cause you to follow after him, and desire to be with him. But one may say, "That is not the case with me; I fear the wolf hath got the straying sheep, and devoured it." Then even that suspicion should make you run to the good Shepherd, abide with him, and keep close by the footsteps of the flock, and beware of straying in the paths wherein destroyers go. When God taketh from you relations whom you dearly loved, he calls you to take your love off the fading creature, and set it on the eternal Creator; when the weak branch is lopped off, then clasp to the body of the tree, which will not fail you.

4. In such trials, study a humble and patient submission to the will of God, who, in his sovereign wisdom and pleasure, hath taken your child or friend from you. Remember who hath done it, even He who gave all men their lives, and hath the absolute power and right to dispose of men's lives as he thinks best. If your fellow-creature do any thing that displeaseth you, you may both ask who did it, and why he did so? But when God doth any thing to you, you must remember he is the Potter and you are the clay, and that he may make or mar his clay vessels, yea, break them in pieces at his pleasure; and there is none can stay his hand, or say to him, What doest thou? "Be still, and know that I am God." Psa. 46 : 10. The master of a family gathers at his pleasure the flowers and fruits of his garden : sometimes he cuts off the buds, sometimes he suffers them to blossom ; sometimes he gathers the

green fruit, sometimes he stays till they are ripe; and every body thinks he may do with his own what he pleaseth; and shall not the Almighty God have liberty much more to dispose of all that grows in his own territories at his pleasure? The master of the family hath not created the trees and plants of his garden, but God hath made and fashioned all the children of men with his almighty hand.

It is the sense of this sovereign right and dominion of God over his creatures, that hath made his people to be silent under the greatest losses. Hence when Aaron lost his two sons by a sudden and extraordinary stroke, it is said of him, "And Aaron held his peace." Lev. 10 : 3. He opened not his mouth, because it was a sovereign God that did it. So holy Job, when he lost all his children by one blow, patiently submits to this absolute Lord : " The Lord gave, and the Lord hath taken away; blessed be the name of the Lord." Job 1 : 21. Job knew that God's relation to them was far nearer than his, and his right to dispose of them was indisputable. It was a holy and excellent speech of that honorable person, lord Duplessis, at the death of his only son : " I could not have borne this from man, but I can from God."

5. Guard against immoderate grief and excessive sorrow for the death of children or near relations; for this is sinful and offensive to God. Grief is sinful and immoderate when it makes you grudge at God's dispensation, murmur at his will, turn unthankful to him for the mercies you enjoy, overlook past favors, or lament a temporal more than a spiritual loss. Alas, there are many who can bewail a dead friend far more than a dead heart, and the loss of a child more than the loss of God's countenance.

Now, for preventing this excessive sorrow, consider these things :

(1.) If you be Christless and impenitent, you have reason to bless God that the stroke was not at your own life, for then you had been eternally miserable, and without hope. What is the temporal loss of a child to the eternal loss of thine own soul? O it is far better to be childless and friendless on earth, than to be hopeless and remediless in hell.

(2.) Consider how little ground you have to complain of any loss or stroke you meet with on earth. If you consider God's *sovereignty and power* over you, you have cause to be thankful that he hath not annihilated you and your relations both long ere now, seeing he hath as full a dominion to reduce you to nothing, as to bring you from nothing. Though God should dash us against the walls, as a potter doth his vessel, no man could have reason to say, What dost thou; or why dost thou use me so? "O house of Israel, cannot I do with you as this potter? saith the Lord." Jer. 18 : 6. Nay, he hath a greater right to deal so with us, than a potter with his vessel, for God hath contributed all to his creature that it hath; but the potter never made the clay which is the substance of the vessel, nor the water that is needful to make it tractable. All that the potter doth, is only to mould the clay into such a shape; besides, the potter's body is no better than the clay he makes his vessel of; nay, perhaps that very clay might once have been some part of the body of a man as good as the potter himself. Now, shall the potter have such absolute power over that which is so near alike to him, and shall not God have it over that which is infinitely distant from him? That word, Dan. 4 : 34, 35, "The Most High doth according to his will," is enough to silence the murmurings of all men under strokes and losses.

If you view the hand of God as most *just and righteous* in what you have met with, you have no good ground to complain. Have you not procured all this to yourself? Is not God most just in all that hath come upon you? Nay, if you consider your sins, and God's absolute dominion over you, you must own he might have dealt with you in a severer way than he hath done: instead of one affliction, you might have had a thousand.

Look to the *mercy* that is mixed with the rod. It is a wonder that this great Sovereign, who is so provoked by us, should allow us any mercy at all; and yet we receive innumerable benefits from him. Whatever be our afflictions, surely they are far less than our iniquities deserve. Hath he cast your child into the grave? he might justly have thrown your soul into hell. It is of the Lord's mercies you are not consumed. Why should a living man complain? a man out of a grave, and out of hell too, hath surely no reason.

If you compare your affliction with the *trials of others* of God's people, yea, even of those saints who have been most eminent, you have no reason to grudge at your loss. You have one child dead, but Aaron, who is called the saint of the Lord, Psalm 106:16, lost two at a stroke; nay, Job, whom God commends above all the saints in his day, had all his children slain by one blow; and both these eminent saints had these losses by an immediate and extraordinary stroke from God. Some godly parents have seen their children live to prove scandals to religion, and a grief of mind to themselves, and would have thought it a mercy if God had taken them away when young. Say not then that there is no sorrow like your sorrow; for the cup which many others have drunk, hath had more bitter ingredients in it than yours.

(3.) Consider that excessive grief cannot better your case; it may well make it worse. If you struggle and contend under God's hand, you act a foolish part—like a bullock unaccustomed to the yoke, that by his struggling galls his neck, and makes the yoke the more uneasy; or like a bird fluttering in a net, that instead of freeing, doth the more entangle itself. Thus by immoderate sorrow and fretting under the stroke, you sin the more against God, and make your burden the more heavy.

(4.) Remember the transactions of your soul with God in the day you entered into covenant with him. When you saw yourself on the brink of hell, and a burden of sin pressing you down, and no hope for you but in Christ, then your cry was, "None but Christ: take children, relations, riches, and all things else from me, and give me Christ. I give up myself, and all I have, to be disposed of at thy pleasure; thy will, Lord, shall be my will." Now, God is taking you at your word, and trying your sincerity in what you said and professed to him so solemnly. He hath disposed of thy dear relation as pleased him: O, believer, dost thou rue the bargain; wouldst thou take thy word again? Where is thy covenanted submission to the will of God, and thy promised contentment with all his disposals?

(5.) Dost thou not believe that a covenanted God is better to thee than all the friends in the world? Cannot God soon make up the greatest loss to thee, if thou turn to him by prayer, and pour out thy heart and sorrows in his bosom? A smile of God's face in prayer can soon sweeten thy bitter cup, and make thee forget all thy sorrows: "In the multitude of my thoughts within me, thy comforts delight my soul." Psalm 94: 19. The author of the Fulfilling of the Scriptures tells us of one Patrick Macilwræ, an eminent saint in the west of Scotland, who having lost his dear and only son, got to his closet, and there poured out his soul to the Lord. When he at length came out to his friends, who were waiting to comfort him and fearing how he would take such a heavy stroke, he returned from prayer with a cheerful countenance, and told some of his friends who asked him the reason of his cheerfulness, that "he had got that in his retirement with the Lord, that to have it afterwards renewed, he would be content to lose a son every day."

(6.) Seriously consider that you are but a few days' journey behind him for whom you mourn, and that you will quickly overtake him and be with him again. This allayed

David's sorrow for his child: "I shall go to him." 2 Sam. 12:23. It is our expecting to live here, to enjoy the comfort of relations, that commonly makes us grieve so much for their death; for if we looked on ourselves as men that were to die in a few days, we should not be so troubled for our friends that are gone but a little space before us.

(7.) If your friends are gone to heaven, you have more reason to rejoice with them than to mourn for them; seeing they are unspeakably happier where they now are, than they could have been with you. It is the most fervent desire and wish of every true Christian to be in heaven; and will you grieve because God hath taken your relations thither, where you desire to be yourself above all things? As Christ said to his disciples before his death, "If ye loved me, ye would rejoice because I said, I go unto the Father." John 14 : 28. So, if your departed friend could speak to you from heaven, he would say, "If ye loved me with a pure spiritual love, ye would rejoice that I am gone to my Father, where I am more happy than you can possibly conceive of me."

OBJECTION. Had I ground to think that my friend is gone to heaven, it would ease me; but, alas, I fear it is otherwise.

ANSWER 1. It doth not belong to us to inquire into the eternal state and condition of those who are gone off the stage. Those secret things belong to God, who exerciseth his mercy or justice towards sinners according to his sovereign will.

2. Supposing the worst, you ought to submit to the uncontrollable sovereignty of God, who hath mercy on whom he will have mercy, and whom he will he hardeneth. "He is of one mind, and who can turn him?" The Lord cut off Aaron's two sons in the very act of sin and rebellion against him, and yet Aaron held his peace, and so ought you.

3. Whatever be the lot of others hereafter, you have reason to be thankful to God. for his distinguishing mercy in

saving you from those flames that others fall into, and giving you good hope through grace of glorifying God above for ever.

DIRECTION 8. Let the sickness and death of others be a warning to you in time of health to make due preparation for the time of sickness and of dying which is before you.

When you see your friends and neighbors in a sickly, weak, or dying condition, the language of the dispensation to you that are in health is, prepare for sickness also. Nay, the feeble voice of the sick doth proclaim this warning as loudly as if they should lift up their voice like a trumpet, and say to you, "Remember that you must lie in the same case ere long; you also must groan under pain, lose your strength and beauty, leave your mirth and company, bid adieu to all the world, and look out for the grim messenger death, that is coming to dissolve your earthly tabernacle, send your body to lie in a putrefying grave, and your soul to stand before God's tribunal, to be sentenced to an endless state." This will be thy case, O young man, strong man, healthful man, as really in a little time as it is of those now before your eyes. O how soon will it come; what thoughts will you then have of the world, of sin, and vain company. Will any thing comfort you then but the favor of God, the love of Christ, and the review of a holy, well-spent life? Wherefore do with all thy might now what thy hands find to do, employ the time of health well in preparing for sickness, and leave nothing to do at that time, which is the most unfit season for a man to do the work of salvation in.

I shall begin with advices to THE FAMILY into which the harbingers of death have come. Surely the warnings of sickness and death ought to be louder in your ears than others, and most diligently hearkened unto by you, that lodge under the same roof with the messengers of the king of terrors.

1. Remember that word, 1 Peter 5:6, "Humble your-

selves therefore under the mighty hand of God." It well becomes guilty sinners, all ye members of the family, to be humble before a holy God, when he is smiting any of them. Humbly acknowledge his sovereignty and absolute dominion over you, saying, "Lord, thou art the author and founder of families, and thou mayest afflict and punish them as thou thinkest fit. Thou settest the solitary in families, and multipliest their number; and thou mayest diminish them, yea, lay them desolate, according to thy pleasure. Thou mightest have made all the members of the family sick, as well as one; thou mightest have given a deadly blow to parents, children, and servants at once, yea, have made the house in which we live a common grave, and buried us all together in its ruins." Humbly acknowledge the justice and mercy of God in the present visitation: "Lord, instead of one, we all deserved to be thrown on sick-beds, and all of us to have been smitten to death. Thou punishest us less than our iniquities deserve." Acknowledge also God's wisdom and love in the present affliction, and humbly submit to take the cup which he hath mingled for you. "The cup which our heavenly Father hath ordered for this family, shall we not drink it? It is a wise and gracious God that doth what is done in the family; therefore it is our part to be dumb, and not to open our mouths to quarrel with it."

2. The command which the king of Nineveh gave to all his subjects, when threatened with ruin, Jonah 3 : 8, is very proper for a master of a family to give to all under his charge, when sickness doth range among them : "Fast, and cry mightily to God, and turn every one from his evil way: who can tell if God will turn away from his fierce anger, that we perish not?" When the destroying angel gets a commission to smite families with mortal and infectious diseases, which sometimes go from house to house like a plague, sweeping many, old and young, off the stage; then especially it should be a time of mighty crying and pleading with

God for mercy, and since our pleading is wholly ineffectual without an atoning sacrifice to incensed justice, let us not forget to bring the all-sufficient sacrifice of Christ's blood along with us, and plead it with God for averting his wrath from our houses and families. As Moses said to Aaron in a time of common calamity, so may I say to you that are heads of families, "Take a censer and incense, and go quickly and make atonement for them; for there is wrath gone out from the Lord; the plague is begun." Numbers 6 : 46. Bring the incense of Christ's satisfaction, that great atonement to divine justice, which was typified by the legal sacrifices and oblations. Humbly and earnestly plead that great sacrifice with God, for turning away the fierceness of his wrath. Get the bunch of hyssop, faith, in order to the sprinkling of your houses with that atoning blood, that so you and your families may be among the preserved in Jesus Christ.

3. Let all the family where sickness is, and especially the head of it, remember that word, "Thou shalt put away iniquity far from thy tabernacles." Job 22 : 23. God hath sent sickness with this message to you: "Search out family sins, whether of omission or commission; mourn over them, turn from them, banish them far away. Let no vice lodge under your roof. Let family worship be no more neglected, nor slightly performed. Let God have both the morning and evening sacrifice." Now, if the members of those families visited with sickness, who are in health for the present, would thus humble themselves, cry to God, plead the blood of Christ, and reform what is amiss among them, the present affliction would be sanctified, and they in some measure prepared for the like trial, when God shall be pleased to put the cup in their hands.

II. In the next place, let me warn all the FRIENDS AND NEIGHBORS of the sick, whether they be of the family or not, to improve the day of health in making ready for the time of sickness. Be much in the exercise of self-examination, humiliation for sin, believing in Christ, renewing covenant with God, mortifying of sin, trimming the lamp, meditating upon heaven, living by faith, denying the world, studying to overcome the love of life and the fear of death—concerning all which I have given directions in the foregoing chapters of this book, when speaking to the sick and distressed. These exercises are not only proper for the sick, but also for those in health; and are suitable preparations for sickness and death, to be studied by all men in every condition. But there are some things further, most necessary to be minded by people in time of their health, in order to prepare them for the time of sickness and of dying, before it come. And,

1. Make your will and keep it by you, that you may not be encumbered with worldly affairs in time of sickness, or at a dying hour. Surely it is great wisdom to attend to this in time of health. But I have spoken largely of this in Chapter I., Direction 6.

3. Take heed in time of health, that you lay not up sad provision against the day of sickness by your careless walk. As it is sin that brings sickness upon us, so it is sin that imbitters it unto us. Oh beware of all known sins, and particularly the sins of earthly-mindedness, unthankfulness for mercies, lukewarmness in religion, neglect to follow Christ, neglect of prayer and formality in it, quenching of the Spirit, falling from your first love, breach of vows, abusing signal mercies, sinning after afflictions, turning to old sins. Guard against these evils now in the time of health, otherwise they will put thorns in your pillow when sickness cometh. Dare not to live in such a course as you would not venture to die in. How do you know but your next step may be into the grave; and would you be willing to lie down there in your sins with earthly, dead, formal, wandering, and unbelieving hearts?

3. Sit loose from the world, and live as a stranger in it, that you may be ready and willing to be gone from it on a short warning. Let death find you dead beforehand—dead to the world. If your affections be glued to the world, it will be a violent rending and sad parting you will have with it when the dying hour cometh. You will be ready, like Lot's wife, to linger, hanker, and look greedily back again.

4. Keep short reckonings with God and conscience, that you may not have old scores to settle when you come to a death-bed. Oh what stinging pain and torment may one sin unmourned for cost you at that time. Let conscience bring in the accounts every day before you sleep, and speedily take up every controversy that may arise between God and thy soul.

5. Dwell much upon the thoughts of death, that you may learn to be acquainted and familiar with it, as Job was, who said beforehand to corruption, "Thou art my father, and to the worm, thou art my mother and my sister." Job 17 : 14. For this cause the Egyptians used to place a dead man's skull in some conspicuous place of their rooms ; the Jews likewise had their sepulchres in their gardens of pleasure, that so in the midst of their delights they might think on their dying time. We read of Philip king of Macedon, that he ordered a page every morning to rouse him from sleep with these words, "O king, remember thou art a mortal man." By this oft-repeated lesson he labored to humble his lofty mind, and make his acquaintance with death, that it might not seem strange or surprising to him when it should actually come and snatch him away.

6. Study to spend every day as if it were to be your last, and perform every duty as if it were the last, always looking on sickness and death as very near. That which makes most men so unconcerned about sickness, death, and eternity is, they view them as things afar off—at thirty or forty years' distance. They think their time will be long here ; why?

they are healthy, of a strong constitution, and their fathers lived so long: which surely are false rules to judge by. It was the expectation of many years that helped on the ruin of that rich fool in the gospel. It were far better for every man to look on himself as standing every day and night at the door of eternity, and hundreds of diseases ready to open the door and let him in. When you lie down at night, leave your heart with Christ, and compose your spirits so as if you were not to awake till the heavens are no more; for certainly that night cometh of which you will never see the morning, or that morning of which you will never see the night. But which of your mornings or nights this will be you know not, seeing your times are not in your own hands.

7. Set apart some time daily for thinking, in a retired way, upon your time that is past, and upon eternity that is to come. The neglect of this duty of meditation and retired thinking is very injurious, both to the godly and ungodly. It was David's practice to think, and to think upon his ways; which engaged him to reform whatever he found amiss in them. Psa. 119 : 59. Oh it is the ruin of many a soul—they are utter strangers to this way of thinking. I have read of a father, who on his death-bed left it as a solemn charge upon his only son, who was a prodigal, that he should spend a quarter of an hour every day in retired thinking, and let him choose any subject he pleased. The son thinks this an easy task, undertakes it, and after his father's death sets himself to perform his promise. One day he thinks upon his past pleasures; another day he contrives his future delights; after a while he begins to think seriously what might be his father's design in laying this task upon him; at length he thinks, his father was a wise and good man, therefore surely he intended and hoped that among the rest of his meditations he would some time or other think of religion. When this had truly possessed his

thoughts, one thought and question comes upon the back of another about his past life and future state, so that he could not content himself with so short a confinement, but was all that night without sleep; yea, and afterwards could have no rest till he became seriously religious. Oh that I could persuade all careless and unthinking souls to go and do likewise. Ah, how many spend their days in a hurry about their worldly affairs, and perish for want of thinking.

8. Among other subjects of your retired thoughts, spend some time in thinking how awful and terrible a thing it must be for a poor Christless soul to make its appearance before an angry God after death. "For who can dwell with devouring fire; who can abide with everlasting burnings?" I have read of a certain king of Hungary, who being at one time extremely sad and heavy, his brother, who was a brisk and gallant man, insisted to know the reason: "Oh, brother," says he, "I have been a great sinner against God, and I know not how I shall appear before his judgment-seat." His brother answered, "These are but melancholy thoughts;" and so made light of them, as most courtiers used to do. The king replied nothing at that time; but the custom of that country was, if the executioner sounded a trumpet at a man's door, he was presently to be led to execution. The king sent the executioner in the dead of the night, and caused him to sound his trumpet at his brother's door, who hearing and seeing the messenger of death, sprang in trembling into his brother's presence, falls down upon his knees, and beseeches the king to let him know wherein he had offended him. "Oh, brother," said the king, "you never offended me, but loved me. But is the sight of an earthly executioner so terrible to thee; and shall not I, who am so great a sinner, fear much more to be brought to the judgment-seat of an angry God?"

9. Think often how religiously men wish they had lived when they come to the time of sickness and death. Those

who have spent their time most carelessly, begin to have other notions of religion when they see the grim messenger approaching.   Go to their bedsides, and ask them whether sloth or diligence, formality or fervency, drinking or praying, loving the world or loving Christ, be the best; would they not tell you, that there are none so wise as they that are most religious?   Think, O man, think with thyself, if thou wert now upon thy death-bed, and sawest thy friends stand mourning about thee, but unable to help thee, what would be thy thoughts and discourse at that time?   Oh, then, let some of the same thoughts and discourse fill up every day and hour of thy life now.   Thou knowest not but this moment thou mayest be as near death, as if thy friends and physicians were despairing of thy life, and had given thee over for dead.

10. Be employed now in fighting the good fight of faith. You have many enemies to contend with, and death is the last of them.   Would you obtain the victory over them? Then get on the Christian armor, and make much use of the shield of faith.   We read in the book of Esther, that king Ahasuerus would not recall the proclamation he had emitted against the Jews, but he gave them full liberty to take up arms to defend themselves and attack their enemies; so here, God will not recall the sentence of death he passed upon all men, in the garden; nevertheless, he allows, yea, commissions all true Israelites to take up arms against death, to conquer and trample it under foot by faith.

11. Be busy now in health, providing and laying up a stock against the time of sickness and affliction, which may contribute to your comfortable living then, when the world's good things will be tasteless and comfortless to you.   As those who have a voyage to make victual their ship, and those who have a siege to hold take in provisions, even so do ye.

Get a stock of *graces* against that time, especially a stock of faith, of patience, of humility, self-denial, etc.   There will

be use for all these then.   A little grace, or a little faith, is
not enough ; for this will faint under afflictions.   We read,
that when the winds began to blow fiercely, Peter's little
faith began to fail.   You have need of a great measure of
patience against that time, that you may wait quietly on
God till he come to your relief.   You know not but he may
lengthen out your trials, and tarry till the fourth watch of
the night before he come with deliverance.

Provide a stock of *evidences of grace*, and of the love of
God, that you may be able to assert your interest in him as
your portion in Christ, and may be persuaded that neither
death nor life will ever separate you from him.

Get a stock of *divine experiences*.   Lay up all the expe
riences you have had of God's loving-kindness, and these
will give great relief and encouragement to the soul in the
day of distress.

Lay up a stock of *sermons*.   Treasure up the counsels
and cordials which they bring you from God's word, that so
you may, according to Isa. 42 : 23, "hear for the time to
come," and especially for the time of sickness, when you
cannot get sermons to hear.   Then it is that you ought to
live and feed upon the sermons you have heard.

Lay up a stock of *prayers*.   Be much in wrestling with
God for help and support in the day of affliction, and so you
may expect gracious answers to your prayer in the day of
calamity.

Provide a stock of *promises*.   Gather now these sweet
cordials from God's word, and lay them up in your heart
and memory, and they will be very refreshing and supporting to you in the day of affliction.

DIRECTION 9. Let those who are in health set about the work of
repentance and turning to God in Christ quickly ; and beware
of delaying this work until the time of sickness and dying.

God's command to you is, to set about the work presently, without any delay : "To-day if ye will hear his voice,

narden not your hearts." Heb. 3 : 7, 8. "Go, work to-day in my vineyard." Matt. 21 : 28. "Remember now thy Creator in the days of thy youth." Eccles. 11 : 1. Well, God's voice to you, O man in health, is, "To-day ;" but the devil's voice to you is, "To-morrow." And which of the two will you hearken to? Surely it is your wisdom to obey the voice of your Creator and friend, and not of your enemy and destroyer. Why? To-day thou art in health—to-morrow thou mayest be in sickness; to-day thou art on earth—to-morrow thou mayest be in hell; to-day Christ is inviting you to come to him—to-morrow he may be sentencing you to depart from him : and consider, that the devil who tempts you to delay this day, will be as ready to tempt you to the same to-morrow, and so the devil's to-morrow will never come. It will still be to-morrow with him to the last hour, that so he may get you cheated out of your whole time and salvation together.

Here I shall endeavor to bring arguments to persuade you to repent and close with the offers of Christ presently, without delay, as God requires ; and to show the evil and danger of delaying till the time of sickness and dying. As to the first, namely, ARGUMENTS FOR PRESENT REPENTANCE, and against delaying the work,

1. Consider the uncertainty of your life and time to repent. Your life is but a vapor—a little warm breath that is going out and in at your nostrils, which may be stopped by death ere you be aware: "Thou knowest not what a day may bring forth." Prov. 27 : 1. It was the saying of a godly man, when invited to a feast upon the morrow, " I have not had a morrow for these many years." It was a bad use the epicures made of this uncertainty: " Let us eat and drink; for to-morrow we shall die." Isa. 22 : 13. It is much wiser to say, " Let us pray, and turn to the Lord ; for to-morrow we shall die." Nay, you have not security for one hour to repent in; for God hath a thousand diseases and ac-

cidents ready to stop your breath and end your days whenever he pleaseth to give them orders. There are many
secure sinners who presume on long life, but there are none
nearer destruction than such, for God is wont to disappoint
those that promise themselves a long life in sin and impenitency, as he did that rich man who was laying up for many
years : "This night thy soul shall be required of thee."
Luke 12 : 19. And O what a dark and dismal night will
it be, if death come before thy repentance. O man, thou
never didst lie down one night with assurance of rising
again ; thou never heardst one sermon with assurance of
hearing another ; thou never didst draw one breath with
assurance of drawing another. What madness then to delay salvation one day or hour longer, and so to leave the
weightiest matter in the world at the greatest uncertainty.

2. Consider that though God in wonderful mercy and
patience should prolong your days, yet the longest life is
short enough for the work you have to do, even if you begin
it now. Nay, had you Methuselah's years to spend, they
would be no more than sufficient to repent and mourn for
the sins and guilt which you have been so long contracting,
to reform and amend the many things that have been amiss,
to perform all the duties incumbent on you, to make sure
your calling and election, and put your soul in a good posture and preparation for an eternal state, and get it made
meet to be partaker of the inheritance of the saints in light.
Now, do you think that all this work can be done in an
instant, or in a time of sickness or old-age, when you are
hardly fit to do any thing ? When a man's spirit is unable
to bear the infirmities of nature, how will he be able to bear
the lashes of a guilty conscience or a wounded spirit ?
When the understanding is weak, the memory frail, the will
obstinately bent the wrong way by a long custom of sinning
and neglecting of duty, will that be a fit time to begin the
work of repentance and conversion to God ? When nature

is decayed, and the candle of life just sinking in the socket, will you begin then to act for God, and make your light shine before men to his glory? O remember your work is long, your time is short, and though you begin this very hour you will have no time to spare.

3. Delay not this work, because it is not of yourself only to do it when you please. It is a delusion of the devil to imagine you may thus repent when you will. No, no; it is God that giveth repentance, and he gives it when and to whom he pleaseth. Acts 5 : 31. And it is a mere peradventure if ever he give it to a delaying sinner. 2 Tim. 2 : 25. When is it that you may have hopes he will give repentance, but when he calls you to it, and prescribes means to be used for that end? Now, that is, to-day, "To-day, if you will hear his voice : now is the day of salvation." To-day, when God is calling and the Spirit striving, is the time of finding the Lord and getting repentance from him. To-morrow it may be too late; the Lord's hand may be closed, and the door of mercy be shut. If you refuse the Spirit when he strives with you, he may leave you and never put in your heart another serious thought of turning to the Lord. O defer not seeking repentance till it be too late ; for there is a time when the Lord will not be found, and then repentance will not be obtained, though you seek it with tears. Indeed God hath promised mercy to penitent sinners, but he hath nowhere promised the aids of his grace and Spirit to them that put off their repentance ; and he hath nowhere promised acceptance to mere grief and sorrow for sin, without faith and fruits meet for repentance. He hath nowhere promised to pardon those who only promise to leave their sins when they can keep them no longer.

4. The longer repentance and closing with Christ is delayed, the difficulty thereof is every day increased. Why? 1. Because of the deceitful nature of sin, which doth daily bewitch and harden the heart more and more in the practice

of it.   2. Custom in any thing hath a strong influence on us; it becomes a kind of second nature and breeds an almost invincible inclination to whatever we have long addicted ourselves to, whether it be in actions natural or moral. Hence even a heathen poet gives this good advice:

"Sed propera, nec te venturas differ in horas;
    Qui non est hodiè, cras minus aptus erit."

Be speedy; put not off till another time:
He who is not prepared to-day, will be less prepared to-morrow.

He that goes on from day to day in sin, will find his indisposition to repent daily increased, the habits of sin strengthened, and himself brought at length under the power of an inveterate custom.   And if it be hard to break any custom, much more a custom in sinning, which is so agreeable to depraved nature.   Hence saith the Spirit of God, "Can the Ethiopian change his skin, or the leopard his spots? then may ye also do good, that are accustomed to do evil."   Jer. 13:23.   3. The longer Satan keeps possession, the more difficult will his ejection prove.   The devils that possessed the man from the womb up, could not be cast out but by some extraordinary way.   4. Delays bring on spiritual judgments from God, such as judicial hardness of the heart, which will make repentance impossible, according to that terrible place, Isa. 6:9, 10, "Make the heart of this people fat," etc., which is quoted no less than six times in the New Testament, as if it belonged only to them that linger and sit impenitent under gospel calls.

5. We should reckon such delays madness in earthly affairs, which are but trifles when compared to salvation. If a man's house were on fire, we should count him mad if he should say it is time enough to quench it to-morrow; or, if he were stung with a venomous serpent, if he should neglect to seek an instant cure.   If he had got poison in his stomach, surely he would never think he could soon enough vomit it up.   If a malefactor were condemned to a cruel

death to-morrow, but had a promise of remission if he should look after it to-day, would he be so foolish as to delay it till next morning? But how much greater madness is it to delay repenting and fleeing to Christ, when God's calls and promises relate to the present time, and our danger in delaying is infinitely greater than in any of the aforesaid cases? Surely there is no sting so dangerous, no poison so deadly as sin; and can we too soon seek after the balm of Gilead, the blood of Christ, for its cure? There is no death like the second death, no fire so dreadful as the eternal fire of God's wrath. Now this fire is already kindled against your souls; and if it be not soon quenched, it will burn to the lowest hell. Lose no time to get it extinguished, by fleeing to the blood of Jesus.

The next thing is to show THE EVIL AND DANGER OF DELAYING this work until the time of sickness and of dying. Alas, it is the common practice of most men. But consider,

1. What wretched ingratitude and baseness there is in it. Is it fit you should give the best of your time to God that made you, or to the devil that seeks your destruction? Is it reasonable that the devil should feast on the flower and prime of your youth and strength, and your Creator have no other but the fragments of the devil's table? When the dregs of your time are come, your strength gone, your senses failed, your understanding and memory weak, your affections spent upon the creature, yea, when you are good for nothing else, will you be so base as to think you are then good enough for God, and for the work of salvation, which requires all your strength and might? But remember, if you be so base as to reserve the dregs of your time for God, you may expect he will be so just as to reserve the dregs of his wrath for you, according to that word, " Cursed be the deceiver, which hath in his flock a male, and voweth and sacrificeth unto the Lord a corrupt thing." Mal. 1 : 14. Your youth, strength, health,

gifts, and talents are the males of the flock; if you give these to the devil, and reserve the weakness of sickness and old-age for God, you draw down his curse upon your head ; and how long will you be able to bear up under the weight of God's curse ?   Now, O delaying sinner, why should you be so ungrateful to God, and injurious to yourself?   God had early thoughts of mercy to you ; and will you have nothing but late thoughts of duty to him ?   Christ did not defer his dying for us till he was old ; and shall we defer living to him till we be old?   Oh, we do not deal with God as we would have him deal with us.   When we need help in trouble, we cry, "Hear my prayer, O Lord; in the day when I call, answer me speedily."   Psalm 102 : 1, 2.   To-day we still make the season of mercy, but to-morrow the season for duty.   When mercy is delayed, we impatiently cry, How long, how long?   We will not wait God's holy leisure. But alas, we would have God wait our sinful leisure.   Oh, let us be ashamed of such disingenuous dealing with our Creator.

2. Death may get a commission to take you off suddenly without giving you any time to repent.   You are not sure to see the evening star of sickness before the night of death overtake you, or that you will have any warning given you before the fatal stroke.   For how many are there who pro-ject long lives and look for time before death to repent, that get a sudden call to flit from the earthly tabernacle, and have not one minute to provide another lodging.   How many are drowned by a sudden storm at sea; and how many killed by outward accidents on land.   Some drop down suddenly in the streets; some die sitting in their chairs ; some go well to bed at night, and never see the morning; some die in a fit of epilepsy or apoplexy, as if shot with a gun.   Thus thousands are hurried into eternity and presented before God's tribunal, without being allowed so much time as to think one serious thought or speak one word—not a moment to

consider where they are going, or to cry to God for mercy. And how know you but this may be your case at death? Must it not be the greatest folly then to delay your repentance to a dying time, when your life may not be one minute longer?

3. Though you may have some time to lie on a sickbed, how know you but your next sickness may be such as shall incapacitate you for spiritual work? Some we see so oppressed with continual slumbering and sleeping, even when death is nearest, that they are in no case to think or speak of those things that belong to their eternal state. Others, in high fevers, are troubled with roving minds, and have no use of their reason, so that they are not capable of settling their worldly affairs; and how much less are they fit to secure their soul's eternal concerns at that time. Some, again, are so racked with pains and agonies, impatient fretting, and bitter uneasiness, that they cannot get one settled thought about their soul's present or future state. Others are so filled with terror and amazement at the view of approaching death and eternity, that they cannot compose their thoughts to examine themselves, confess their sins, act faith in a Saviour, or follow any direction that is given them; but go off the stage in distraction, being incapable of doing any thing to purpose for their souls. Some are brought to a great strait between the word of God and the physician. The word of God and his ministers tell them, if they do not mourn for their sins and wrestle for mercy, they cannot be saved; but saith the physician, if you trouble yourself with sad and melancholy thoughts, you prejudice your health and hazard your life. Oh, is this a fit time to begin your preparation for another world?

4. The Spirit of God being long resisted and vexed by many in the day of health, is provoked to leave them on death-beds to the hardness of their own hearts; and so they remain like stocks and stones, dead and stupid to the last.

5. The devil, who was busy all your life to keep you from repentance, will not be idle at this time; nay, he will be more active than ever to ruin you, by causing you to split on the rock either of presumption or of despair. He will sometimes tell sinners, " You need not trouble yourselves about your souls; God is more merciful than to damn you; the repentance you have already will serve the turn." But if this will not quiet them, he will study to drive them to despair, by telling them, " You have lost the season of repentance and closing with Christ; and now there is no remedy and no hope for you, and it is in vain to use any further means." O then, do not hearken to Satan now, when he tempts you to delay your repentance.

6. Whatever appearance of repentance some dying persons may have, let that be no encouragement to put off the work till that time. Why? There lieth a just suspicion upon a late repentance, that it is seldom sound and sincere. It is no sound work that ariseth more from fears of hell than from any real hatred of sin—more from love to self than love to God. And it is to be feared that death-bed repentance is mostly of this sort, seeing ordinarily it consisteth more in grief and fear, prayers and promises, than in a hearty loathing of sin, love to holiness, or willingness to accept of Jesus Christ; for have we not seen many of those penitents, who, in the view of death, have professed great sorrow for their wicked lives, and made solemn promises of amendment, yet when they have happened to recover, all their righteousness hath vanished, and they have returned to their former sins as greedily as ever? And O, delaying sinner, what ground have you to think that your death-bed repentance will be any better than theirs? Be wise then in time; set heartily about securing salvation in the day of your health, and do not leave the weightiest work to the weakest time.

OBJECTION 1. But hath not God promised mercy to them that repent of their sins at any time?

ANSWER. Yes, to them that repent truly and sincerely: but do not think that it is in your power to repent so at any time you please; no, it is impossible you can do it without the influence and assistance of the Spirit of God. And God hath nowhere promised this to those who put off their repentance to a death-bed. There is a great difference between a sick man's howling upon his bed, and sincere gospel repenting. I grant true repentance is never too late; but O, late repentance is seldom true. True repentance is that which hath a care to walk holily, or hath works meet for repentance joined with it. Hence repentance is not only called METANOIA, a change of mind; but also METAMELEIA, an after-care. Now, for a death-bed repentance, that hath no such holy care or good works, I know no promise in the Bible that annexeth salvation unto it.

OBJECTION 2. Do not we read in Christ's parable of the laborers, Matt. 20, that some were hired and brought into the vineyard at the eleventh hour, and got the same reward with those that were hired at the first and third hours?

ANSWER 1. Those that were brought in so late, could say for themselves, verse 7, that no man had hired them, or had offered to hire them before; the gospel call and offer of salvation through Christ had not been tendered to them. But O, this will not stand you in stead, who have had many a call and offer made you at the third, sixth, and ninth hour, and have resisted and refused them: you will not have it to say at the eleventh hour, as these had, "No man hath hired us."

2. Those men, though they came in but at the eleventh hour, not being sooner hired, yet they were laborers in the vineyard, and wrought one hour therein faithfully, in obedience to their Lord's command, and so brought forth some fruits meet for repentance, and were accepted. But this is no encouragement to any to expect to be brought in at the twelfth hour, when there is no time to work, nor

bring forth any fruits to testify the sincerity of their repentance; we have no promise of acceptance made to such.

OBJECTION 3. The penitent thief on the cross sought
mercy from Christ at the last hour, and got it.

ANSWER. That is a single instance, and gives no encouragement to delaying sinners. The Scriptures contain a history of more than four thousand years, and yet during all
this time we have but one example of a man that truly and
sincerely repented when he came to die. And in this man's
case there was such an extraordinary conjunction of circumstances as never happened before, and can never fall out
again to the end of the world. This man had the happiness
to die close by the newly pierced and bleeding wounds of a
crucified Jesus, when he was lifted up from the earth in the
height of his love, drawing sinners to salvation; which was
the juncture that can never have a parallel. Again, the
man never had any offer of Christ nor day of grace before
now; he surrendered himself upon the very first call; and
his faith in Christ at this time was truly singular and mirac-
ulous. He was designed by heaven to be made a rare monument of the power of Christ's grace, and a special trophy
of his victory over devils and wicked men, at a time when
they seemed to triumph over him, as one crucified through
weakness.

From all which we may see that this example was extraordinary, and affords no ground for the presumption of
delaying sinners. You may as well cast yourselves into the
sea in hopes of preservation by a whale, from the example of Jonah, as defer repentance now in hopes of repenting on a death-bed, from the example of the thief on the
cross. Your way of sinning differs vastly from his. He was
not guilty of presumption, as you are; he did not slight
Christ's call and offers in the day of his health, and delay
his repenting and closing with Christ, in hopes of an oppor
tunity for them at the hour of death, as you do. Do you

know what God determines concerning presumptuous sinning? You may see it in Numbers 15 : 28, 30, 31. "And
the priest shall make an atonement for the soul that sinneth
ignorantly. But the soul that doeth aught presumptuously,
whether he be born in the land or a stranger, the same re-
proacheth the Lord; and that soul shall be cut off from
among his people, because he hath despised the word of
the Lord." O presumptuous, delaying sinner, let this word
of the Lord awaken you to a speedy, an immediate resolution to obey his voice. "Return ye now every one from his
evil way, and make your ways and your doings good." Jer
18 : 11. Now is the accepted time: if you will hear his
voice, it must be to-day. Lord, save us from hardening our
hearts. Amen.

CPSIA information can be obtained at www.ICGtesting.com
Printed in the USA
LVOW100722261111

256536LV00001B/1/P